The Social Sciences

Foundations of the Social Studies

Contributors

Ralph W. Haskins
Lillian W. Stimson
Vernon R. Iredell
Ronald H. Wolf
Alfred K. Guthe
William E. Cole
E. Ohmer Milton
John W. Davis

THE UNIVERSITY OF TENNESSEE

The Social Sciences
Foundations of the Social Studies

Edited by John U. Michaelis
THE UNIVERSITY OF CALIFORNIA, BERKELEY

and A. Montgomery Johnston
THE UNIVERSITY OF TENNESSEE, KNOXVILLE

ALLYN AND BACON, INC.   1965

Preface

THE CURRENT TREND TOWARD BUILDING THE SOCIAL STUDIES CUR-
riculum on the social sciences has created new responsibilities for
teachers and curriculum specialists. Of first importance is the
responsibility of school personnel to ground themselves in the nature
of the disciplines that are most useful in curriculum planning. The
discharge of this responsibility is especially difficult in the social
studies because of the variety of disciplines that are drawn upon in
curriculum planning. Further difficulties arise because of the diversity of points of view that exist within each of the social sciences.

The central purpose of this volume is to aid teachers and curriculum specialists in their efforts to gain a deeper understanding of
the nature of the social sciences. Basic information is presented on
eight disciplines in order to answer such questions as: What is history? What is geography? How are other pertinent disciplines
defined? What points of view are dominant at the present time?
What key concepts and generalizations are of first importance?
What methods of inquiry are employed by scholars in each discipline? These and related questions must be considered before
decision-making can go very far in dealing with methodological and
substantive aspects of the social studies curriculum.

This volume is not intended to be a methods book. Rather,
it is viewed as a supplement to the many fine social studies methods
books currently available for use in courses for prospective elementary
and secondary school teachers. The assumption has been made
that teachers and curriculum workers at both the elementary and
secondary school levels need to be grounded in the nature of the
social sciences. This assumption is in keeping with the current trend

51354

to plan the overall social studies program in a Kindergarten through Grade 11 or 12 sequence. Sincere efforts have been made to include material that is relevant to the needs of teachers at all levels.

Grateful acknowledgment is made to the eight scholars who contributed the chapters on the disciplines that are treated in this volume. The editors are deeply appreciative of their constructive concern for the improvement of the social studies curriculum. Each scholar gave freely of his time in presenting ideas to teachers, getting reactions, and conferring with the editors. It was only through the cooperation of these distinguished scholars that a volume such as this could be produced. And it is only through such cooperation that continuing improvement of the social studies program can be achieved.

Acknowledgment also is made to the many individuals who contributed ideas and offered suggestions during the preparation of the manuscript. Of particular importance were those ideas and suggestions related to ways in which concepts, generalizations, and methods of inquiry from the social sciences can be incorporated in the social studies. The ideas drawn from current social studies projects, curriculum guides, and new instructional materials were especially helpful.

John U. Michaelis
A. Montgomery Johnston

Contents

vii

I

The social sciences: foundations of the social studies

John U. Michaelis
School of Education
University of California, Berkeley

A. Montgomery Johnston
College of Education
University of Tennessee

FUNDAMENTAL CHANGES ARE TAKING PLACE IN THE SOCIAL STUDIES. The primary factor contributing to these changes is the emphasis on the social sciences as the foundations of the social studies. Intensive efforts are being made to identify the basic ideas that scholars believe to be of greatest importance in their areas of study and to organize these ideas in ways that will promote depth of learning. Special attention is being given to the development of programs based on the structure of the social sciences—the concepts, generalizations, themes, and methods of inquiry that are fundamental in each discipline. Teams of scholars, teachers, curriculum coordinators, and social studies specialists are involved in a variety of projects and activities, the impact of which is felt in curriculum revision, the production of teaching materials, and classroom instruction.

Why is there renewed emphasis on the social sciences as the foundations of the social studies? Knowledge from the social sciences and data on societal problems and the nature of human development and learning have long been used to make curriculum decisions. But new knowledge is being produced at an unprecedented rate. A critical selection of this new knowledge needs to be incorporated in the social studies in ways that will promote excellence of learning, focus on fundamental ideas, and give insights into modes of inquiry. Social scientists, teachers, and curriculum specialists have observed a variety of activities designed to update mathematics and science education. New curriculum projects have been instituted to devise new approaches to instruction. Special attention is being given to the nature of the fields of study that are fundamental to curriculum planning. There is no sound reason for failing to give similar attention to the foundations of the social studies. A systematic review of the nature of modern social sciences is needed to facilitate continuing improvement of social studies instruction.

New Responsibilities for School Personnel

As is typical of curriculum changes, new developments in the social studies have created new responsibilities for school personnel. Heading the list of these responsibilities is the need for an understanding of the structure of the social sciences that can be used to improve curriculum planning and teaching in the social studies. Essential to knowledge of the structure of the social sciences is an understanding of the nature of the social sciences as disciplines, the key concepts and generalizations in each field, and the methods of inquiry that are employed. Herculean though the task may seem, its accomplishment can be aided by a consideration of what social scientists themselves believe to be the most significant characteristics of their disciplines. The task can also be facilitated by examining the views of social scientists regarding the place of their disciplines in the social studies program.

This volume is designed to help teachers and curriculum specialists carry out this task. No other book for school personnel has dealt directly with the nature of those disciplines which are the foundations of the social studies. While reports are available on what social scientists believe high school graduates should study in their disciplines,[1] none deals directly with such questions as, What

[1] For example, see *The Social Studies and the Social Sciences* (New York: Harcourt, Brace & World, 1962); *High School Social Studies Perspectives* (Boston: Houghton Mifflin, 1962).

is history? What is geography? What is economics? What is the nature of these and other social sciences? What key concepts and methods of inquiry are of basic importance?

A consideration of those disciplines which are used as bases for instructional planning provides a background of understanding that is helpful in several ways. Goals of instruction can be clarified, patterns of organization can be improved, and content can be selected with greater discrimination. As attention is given in the classroom to key concepts, ideas, and modes of inquiry characteristic of different disciplines, students can begin to understand the styles of thought, domains of study, special interests, and current issues in the social sciences. It is possible to develop an understanding of why different answers may be suggested to the same questions, why different solutions may be offered for the same problems, and why different points of view may be expressed on the same issues. What to expect and what not to expect from historians, economists, and other social scientists may also be clarified. In short, it is the thesis of this volume that curriculum planning and teaching in the social studies will be improved as school personnel develop deeper insight into the nature of the social sciences. Let us begin by viewing the social sciences as a broad domain of knowledge.

The Social Sciences as a Broad Domain of Knowledge

In the academic world, knowledge may be classified into four major divisions. Mathematics is a domain of inquiry in its own right and at the same time is an essential part of many other domains of knowledge. The natural sciences include physical sciences such as physics and chemistry, and life sciences such as botany and zoology. The social sciences include such disciplines as sociology, human geography, and political science. The humanities include literature, languages, art, music, and philosophy.

The social sciences are in a middle position in an academic classification of knowledge between the natural sciences and the humanities.[2] Given birth by distinguished mothers—history and

[2] A social science as a science is concerned with the study of selected aspects of human relationships, e.g., economic, political, social, and cultural aspects. A helpful way to view science in this context is in terms of (1) purpose—to produce knowledge that can be used to describe, explain and predict

philosophy—the social sciences have applied scientific modes of inquiry to the study of human relationships. At times in the past, some "obstreperous offspring" have forgotten the breadth and depth of "mother's understanding," and have tried to "show mother how a new scientific boy should behave" if he is to emulate the physical sciences and discover natural laws. Such behavior has been met with patience (and an occasional spanking) by history and philosophy, which, like all good mothers, must have felt that a period of maturing would bring greater wisdom to the study of the human condition. Today the offspring realize that scientific methods of investigation are helpful but that the study of subjective-qualitative dimensions of the human condition may call for modes of inquiry beyond the present purview of science. As suggested by a scientist, science and humanism working together are "a powerful instrument for understanding the world." [3] The social sciences reflect in varying degrees both a scientific and humanistic emphasis.[4] The social sciences are marked by the use of both quantitative and qualitative approaches to the study of man in society. Canons of scientific scholarship are prized as guidelines to free inquiry. Reflective analysis of issues and problems is recognized as essential in many areas of study. There is a high regard for reasoning and for intuitive thinking.

What are the social sciences?

The social sciences embrace those disciplines that deal primarily with the study of human relationships. Listed in most classifications are sociology, cultural anthropology, and social psychology—three behavioral sciences which focus directly on the study of man's be-

---

group behavior; (2) methods—precise, rigorous, systematic, replicable; and (3) characteristics—a body of established facts organized within a structure of concepts, generalizations, theories, or models that are useful in providing explanations, making predictions, and guiding further study.

[3] Harold G. Cassidy, *The Sciences and the Arts* (New York: Harper & Row, 1962), p. 3. For a provocative discussion of the sciences and humanities as two cultures, see C. P. Snow, *The Two Cultures: And a Second Look* (New York: New American Library, 1963).

[4] For a stimulating discussion, see Robert A. Nisbet, "Sociology as an Art Form" in *Sociology on Trial,* ed. Maurice Stein and Arthur Vidich (Englewood Cliffs, N.J.: Prentice-Hall, 1963), pp. 148–161.

havior in groups. Also included are political science and economics, parts of which are sometimes referred to as "policy sciences" because of their contributions to decision-making in two basic realms of human endeavor. History may be placed in either the social sciences or the humanities, although some scholars agree with curriculum workers that it is a social science.[5] It should be recognized, however, that history with its imaginative re-creation of the past, a re-creation based on historical facts, "is much closer to the arts than other *sciences* are" [6] (italics added). Geography may be placed in either the physical sciences or the social sciences, depending on the major emphasis, although it is generally recognized that human geography is properly classified as a social science. Philosophy is usually classified with the humanities, but it is included in this volume because it deals with questions of significance in the social studies; and there is increasing recognition of its importance by curriculum workers.[7] Philosophy (the root meaning is love of wisdom) deals with meanings, values, standards, and many other qualitative dimensions of experience and it has in some respects "more kinship with art than with science." [8] But philosophy's kinship with science in general and social science in particular is evident in the logical processes it employs and its deep concern with exploring the human condition. For example, in a discussion of sociology as a humanistic discipline, sociologists have been urged to maintain ongoing communication with other disciplines that focus on the human condition. "The most important of these are history and philosophy." [9] The close relationship of sociology to these two disciplines is illustrated by the common emphasis on the fundamental questions, What does it mean to be a man? and What does it mean to be a man in a particular situation? [10] Similar statements are applicable to the other social sciences included in this

[5] Maurice Boyd and Donald Worcester, *American Civilization: An Introduction to the Social Sciences* (Boston: Allyn and Bacon, 1964).

[6] Abraham Kaplan, *The New World of Philosophy* (New York: Random House, 1961), p. 11.

[7] See the Appendix for a statement from a recently developed social studies guide.

[8] Kaplan, *op. cit.*, p. 369.

[9] Peter L. Berger, *Invitation to Sociology: A Humanistic Perspective* (New York: Doubleday, 1963), p. 168.

[10] *Ibid.*, p. 166.

5

volume.[11]   In fact, a good case can be made for the argument that many of the fundamental problems of any science are philosophical problems.

Another way of viewing knowledge in general and the social sciences in particular is in terms of two broad categories, namely, the arts and the sciences.   The arts, or humanities, deal with man's imaginative and subjective expressions through different forms of art, music, philosophy, and literature.   They tend to focus on individual awareness and experience and to include creative and subjective expression of thoughts and feelings.   The arts as disciplines are concerned more with man's ideas of *what ought to be* rather than with *what is*.   The sciences, on the other hand, deal with *what is* and may be grouped into three subdivisions: (1) physical sciences, which deal with relationships between things and events in the inanimate world, (2) life sciences, which deal with the nature of living things, and (3) behavioral sciences, which focus on human and animal behavior.   In a recent volume, the behavioral sciences, which include the social sciences, have been classified as follows: [12]

Older Fields:	*Anthropology, Sociology, History, Economics, Political Science,* Jurisprudence, *Psychology,* Education
Newer Fields:	Communication Theory—Information Theory, Cybernetics, Linguistics, Sign Behavior
	Preferential Theory—Game Theory, Decision-Making Theory, General Systems Theory

Note that only six of the fields included in this book are listed above under "older fields" (in italics); geography and philosophy are omitted.   Note also that jurisprudence and education are listed above but are omitted from this volume.   Geography and philosophy are included in this volume because human geography contributes much to the essential content of the social studies and philosophy contributes much to the methods of dealing with meanings, values, issues, and problems.   Jurisprudence and education are omitted because their relationship to curriculum planning is different from

[11] For examples see Robert A. Dahl, *Modern Political Analysis* (Englewood Cliffs, N.J.: Prentice-Hall, 1963); D. G. Mandelbaum, G. W. Lasker, and E. M. Albert, *The Teaching of Anthropology* (Berkeley: Univ. of California Press, 1963).
[12] Rollo Handy and Paul Kurtz, *A Current Appraisal of the Behavioral Sciences* (Great Barrington, Mass.: Behavioral Research Council, 1964).

that of other social sciences. The focus in this volume is on the nature of those social sciences from which the substantive portions of the social studies are drawn. Content related to education and jurisprudence that should be included in the curriculum may be treated from the perspective of the political scientist, anthropologist, economist, historian, or sociologist. Scholars in these disciplines typically include relevant content from education and jurisprudence as well as from other disciplines. However, it is hoped that in the near future, education and jurisprudence will be reviewed in the same fashion as have the disciplines that are included in this volume.

Another question is whether or not the newer fields should be included in a volume such as this. At the present time, we do not think so. Psychologists, sociologists, and other scholars in the older fields are in close touch with the newer fields. It is assumed that they will select from the new fields that which is most pertinent to problems in their own disciplines and in turn most appropriate for use in the social studies. The time may come when one or more of the newer fields will have much to offer that cannot be properly synthesized in the older disciplines, but for the present it seems wise to give primary attention to those disciplines which currently are most directly related to the social studies.

Distinctive Characteristics of the Social Sciences

The study of man as a unique living creature may be viewed in two fundamental dimensions: man as an individual and man as a social being. In such disciplines as physiology, physical anthropology, and physiological psychology, some scientists study man as an individual in order to clarify the physical nature of the species *Homo sapiens*. Social scientists study man as a social creature in order to clarify the nature of the group life of man. While the two dimensions overlap in many ways, each is distinctive in its emphasis.

The distinctiveness of the social sciences can be further clarified by considering the broad areas of study which they encompass. As pointed out by social scientists cited at the end of this chapter, the social sciences are focused on the study of:

1. The nature of societies and cultures, and the interactions of people with each other and their social and physical environment.

2. Changes in human relationships, and reinterpretation of relationships between present and past events.
3. Human activities in spatial distributions and the interaction of cultural, biotic, and physical elements.
4. Basic social systems, institutions, and processes.
5. Relationships between individuals and institutions, and among political, economic, and social institutions.

Notice in the previous list that social or group aspects of living are stressed. Notice also the breadth of inquiry which encompasses society and culture, human relationships and institutional relationships, time and space dimensions, social structures and processes, in short, the whole of man in society. This breadth of inquiry requires the use of multiple modes of inquiry, ranging from the purely scientific to the philosophic, in order to provide systematic and rational explanations of human relationships. Because of the breadth of inquiry, the use of multiple modes of inquiry, the complexity of problems which are studied, the difficulty in setting up controlled studies, and the relation of the observer (or researcher) to the observed, the social sciences are among the most difficult and the most challenging areas of study.

In some ways the social sciences are a human counterpart of those life sciences which focus on nonhuman living creatures. Botanists, zoologists, and other life scientists investigate life in the natural world. Social scientists investigate the social world of man, who is unique among living things because he is a thinking, learning, reasoning, communicating, tool-using, tradition-building, worshipping, and culture-bearing creature. The study of this unique creature, man, and the societies in which he lives is marked by both unity and diversity.

Unity and Diversity in the Social Sciences

A tendency toward increasing unity of the social sciences is evident in the common purposes, concepts, and methods of inquiry which may be found in the writings of scholars in different disciplines. For example, a central purpose of many social scientists is to investigate human activities in order to produce descriptions and explanations of group behavior. Illustrative of commonly used concepts are culture, structure, function, social interaction, socialization, input and output, motivation, role, internalization, evolution, adaptation, and ethnocentrism. Methods of inquiry used in the social sciences include the logical procedures involved in defining problems, formulating hypotheses, analyzing and synthesizing data, making comparisons, and drawing and checking conclusions, as well as such techniques as observation, survey, case study, content analysis, interviewing, and field work.[13]

Diversity is evident within each of the social sciences as well as among the social sciences. The interest of each scholar is a prime factor in this diversity and is reflected in his chosen specialization and in his methods of inquiry. Some scholars prefer to engage in studies that require systematic observation and theory building in the mode of the experimental scientist. Other scholars prefer studies that deal with questions and problems not subject to quantitative analysis, studies that require critical reflection and reasoning more in the mode of the humanist. Between these two extremes are scholars who prefer to do studies in the middle range that may not be experimental in nature but which do meet canons of scientific investigation.

Within the social sciences one finds differing points of view, approaches, and theories. Unlike a discipline such as physics in which there is general agreement on basic theory, the social sciences are marked by a variety of theories. Illustrative of this variety are the different theories of learning, personality, historical explanation, economic development, political behavior, and social systems. While a few individuals lament this variety, others believe that it is to be expected because of the late emergence of the social sciences, the complexity of the problems investigated, and the many difficulties involved in studying human behavior in groups.

Within each discipline, however, there are styles of thought, modes of expression, areas of content, and rules of evidence that have distinctive characteristics and set one discipline apart from others. For example, historians as a group place high value on chronology, criticism of source materials, distinctive features of events, and synthesis of data to interpret events and their relation-

---

[13] For a discussion of general methods, see Elgin F. Hunt, *Social Science* (New York: Macmillan, 1961), pp. 20–34; and Bernard Berelson and Gary A. Steiner, *Human Behavior: An Inventory of Scientific Findings* (New York: Harcourt, Brace & World, 1964), pp. 15–35.

ships. Geographers focus on spatial relationships, using concepts from a variety of disciplines to describe and explain distributions within regions and to develop generalizations and theories related to climate, land use, and other topics. Cultural anthropologists place high value on holistic or complete studies of cultures and on the use of participant-observation as a means of gathering first-hand data. Similarly, each of the other disciplines has distinctive features or emphases that give a feeling of community of scholarship to its disciples.

Social Scientists as Scientists

Social scientists as scientists place high importance on public or open review of findings, precise definition of terms, objective collection of data, replicability of findings, use of systematic and cumulative procedures, and development of theories that have explanatory and predictive power.[14] In the role of scientists studying behavior in groups, social scientists investigate *what is* in contrast to *what ought to be* (the categorical in contrast to the normative). The general and abstract levels of inquiry are favored over the concrete and particular in that social scientists want to generalize about the form and pattern, or structure and function, of human interaction.[15]

The data provided by social scientists may be used to make value judgments about human affairs. But when this is done, it is carried on in the mode of the ethicist, classicist, or critic, not in the mode of the scientist. Data from the social sciences also may be used for propaganda purposes by governments, patriotic groups, and others concerned with acceptance or rejection of a particular point of view. In the social studies program, one can find information drawn from the social sciences that has been refashioned for the purpose of developing attitudes and points of view compatible with the values and ideals we cherish. This should be recognized as a

[14] Berelson and Steiner, *Ibid.*

[15] Robert Bierstedt, Eugene J. Meehan, and Paul A. Samuelson, *Modern Social Science* (New York: McGraw-Hill, 1964), pp. 10–11. The opposing terms used in this reference to describe sociology are helpful in describing other disciplines: social vs. natural, categorical vs. normative, pure vs. applied, abstract vs. concrete, generalizing vs. particularizing, rational vs. empirical, general vs. special.

transformation of data, not as social science data in their scientific form. There is no scientific warrant for any form of propaganda or indoctrination in the social sciences if one accepts the view that science consists in objective, ethically neutral, free, and open inquiry.[16] But it is the task of those scholars concerned with ethics, social and political philosophy, or religion to make value judgments. While some social scientists may assume such a role, they do not do so as scientists.

Another feature of social science as science is evident as one considers the emphasis given to pure science as distinct from applied science. Social scientists are primarily interested in pure science. In fact, theory builders in the social sciences stress the importance of pure science and typically avoid applied science even though their theories may contribute to the solution of policy problems, as in economics or political science. Applied science deals with the use of knowledge to solve problems and is represented by such fields as engineering, medicine, nursing, education, and agriculture. In applied fields the emphasis is on applications of ideas, although some contributions may be made to the advancement of pure science by practitioners in applied disciplines. In general, the social scientist as scientist wants to advance knowledge in his domain of study, leaving applications to others.[17]

The search for general principles and the development of theory are characteristics of science that are valued by many social scientists. There is a great range in the social sciences: at the extremes are economics with a large body of theory and so-called laws and political science with only limited theory based on scientific data; in the middle are psychology, sociology, and anthropology. On the other hand, history deals with the unique and particular, and historians usually avoid the development of general laws and principles to explain changes in the past or to predict the future.

Several qualities characterizing the activities of scientists are valued by social scientists. Objectivity, in the sense of basing conclusions on evidence rather than on personal desire or bias, and open-mindedness in considering new evidence are given high priority. A spirit of free and open inquiry is paramount in all of

[16] *Ibid.*
[17] For a good discussion of applications, or reduction to practice, see Cassidy, *op. cit.*, pp. 129–156.

the sciences and it is recognized that critical review by other scientists is essential to the advancement of knowledge. Relativism in the sense of rejecting absolute truths and avoiding authoritarian and ethnocentric tendencies is a hallmark of the social sciences. Skepticism in the sense of questioning conclusions and checking them against evidence is viewed as being essential to the correction of mistakes and the development of valid generalizations. Precision in the use of language is valued and special attention is given to the definition of terms. Both the empirical collection of facts and the rational structuring of theories are recognized as important elements in the study of human relationships. And fact and theory are interrelated as theories are created to bring relevant facts into an explanatory system.

Humanistic Approach

Granted that the emphasis in the social sciences is upon the use of scientific methods to produce knowledge, it is generally recognized that humanistic approaches to knowledge are involved in varying degrees. The humanistic approach is the reflective, critical, subjective study of problems in the modes of the ethicist, classicist, or critic, in contrast to the objective, quantitative, systematic modes of scientists. In considering the social sciences on a scientific-humanistic continuum, most authorities would agree that economics has developed considerable maturity as a social science and would cite as evidence such practices as theory-building, use of models, and quantification of concepts. Similarly, certain areas within psychology, sociology, and anthropology are near the scientific end of the continuum. Toward the humanistic end of the continuum is history, which, as noted earlier, has more kinship with the arts than do other behavioral sciences. Some parts of sociology, anthropology, and political science must certainly be placed on the humanistic side of the continuum.[18]

A major point of confusion has resulted from the failure to recognize the role of imagination, intuitive thinking, or creative thinking in the work of both the scientist and the humanist. Illuminating concepts and seminal ideas are outcomes of the creative

[18] Berger, *op. cit.*; Dahl, *op. cit.*; Mandelbaum, and others, *op. cit.*

thinking of man whether he is working in a laboratory or studio. Flashes of insight are experienced by both scientists and artists. They do not produce new ideas by routinely following research procedures or accepted standards for expressing thoughts and feelings. Through intuitive or creative thinking the great idea is born, and it may be tested in the laboratory or studio through the application of techniques at the command of the scholar. As Nisbet has pointed out, both the scientist and the artist are motivated to understand and interpret reality and to share their understanding and interpretation with the world.[19]

Special, General, and Synthesizing Disciplines

Another way of viewing the social sciences is in terms of the degree of specialization, breadth of inquiry, and emphasis on syntheses of material from other disciplines. Most specialized of all is economics, in which a body of theory has been developed as a relatively distinct area of knowledge. Economics is, of course, intertwined with political science in certain ways and has links to other disciplines, but it is clearly the most independent of the social sciences. Political science, although linked to other disciplines more closely than is economics, is more specialized than cultural anthropology, sociology, history, and social psychology.

Far broader in focus and far more integrating in nature are history, philosophy, and cultural anthropology. History is one of the major synthesizing disciplines.[20] For example, a historian may draw relevant content from various social sciences, and from art, drama, biography, or other sources that contain data needed to recreate and interpret past events. History is indeed a prime integrator of content from the social sciences and the humanities. Cultural anthropology is holistic in scope, dealing with economic, political, and other aspects of culture. It has been characterized as "the generalizing science about all varieties and all aspects of mankind." [21]

[19] Robert A. Nisbet, *op. cit.,* p. 151.

[20] Philip H. Phenix, *Realms of Meaning* (New York: McGraw-Hill, 1964), pp. 233–264.

[21] Douglas L. Oliver, "Cultural Anthropology," in *The Social Studies and the Social Sciences* (New York: Harcourt, Brace & World, 1962), p. 141.

In fact, it has been stated that anthropology is assuming an integrative role for the behavioral sciences, a role that was assumed in the past by philosophy for all of the sciences.[22]   Even the most staunch proponent of integration of the social studies could hardly ask for more.

Human geography is also a synthesizing discipline which, like history, draws much from the social sciences. Unlike history, geography has deep roots in the physical sciences but little or no kinship with the arts. As has been pointed out by an eminent geographer, geography is a prime integrator of the natural and social sciences.[23]

Sociologists recognize the importance of interrelationships as they seek to develop a general science of society. In fact, it has been recommended by a sociologist that students in the schools should develop "an integrated view of society, no matter how elementary this view may be." [24] This recommendation is based on the premise that students should gain an understanding of sociology as "a coherent body of thought," [25] a premise that should not be misconstrued to mean an undisciplined kind of integration.

Psychologists, like sociologists, endeavor "to integrate findings into a coherent body of concepts and principles." [26] Content may be drawn from the biological sciences and from various social sciences in order to secure data essential to an understanding of behavior. Social psychology overlaps sociology to such an extent that it is sometimes difficult to differentiate between the investigations of social psychologists and sociologists. The many common concepts and methods of inquiry used in psychology, cultural anthropology, and sociology are indicative of the interrelationships and broad scope of these three behavioral sciences.

School personnel should recall the general and integrative nature of the disciplines discussed previously as questions arise regarding interrelationships in the social studies. Modern geography and

[22] Mandelbaum, and others, *op. cit.*, p. 589.

[23] George B. Cressey, "Geography," in *High School Social Studies Perspectives* (Boston: Houghton Mifflin, 1962), pp. 84–85.

[24] G. S. Sykes, "Sociology," in *The Scholars Look at the Schools* (Washington, D.C.: National Education Association, 1962), p. 29.

[25] *Ibid.*

[26] W. J. McKeachie, "Psychology," in *The Social Studies and the Social Sciences* (New York: Harcourt, Brace & World, 1962), p. 181.

history are not the *separate and isolated* treatments of human relations that some individuals believe them to be. Similarly, units of instruction that are primarily anthropological or sociological in orientation are not *isolated and separate* studies that provide little or no opportunity for the discovery of relationships. The synthesizing and integrating nature of various social sciences should make it possible to discover interrelationships in the context of the structure of the disciplines. Furthermore, it should be recognized that expertness in the synthesizing of ideas is a scholarly and disciplined activity. When curriculum planners who are not grounded in the disciplines attempt to bring ideas together in integrated form, they may miss truly fundamental interrelationships or create obstacles which will prevent students from gaining insight into the coherent structures in the disciplines—structures that highlight relationships. This is a cogent argument for viewing the social sciences as the foundations of the social studies, a view that is in need of clarification.

The Social Sciences as Foundations of the Social Studies

The social sciences are foundations of the social studies in three distinctive ways.[27] First, the social sciences are primary sources of the content of the social studies: the concepts, generalizations, and methods of inquiry. Second, the social foundations of curriculum planning in the social studies draw data from the social sciences related to societal values, problems, changing conditions, and our democratic heritage. Third, the psychological foundations of curriculum planning in the social studies draw data from the social sciences related to social processes, learning, child development, and other psychological-methodological aspects of instruction.

The fact must not be overlooked that the social sciences are foundations of the social studies in these three ways, but are foundations of other areas of the curriculum in only the latter two ways.

[27] For a detailed discussion, see John U. Michaelis, *Social Studies for Children in a Democracy*, 3d ed. (Englewood Cliffs, N.J.: Prentice-Hall, 1963), pp. 34–67.

Science education, for example, is based on content drawn from the natural sciences but looks to the social sciences for data related to the social and psychological foundations of science education. Similarly, the language arts, mathematics, and other areas of the curriculum have substantive roots in related disciplines but look to the social sciences for data related to the social and psychological foundations.

Difficulties have arisen in the past in social studies planning because of the failure to differentiate the substantive foundation from other foundations of the program. For example, views of the content of the social studies have sometimes been blurred by the admixture of material from the other two foundations. When this occurs, the structure of the curriculum is poorly defined and the substantive portions of the social studies are not rooted solidly in the social sciences. Furthermore, inordinate attention may be given to personal or social problems, fleeting local events, superficial problem solving, or life situations. As a consequence, inadequate attention may be given to fundamental concepts and ideas from the social sciences. What is needed is systematic attention to all three foundations, with relationships among them kept in view, but certainly not any failure or neglect in shaping up the substantive foundations which give the curriculum its basic structure. With this basic structure clearly defined, it is possible to achieve maximum value from the social and psychological foundations in attuning the basic program to societal and individual needs and conditions. The emphasis in this book is clearly on the social sciences as the substantive foundation of the social studies. The other foundations are treated in detail in standard works on the social studies curriculum.

Curriculum Revision Problems

The current trend to ground the social studies firmly in the social sciences has created several problems of concern to teachers and curriculum specialists. A major problem is how to use generalizations from the social sciences in planning the social studies program. Generalizations may be viewed as goals of understanding, long-range outcomes of instruction, and key ideas which students should have on completion of their schooling. Related information, concepts, and subgeneralizations must be identified and incorporated in units of study at different levels of instruction so that there will be continuing progress toward the attainment of generalizations. For example, the generalization "Interdependence is a key factor in human relationships" focuses on the selection of content related to interdependence in studies of the home, neighborhood, and community in the early grades and studies of our state, our nation, and other lands in the later grades. Teaching plans, units of study, and the course of study should be synchronized to keep instruction centered on the development of the generalizations.[28]

Of special concern to teachers is the problem of how to develop concepts and generalizations. Specific procedures for doing so have been outlined in detail.[29] A fundamental principle to remember is that each teacher should provide instruction that contributes to increasing depth and breadth of understanding of the generalizations. Inductive approaches, in which students clarify questions and problems, gather and organize pertinent information, and formulate and check generalizations, are generally preferable to deductive approaches in which efforts are made "to prove generalizations." To be avoided is the teaching of generalizations as conclusions to be memorized. Rather, students must be provided opportunities to study, organize, and interpret information and to develop concepts that add dimensions of meaning to the generalizations. Generalizations of the type included in the following chapters and in the Appendix are high-level abstractions which call for a thorough grounding in the facts and concepts from which they have been derived.

A problem of long standing is the subject matter that should be selected to develop basic generalizations. The authors of the following chapters have not specified a certain body of content for the simple reason that a variety of carefully selected content can be used. For example, in the early grades, pupils may use content related to their own families, communities, and states, different though they may be, and still develop basic generalizations that include such concepts as interdependence, use of resources, and influence of climatic factors. As other lands and peoples are studied, curriculum workers may select from a broad range of countries in Europe, Asia,

[28] *Ibid.,* pp. 40–48, 209–255.
[29] *Ibid.*

the Middle East, Latin America, and Africa. Social scientists or social studies specialists are not in agreement as to the specific content to develop basic concepts and generalizations. But there is agreement on the fundamental principle that related subject matter should be selected and organized so that basic generalizations will be developed as students progress through the instructional program. It is also important for teachers and curriculum workers to understand the nature of the fields of study that are the foundations of the social studies. The primary purpose of this volume is to help school personnel develop this understanding.

In no way should the foregoing statement be misinterpreted to mean that knowledge *of* each social science is less important than knowledge *about* each social science. Both are important! But up to the present time there is no single publication for school personnel that deals with knowledge *about* the social sciences. It is hoped that this book will meet this critical need.

Knowledge *of* each discipline can best be obtained through basic study in the preservice and inservice teacher education programs. To be most helpful this knowledge should be related directly to the units of study in state and local social studies programs. To attempt to meet this need in a single publication designed to acquaint school personnel with the nature of the social sciences would result in a superficial treatment of content which would be of little help to teachers and curriculum specialists.

Another key problem arises as attempts are made to incorporate methods of inquiry from the social sciences in the social studies program. This book should be helpful in meeting the problem because each author suggests methods that are most widely used in the discipline he discusses. The reader will discover that many of them are familiar, e.g., observation, field studies, mapping, interviewing, experimentation, and critical analysis of documents. In addition, the general pattern of inquiry outlined in different chapters is closely related to problem-solving techniques, critical thinking processes, and study skills as they are used in the social studies.[30]

Closely related to the problem of incorporating methods of inquiry in the social studies is the development of those skills and

[30] For example, *Ibid.,* 313–524; and Helen M. Carpenter, ed., *Skill Development in the Social Studies,* Thirty-third Yearbook (Washington, D.C.: National Council for the Social Studies, 1963).

abilities essential to the effective use of instructional materials. For example, the interpretation of maps calls for such abilities as orienting maps, using the legend, using symbols, and making inferences. The critical analysis of documents calls for the use of reading and study skills. Because these skills have been treated in detail in other works, they are not included in this book.[31] The reader will quickly recognize how closely linked they are to the methods of inquiry reported in the following chapters.

Eight Foundation Disciplines

In the chapters that follow, the eight disciplines are discussed that are believed to be essential in planning the substantive foundations of the social studies. Each author has given attention to definitions, major branches, basic concepts, and methods of inquiry of the discipline under review. Brief comments appear at the end of each chapter on the place of the discipline in the social studies. These comments are designed to stimulate discussion in which further implications will be drawn as appropriate in different communities and states.

In addition, each chapter contains highlights that should be noted. These range from specific concepts and significant facts to broad goals of first importance in the discipline. There are sections that contain examples which may be used as models for developing concepts, handling issues, and correcting misconceptions in the social studies. Other sections contain ideas that can be transformed into principles and procedures for use in clarifying the styles of thought of scholars in different areas of study. In several instances, issues and differences in viewpoints that exist within each discipline are reported.

The order of the chapters has been deliberately planned. History is presented first because of its broad perspective, emphasis on relationships, methods of study, and basic importance in the social studies. Geography follows because, like history, it is a synthesizing discipline of basic importance in the social studies. Political science and economics are presented next because they are more

[31] *Ibid.*

specialized than other social sciences, have many links to history and geography, are intertwined in significant ways, and have a solid place in the social studies. Anthropology, sociology, and psychology —three fundamental behavioral sciences—follow. These broad-ranging sciences, with their focus on human behavior, are contributing much to other disciplines and to the social studies. Philosophy is presented last in order to give breadth of perspective to views of knowledge, modes of inquiry, and relationships among disciplines, as well as insights into the nature of philosophy as a discipline. Thus we begin and end the main portion of this volume with the two oldest, synthesizing, disciplines, which employ modes of critical, reflective inquiry and reasoning of central importance in the social studies. The final chapter is a concise review of new developments in the social studies which are illustrative of ways in which programs of instruction are being built on the foundation disciplines.

A special comment should be made about the Appendix, which contains a summary of generalizations prepared as part of a state-wide curriculum project in which attention was given to the same eight disciplines included in this volume. The statements were prepared by teams of scholars and critically reviewed in meetings with school personnel and social studies specialists. The statements are designed to serve as a source of information on generalizations that can be used to plan the social studies curriculum. As each chapter is read, be sure to check the appropriate section of the Appendix and note the similarities and differences in the concepts and generalizations.

It is hoped that the order of presentation will help to clarify the humanistic and scientific features of the social sciences and the many relationships among them, and reveal features that give them distinctiveness. A point to keep in mind as the chapters are read is that the social studies, like the social sciences, should have dimensions and perspectives that bring together the finest of man's intellectual endeavors in both the scientific and humanistic traditions.

The writers were reminded of this point in a recent conversation with a social scientist who reacted to comments about new developments in the social studies as follows:

It seems to me that the current emphasis on basic ideas and methods of inquiry from the social sciences is a good one. But I am concerned about the danger of emphasizing them in a way that does not give students insight into the *spirit* of inquiry and the styles of thought that are so important in the social sciences. For example, I hope that teachers won't shift from one concept or generalization to another in a disconnected manner and use techniques of inquiry as isolated activities. Rather, I hope that they will view concepts and methods of inquiry as interrelated tools of investigation and learning. And above all, I hope that they will help students to appreciate the spirit of inquiry that is characteristic of the social sciences—a unique combination of scientific attitudes and deep concern for the human condition.[32]

The authors of the following chapters have been eminently successful in revealing the spirit of inquiry that characterizes the disciplines with which they are dealing. Each chapter conveys a feeling for the deeper concerns of social scientists and for the attitudes and styles of thought that are characteristic of scholars at work in their areas of special interest. The manner in which the spirit of inquiry is interfused with concepts, themes, generalizations, and methods of inquiry is an outstanding feature of this volume. The reader is urged to identify himself as closely as possible with the styles of thought presented in each chapter so that he can better guide his students "to appreciate the spirit of inquiry that is characteristic of the social sciences—a unique combination of scientific attitudes and deep concern for the human condition."

SUGGESTED READINGS

The following readings have been selected with the special interests of teachers and curriculum specialists in mind. More detailed and technical references are given at the end of following chapters. (Starred items are paperbacks.)

REFERENCES ON SEVERAL SOCIAL SCIENCES

BERELSON, BERNARD, ed., *The Behaviorial Sciences Today* (New York: Basic Books, 1963). A review of present interests in the behavioral sciences.

BERELSON, BERNARD AND GARY STEINER, *Human Behavior: An Inventory of Scientific Findings* (New York: Harcourt, Brace & World, 1964). A summary of generalizations drawn from the behaviorial sciences.

[32] Personal comment to the authors, 1964.

CASSIDY, HAROLD G., *The Sciences and the Arts* (New York: Harper & Row, 1962). Similarities and differences between sciences and arts; relationships among the disciplines.

HANNA, PAUL, and others, *Beyond the Americas,* pp. 14–34 (Teacher's Edition) (Chicago: Scott, Foresman, 1964). Descriptions by social scientists of ways in which geography, history, anthropology, sociology, economics, and government may be incorporated in studies of other lands and peoples.

* *High School Social Studies Perspectives* (Boston: Houghton Mifflin, 1962). Essays on the social sciences and area studies; suggestions for secondary school social studies.

PHENIX, PHILIP H., *Realms of Meaning* (New York: McGraw-Hill, 1964). The social sciences and other disciplines in relation to six realms of meaning; implications for curriculum development.

The Social Studies and the Social Sciences (New York: Harcourt, Brace & World, 1962). Essays on the social sciences and area studies; suggestions for secondary school social studies.

* SOWARDS, WESLEY G., ed., *The Social Studies: Curriculum Proposals for the Future* (Chicago: Scott, Foresman, 1963). Stimulating essays on the social sciences, elementary and secondary social studies, structure in the social sciences, and future needs.

WHITE, CARL M. and Associates, *Sources of Information in the Social Sciences* (Totawa, N.J.: Bedminster Press, 1964). Concise descriptions of selected social sciences accompanied by detailed guides to the literature on social science, history, economics and business administration, sociology, anthropology, psychology, education, and political science.

* ZNANIECKI, FLORIAN, *Cultural Sciences* (Urbana: Univ. of Illinois Press, 1963). The origin, development, and status of social sciences with emphasis on sociology.

HISTORY

* CARR, E. H., *What Is History?* (New York: Alfred A. Knopf, 1962).

SMITH, PAGE, *The Historian and History* (New York: Alfred A. Knopf, 1964).

* NEVINS, ALLAN, *The Gateway to History* (Garden City, N.Y.: Doubleday, 1962).

GEOGRAPHY

HARTSHORNE, RICHARD, *Perspective on the Nature of Geography* (Chicago: Rand McNally, 1959).

PATTISON, WILLIAM D., "The Four Traditions of Geography," *Journal of Geography,* 63:211–216, 1964.

WARNTZ, WILLIAM, *Geographers and What They Do* (New York: Franklin Watts, 1964).

POLITICAL SCIENCE

BIERSTEDT, ROBERT, E. J. MEEHAN, AND P. A. SAMUELSON, *Modern Social Science* (New York: McGraw-Hill, 1964), Part 2, The Political Order.

* DAHL, ROBERT A., *Modern Political Analysis* (Englewood Cliffs, N.J.: Prentice-Hall, 1963).

* HACKER, ANDREW, *The Study of Politics: The Western Tradition and American Origins* (New York: McGraw-Hill, 1963).

ECONOMICS

* COMMITTEE FOR ECONOMIC DEVELOPMENT, *Economic Education in the Schools* (New York: Joint Council on Economic Education, 1961).

SAMUELSON, PAUL A., *Economics: An Introductory Analysis,* 6th ed. (New York: McGraw-Hill, 1964).

WRONSKI, STANLEY P., and others, *Modern Economics* (Boston: Allyn and Bacon, 1964).

ANTHROPOLOGY

* ASHLEY MONTAGU, M. F. *The Science of Man* (New York: Odyssey Press, 1964).

HOEBEL, E. ADAMSON, *Man in the Primitive World,* pp. 3–13 (New York: McGraw-Hill, 1958).

* OLIVER, DOUGLAS L., *Invitation to Anthropology* (Garden City, N.Y.: The Natural History Press, 1964).

SOCIOLOGY

FARIS, ROBERT E. L., *Handbook of Modern Sociology* (Chicago: Rand McNally, 1964).

* INKELES, ALEX, *What Is Sociology?* (Englewood Cliffs, N.J.: Prentice-Hall, 1964).

* STEIN, MAURICE AND ARTHUR VIDICH, eds., *Sociology on Trial* (Englewood Cliffs, N.J.: Prentice-Hall, 1963).

PSYCHOLOGY

ENGLE, T. L., *Psychology: Its Principles and Applications,* 4th ed. (New York: Harcourt, Brace & World, 1964).

McKEACHIE, W. J., "Psychology," in *The Social Studies and the Social Sciences,* pp. 171–190 (New York: Harcourt, Brace & World, 1962).

RUSSELL, ROGER W., *Frontiers in Psychology* (Chicago: Scott, Foresman, 1964).

PHILOSOPHY

HULLFISH, H. G. AND P. G. SMITH, *Reflective Thinking: The Method of Education* (New York: Dodd, Mead, 1961).

KAPLAN, ABRAHAM, *The New World of Philosophy* (New York: Random House, 1961).

NATANSON, MAURICE, ed., *Philosophy of the Social Sciences: A Reader* (New York: Random House, 1963).

2   History

Ralph W. Haskins
Department of History
University of Tennessee

What Is History?

"HISTORY," WROTE EDWARD GIBBON, IN ONE OF HIS MORE CYNICAL moods, "is indeed little more than the register of the crimes, follies, and misfortunes of mankind." [1]   "History," declared a schoolboy, "is hard work."   The one remark was plain exaggeration, the other sheer realism.   But the views of the author of *The Decline and Fall of the Roman Empire* looking down from his lofty summit and of the student standing at the bottom of the hill suggest the vast compass of the word "history."   Even the most casual examination of opinion past and present shows that the term has meant many things to many men.   Our inquiry into the meaning of history might be prefaced by a series of questions: What does the dictionary say about it?   How do the historians themselves define it?   What is "history" in college courses?   What are the main goals of the historian?   With what kinds of data does he work?   And what things lie outside the scope of history?

---

[1] Edward Gibbon, *The Decline and Fall of the Roman Empire* (London: 1776–1788). See also Modern Library Edition (New York: Random House, 1932), p. 59.

Some definitions of history

In one sense, history is a narrative of events, an exposition which tells how these events unfolded. History can be the annals of a nation, a society, or a social group. History is also a systematic written account of events which affect a nation, an institution, or a social group, and an account usually connected with a philosophical explanation of causes. Thus, it can be both narrative and interpretative. In still another way, history is described as the branch of knowledge that records and explains past events as an aggregate or as steps in human progress. In short, the dictionary defines history as a descriptive or analytical record of the human past.

Concepts of history have varied through the ages. To the Greeks, who originated the word *historia* (information or research) in Western culture, it first signified an inquiry or investigation. They subsequently identified it as both the inquiry and the record of its results. The Chinese of antiquity likewise appear to have conceived of history as a record of events. In the Middle Ages, when men placed more emphasis upon the future than upon the past, history was less an account of nations, societies, or individuals than the unfolding of a divine plan. In more modern times, it has become once more the study of the human past.

Ironically enough in an age which demands precise terminology, historians continue to disagree about the meaning of history. A few avoid any definition, while others speak in very general terms. For one it is the knowledge of things said and done, while another calls it "the past of mankind," and a third asserts that "the only possible answer is that history is the study of all past human activities." [2] Of course there are more elaborate explanations. "The object of the study of history," says the French scholar Henri Pirenne, "is the development of human societies in space and in time." [3] And Edward H. Carr, in a series of lectures called *What Is History?*, describes it as both the investigation conducted by the

[2] Louis Gottschalk, *Understanding History: A Primer of Historical Method* (New York: Alfred A. Knopf, 1950), p. 41; Joseph R. Strayer, ed., *The Interpretation of History* (New York: Peter Smith, 1950), p. 6.

[3] Quoted in E. R. A. Seligman and Alvin Johnson, eds., *Encyclopaedia of the Social Sciences* (New York: Macmillan, 1930–1935), Vol. VII, p. 358.

historian and the series of past events which he investigates, "the serious process of enquiry into the past of man in society, an unending dialogue between the present and the past." [4] Let us say that history, the study of the evolution of human society, investigates, records, and interprets for the present events of social significance. Thus, history is event, record, and process.

History in the college

The variety of college courses, ranging from the survey to the seminar, shows the broad scope of history. At the lowest level are the elementary surveys which deal with Western civilization, the United States, the Americas, Africa, or Asia, and which reflect a common method of organization around continents. Africa and Asia are comparative newcomers here, a testimony to their increasing significance in the world. Some institutions offer "intermediate" surveys concerned with "families" of nations (the Atlantic community) or with areas which share an important relationship if not necessarily a common heritage (the West and the Far East). In general, the survey emphasizes breadth rather than depth, an overview rather than a detailed treatment.

The advanced course, a more intensive examination of a segment of the field, may consider large time spans (ancient, medieval, or modern history), shorter periods (the United States in the nineteenth century, the French Renaissance, or the English Reformation), countries, institutions (the medieval Church, the Hapsburg Monarchy), and peoples (interpretations of the American character, history of the Jews in Europe). The degree of specialization is indicated by constitutional history, a study of government which is focused on institutions; diplomatic history, the story of relations between states; military and naval history, the analysis of warfare and its related problems; colonial history, the expansion of nations beyond their normal boundaries; social history, which places more emphasis on the history of the people in general and less upon the role of politics and the state; economic history, a close relative but one which pays particular attention to the material basis of life; and various titles

[4] Edward Hallett Carr, *What Is History?* (New York: Alfred A. Knopf, 1962), pp. 35, 59.

such as cultural history, intellectual history, or the history of ideas, all of which center on the evolution of thought. Now and then a course in biography reminds one of the "great man" theory of history. In the United States, regional studies (the West, the South, the Pacific Northwest, the old Northwest, or New England) are common fare. These are based upon the geographic concept of the region with its interdependence, as well as upon the historical concept of sectionalism with its rivalries. Courses in state history reflect another American heritage and the recognition of urbanism is shown in Columbia University's course, History of the City of New York. Far too seldom does one find undergraduate courses, such as Interpretations of History, which delve into the meaning and nature of the subject. Increasing awareness of the link between history and other disciplines is demonstrated by courses like History of Science, History of Religion, History of Education, and History of the Social Sciences, as well as in various "area" programs which involve a number of fields and are generally called American, Latin American,[5] Asian, African, or Slavic studies.

The most typical graduate course, usually known as a seminar, stresses first-hand investigation of historical materials under professorial direction, and may be an intensive study of historians, historical method, or theory of history, or may center on a phase of one of the myriad of subjects mentioned previously. Edward Freeman's announcement that "history is past politics and politics is present history," so appealing in its own time, seems clearly dated. In one way or another, college history courses touch most aspects of the human past.

Main goals of the historian

The historian's primary purpose is to interpret the present through an understanding of the past and in so doing to chart a general course for the future. Other goals follow from his interest in these time spans. At this point we are concerned with a general statement designed to shed further light on the meaning of history and

[5] The program of Latin American studies at the University of California at Los Angeles, for example, includes history, Spanish and Portuguese, geography, anthropology, economics, political science, sociology, folklore, linguistics and philology. Some of these courses are requirements, others optional.

to serve as an introduction to a later discussion of the importance of the field.

In his analysis of the human record, the historian hopes to describe the past as accurately as possible. Ideally, he may search for the truth *wie es eigentlich gewesen ist,* or "as it really happened," to use the classic statement of Leopold von Ranke, the "father of scientific history." Ranke and his school believed in letting the facts speak for themselves. Yet it is a goal never realized, for the past is a complexity of the true, the near-true, and the false. All the historian can hope to do is to approximate the truth through a comprehensive account based upon his research and his interpretations. But Ranke's bright vision remains an ideal and the pursuit of truth an obligation.

Closely akin is the goal of objectivity, the impartial reporting of the past, and like the passion for truth a heritage of the nineteenth century. But historians, like other human beings, are subjective; they cannot "extinguish the self." They have an interest, a point of view, a frame of reference. The dictum that each generation rewrites its own history has been verified countless times. And the dry bones of fact mean nothing unless they are clothed with the imagination of the historian. Yet he must try to be as objective as possible by recognizing and trying to control the effects of subjectivity.

One of the historian's chief tasks is the analysis of change over periods of time. He is not interested in chronology as such, for chronology means little without interpretation. By exhibiting successive societies in action, history gives us definite impressions of society in the past, of its processes, and of the role of social problems as a factor in producing change. Thus, the historian contributes to an understanding of human nature in history.

In interpreting the past the historian tries to achieve a balance, a happy medium between facts and interpretation, between the individual and the group, between societies and civilizations, between the familiar and the strange, and between thought and action. If history is to be a practical science, it cannot be content with mere narrative, the what, when, and where; it must also interpret the how and why, the cause and effect. The individual is not to be submerged in the stream of history; yet history is far more than collective biography. A broadening point of view is seen in the increasing study of whole civilizations as well as particular countries. Change is an inescapable force in our lives; but with change we must recognize elements of the past and present as they are projected into the future. Most historians would not accept R. G. Collingwood's thesis that all history is the history of thought; [6] but they realize that what contemporaries *thought* about their own times may often be as important as what they *did*. The War of 1812 was not quite the glorious triumph acclaimed by that generation; yet the psychology of victory was a vital element in postwar nationalism.

Is the historian a prophet? Can history be used to foretell the future? Employed with care, it is a valuable guide. It offers analogies between wars: the Peloponnesian War of the Greek world, the international conflicts of the eighteenth century, and the global wars of the present. There is a cold war nowadays but there was also a "cold war" between North and South, a conflict which began many years before 1861 but was also the dominant theme of the period between the secession of South Carolina in December 1860, and the firing on Fort Sumter in April 1861. For the Negro slave, the outcome of the Civil War was the "day of jubilo"; yet even a contemporary observer might readily have predicted that it would be many years before the Negro reached a status of equality. The analyst of the Progressive Movement, knowing the historic attitudes of the bourgeoisie and seeing the middle-class orientation of reform in the early twentieth century, could have suggested that its legislation would be moderate rather than radical.

Still, prediction in history had greater possibilities in earlier times, when the basic order of the past resembled that of the present and was more likely to extend into the future. The twentieth century is revolutionary in nature, its tempo infinitely faster, its time span of continuity shorter; so the use of history in long-range forecasting is much less practical. Those who dream the dream of prophecy would do well to heed Toynbee's observation that history can perhaps show us possibilities or even probabilities but never certainties.[7] The future is a tortuous path with some familiar signposts but never a broad, well-marked avenue.

[6] R. G. Collingwood, *The Idea of History,* ed. T. M. Knox (New York: Oxford Univ. Press, 1956), p. 231 *passim.*

[7] Pieter Geyl and Arnold Toynbee, "Can We Know the Pattern of the Past?—A Debate," in *Theories of History,* ed. Patrick Gardiner (New York: The Free Press of Glencoe, 1959), p. 317.

Finally, although the historian's research leads him naturally toward the concrete and the particular, eventually he cannot help generalizing about his findings; and the result is the evolution or reiteration of some larger theme of history. But the search for a synthesis is more than idle speculation; a principle of utility is involved. Joseph Strayer reminds us that "history must be a guide to action, not an excuse for contemplation." [8] Raising fundamental questions about the nature of history in the interest of interpreting human society is indeed a legitimate goal of the historian.

The historian and his data

"What a very curious and instructive study it is to note some of the materials of which History is made," observed a North Carolinian nearly a century ago. Intent upon turning her readers into writers of history, she went on to say that "a fragment of a letter, a street ballad, an obscure and anonymous pamphlet,—the fag-end of a sonnet or a satire,—and in one case at least, a rude description on the bark of a tree, have furnished suggestions, hints, and dates, and have supplied what was wanting to legislative summaries, official acts and correspondence and formal State papers." [9] That such a statement appeared in the "Young Lady's Column" of a religious journal is in itself a curious and instructive study. Here was a woman with a sense of history.

For the most part, she was speaking of written records; but the historian works with materials of all kinds. There are human remains, the "archives of the earth," which belong more properly, but not exclusively, to the archaeologist and the anthropologist. There are the physical remains created by man: roads, bridges, fortifications, buildings, tools, pottery, coins, and weapons. A third type of record might be called institutional, representing an enormous mass of customs, habits, games, ceremonies, and religions—all of them examples of the continuity of history. The modern Olympic Games perpetuate an ancient Greek tradition; four days of the week are named for Norse gods; and the practice of carrying a bride across the threshold reminds us of the days when brides were literally stolen. There are orally transmitted records in the form of myths, legends, ballads,

[8] Strayer, *op. cit.*, p. 5.
[9] Louis R. Wilson, ed., *Selected Papers of Cornelia Phillips Spencer* (Chapel Hill: Univ. of North Carolina Press, 1953), p. 124.

folklore, and superstitions. Originating as a series of tales passed on from mouth to mouth, the story of the Trojan War eventually became Homer's *Iliad,* so inspiring that Heinrich Schliemann realized a boyhood dream by unearthing not one but several Troys, layers of civilization. In our own history the southern legend of the Lost Cause seems but an abstraction of the mind; but no serious historian can deny its significance since Appomattox. The forest of myth that has grown up around the towering figure of Lincoln once prompted a college student to declare that Lincoln was born in a log cabin which he built with his own hands.

The evolution of the art of writing, one of the common dividing lines between history and prehistory, opened up a store of materials ranging from the papyrus and other writing of antiquity to the letter and other manuscripts of a later day. A second great change came with the perfection of printing in the fifteenth century and the multiplication of books and papers. Among the written records are chronicles, annals, biographies, memoirs, and diaries, as well as letters, public documents, and private papers such as those of business firms. Though the classification is not always hard-and-fast, the historian divides his materials into primary and secondary sources. The former are accounts by eyewitnesses or contemporaries, surviving objects from the time, diaries, letters, and newspaper reports of current events. Secondary materials include historical accounts written by persons who have either studied the primary sources or have used the works of those who did. In this category are monographs, textbooks, and the histories of countries. In our day another revolution in communications has invested orally transmitted records with a new significance. The historian can now avail himself of the data provided through radio, television, and tape recording. A pioneer effort in the field of tapes and one worthy of emulation, is the Oral History Project of Columbia University.

Upon occasion the historian uses personal observation in the form of an interview or a visit to a historic site. The late Herbert E. Bolton of the University of California was famous for his trips on horseback, pioneer journeys in which, equipped with map and diary, he traced the footsteps of Spanish explorers. Just as remarkable was Samuel Eliot Morison's preparation for his *Admiral of the Ocean Sea.* In 1939, the Harvard historian, carrying with him the records of Columbus and others, undertook to follow as nearly as possible the exact routes taken by the great discoverer. Of course, such field work, resembling that of the geographer or the geologist, cannot recapture the past as it was; but how much greater the historian's feeling for his subject and how much richer the approximate truth that he reaches.

In the last two centuries the historian's materials have been multiplied by the emergence of public archives, the increase of private collections, the work of historical societies, and government assistance to history. Fellow scientists have contributed almost immeasurably to an enrichment of the historian's sources and have added significantly to his techniques, sometimes even to the point of contributing their own appraisals of history. At one end of the scale, our knowledge of prehistory has been increased by the archaeologists, the anthropologists, and others; at the opposite end, the student of the twentieth century is confounded by the vast mass of documentation available. He may well envy the historian of bygone days his relative ignorance of his subject. Letter and pamphlet, ballad and book, satire and sonnet are but a part of the bottomless reservoir of history.

The limited scope of history

In saying that the essence of history is its involvement with the past, we have sketched a heroic canvas. The average man can know only an infinitesimal fragment of history and the historian can know relatively little more. It staggers the mind to conceive of the events that take place within the space of a single hour. History is indeed a mosaic beyond the imagination—but it is not everything.

Is history the whole past, the study of all events? Do natural phenomena, such as geological changes, earthquakes, and tidal waves, come within its scope? In general, no; unless they affect man they are mainly of interest to the geologist, the geographer, and others. On the other hand, such a natural catastrophe as the Black Death, which spread over Europe in the fourteenth century and affected great masses of humanity, comes within the domain of history. History is concerned mostly with the changing *human* past.

How far back in time does history go? Are Darwin's organisms, wriggling in primordial slime and man's ancestors in the evolutionary process, part of the stuff of history? It is doubtful. Though the life of earlier cultures was often exceedingly complex, the eras prior to the appearance of written records are prehistory and lie primarily within the domain of the archaeologist and the anthropologist. History is essentially the story of *civilized* man.

Is history a science or an art? J. B. Bury's assertion that it is "simply a science, no less and no more," [10] represents one point of view in a time-worn controversy. It might be called "a science of reasoning" rather than an exact science. It cannot reproduce events at will. Unlike the scientist, the historian must rely on evidence originating beyond his own experience. The element of humanity makes history far less predictable than science. And history lacks fixed terminology. Even though it has borrowed words and phrases from the other sciences, it speaks the language of the average man in an age of "special and private languages and sub-languages." [11] "Civilization," "liberty," and "progress" are flexible in their application. Nor are there "laws" in history in the sense that there are laws in science.

Yet history does use the scientific method. President Truman once commented that "if science is defined as a methodological effort to find the facts, then history is the greatest of the sciences." [12] The historian's process is empirical, involving the framing and testing of hypotheses as well as the collection, systematic observation, and classification of facts. If the historian is concerned with such elusive entities as nations, societies, classes, and eras, the scientist is occupied with his own imponderables. If the scientist in his laboratory deals concretely with materials, the historian also deals with individuals and specific events. Though there are no "laws" of history, historic events follow the same natural laws as the objects of science.

History is in a number of ways both a science and an art. As Jacques Barzun says, "the historian is an exact reporter working in the realm where the concrete and the imponderable meet." [13] Spec-

[10] J. B. Bury, "The Science of History," in *Selected Essays,* ed. Harold Temperley (New York: Cambridge Univ. Press, 1930), pp. 3–22.

[11] Philip Graham, quoted in Washington *Post,* August 11, 1963.

[12] R. G. Cowherd, "Mr. Truman's Uses of History," in *Social Studies,* L (April), 147, 1959.

[13] Jacques Barzun and Henry F. Graff, *The Modern Researcher* (New York: Harcourt, Brace & World, 1957), p. 15.

ulation on the subject proves once more that history is controversy; and nowhere is this more apparent than in the domain of ideas.

Ideas and History

As one reviews the events of the past, it is natural to generalize and to draw conclusions. They may be an evaluation of one's school experience, residence in a certain locale, or even one's whole life; or one may view one's own generation in perspective. Such conclusions may be merely contemplative or they may have a practical meaning. The historian follows a similar process in posing his hypotheses, collecting and arranging his materials, and interpreting his findings. Eventually he reaches a synthesis: he sees general and specific history as a part of universal history. He may view the past through rose-colored glasses or he may become a prophet of doom. A Benedetto Croce hails liberty as the great impulse of history, an Oswald Spengler composes a requiem for Western civilization. Ideas, large or small, are "the threads which bind the minds of men together sufficiently for joint action to occur." [14]

As a general guide to the multitude of ideas from antiquity to the present day, let us say that they vary as the life and spirit of different ages vary: each nation and age is dominated by its prevalent set of ideas. An era in which religion is the all-pervading theme will most certainly demand a religious rationale; a people drawn by the lodestone of nationalism may stress the role of great leadership; a century marked by a scientific revolution will very likely view history in scientific terms. We have an enormous backlog of "key ideas." With the passage of time, such central themes are often abandoned but just as often they persist, like legends, as relics of the past. Like legends, they have their value.

Some older ideas

Jacques Barzun points out that the common man, with his basic concept of "popular history," tends to oversimplify ideas; [15] but it is also

[14] Carl G. Gustavson, *A Preface to History* (New York: McGraw-Hill, 1955), p. 153.
[15] Jacques Barzun, "History, Popular and Unpopular," in Strayer, *op. cit.*, p. 31 *passim*.

interesting to observe that historians and other thinkers have found it difficult to resist the same temptation. For centuries it was widely believed that history represented the unfolding of a divine plan. Of a later vintage was the idea that men, and particularly outstanding men, determine the course of history. A never-ending polemic has centered around the question of which is more important, man or nature. Still other points of view have seen history as determined chiefly by economics or politics or some other single factor. Twentieth-century thought is skeptical of the one-factor approach but such ideas have contributed significantly to the fabric of history and we shall return to some of them in discussing historical theories. As a sample of these deterministic ideas, let us devote some brief space to the question of laws in history.

An incidence of the scientific revolution in the eighteenth and nineteenth centuries was the idea that history operated according to fixed scientific laws. The findings of Newton and others had established the existence of laws in nature; and what was true in nature must be true of the affairs of mankind. In the wake of the Age of Reason, with its search for a "natural order" in economics, in religion, in government, and in society as a whole, such theorists as the Englishman Henry Thomas Buckle predicated a series of "laws" of historical development. Laws of nature, said Buckle, not altogether illogically, were strongest in primitive society and weakest in advanced civilizations.[16] In the same century, the pessimist Brooks Adams wrote a book entitled *The Law of Civilization and Decay*. These and other attempts to formulate laws were based upon the fallacy that history is an exact science.

However, both technology and our broadened knowledge of man and his tendencies are making history more and more scientific. We can now ascertain general tendencies or patterns in religious movements and in the course of revolutions. Though the specific events of the English, American, French, Russian, and other revolutions are not exactly alike, general patterns which resemble "laws" are apparent. If we do not insist upon exactness but rather approximation, the idea has some validity. This is not the same as saying that history repeats itself. Frederic L. Paxson once suggested

[16] Harry Elmer Barnes, *A History of Historical Writing*, 2d ed. (New York: Dover Publications, 1962), p. 202.

that "history just staggers and *thinks* it repeats itself." One must always remember that the historian's theme is humanity and that he must always take into account the vagaries of free will and the fortuitous. That France went from Bourbon absolutism seems to be a case of history repeating itself; but the France of Napoleon was not the France of Louis XVI. And who could have foreseen that the new despot would come from the rocky isle of Corsica? History has its recurring patterns but it is no treadmill.

Ideas now in vogue

Our own age is one of introspection and historical self-criticism, a period somewhat analogous to that which followed the upheavals produced by the French Revolution and the Napoleonic Wars. One factor which has contributed to the self-searching of the present day is the broadening and deepening of knowledge. Because of the progress of technology, we know more about human affairs than at any other time in history. Yet it is widely believed that the human mind has not been able to keep pace with the march of science. In trying to explain the confusion of present thought, one must also consider the shattering effect of cataclysmic events: two world wars, a great depression, and the cold war. For the world in general and for historical thinking in particular, ours is a period of crisis, and a period all the more challenging because the public is more conscious of history than ever. It is in this context that we must view some of the ideas now in vogue.

Perhaps one reflection of the instability of the present day is the belief that history seems to be governed by chance and fate rather than by providence and reason. Despite all that has been said and written about the logic of history, its focus on humanity makes it uncertain. So much are historians given to speculating about chance that a critic once asked facetiously: "If Cleopatra's nose had been shorter, would the course of history have been different?"

In much the same tenor is the idea that history is relative. "Whatever a given age or people believes to be true *is* true for that age and that people," said William A. Dunning many years ago,[17]

[17] William A. Dunning, *Truth in History and Other Essays* (New York: Columbia Univ. Press, 1937), p. 17.

and such writers as Carl Becker, Charles A. Beard, and others have also subscribed to this theory.[18] The relativist position has been summarized by Harry Elmer Barnes in his *History of Historical Writing:* (1) Historical events are so complex that no one can reconstruct the past exactly as it was; (2) accepted historical truth at any one time depends as much upon the mental climate of that particular period as upon the facts to be interpreted; (3) each generation rewrites its own history; and (4) truth will shift from time to time because of emotional factors.

A glance at interpretations of American involvement in World War I demonstrates that there is much to be said for this viewpoint. The immediate reason for our entry was Germany's resumption of unrestricted submarine warfare but the underlying causes admit of no simple generalization, and interpretations since have varied with the times. A historian writing against the immediate background might stress the role of idealism and the mission of America; but some interpreters during the cynical twenties and early thirties focused their attention on the part played by British propaganda. In the throes of the Great Depression, when capitalism itself seemed to be on trial, some writers turned to the role of Big Business and the "merchants of death." A historian of the present day, given our preoccupation with security, might regard security as the prime reason; or, in the light of our investigations into the human mind, he might see attitudes as more important.

A contrasting dictum holds that the study of history reveals truth, continuity, and progress. Of course, the idea of progress is not new. It was a part of the glow of optimism produced by centuries of advance in Western civilization. The Age of Discovery had broadened the horizon and projected the expansion of Europe over the globe; the achievements of science had ushered in the Age of Reason, with its unlimited faith in the capabilities of man; and the giant strides of the Industrial Revolution had contributed to his material well-being. It was a time of peace, for there were no gen-

[18] For example, see Carl Becker, "Detachment and the Writing of History," in *Atlantic Monthly,* CVI (October), 425–436, 1910, and Charles A. Beard, "Written History as an Act of Faith," *American Historical Review,* XXXIX (January), 219–229, 1934. For strictures on the theory, see James C. Malin, *On the Nature of History* (Lawrence, Kansas: The Author, 1954), Ch. 1.

eral wars after the fall of Napoleon. The theories of Darwin, though disturbing, seemed upon reflection to be further proof that history was evolving toward the perfection of man's estate on earth. By 1900 the doctrine of progress had become a cult.

The storms of the twentieth century have clouded the rosy visions of the past. Progress no longer appears to be inevitable; indeed, it is fashionable to substitute "change" for "progress." Yet history is not exclusively chaos or change; on the contrary, it shows a degree of observable order and pattern.[19] Relativism does not prevent us from sharing common assumptions with other peoples. For example, a comparative appraisal of civilizations shows certain constants, not only in moral codes but in notions of justice and in the use of such basic social functions as education, transportation, and communication. And progress has never advanced in a straight line toward some clearly defined goal; the ground gained by one generation may be lost by another. Yet there has been progress through the transmission of acquired skills from one generation to the next. The historical record demonstrates biological and cultural evolution from a bestial state. And if everything is relative, what of our values and standards?

As significant as any idea today is the belief that history is determined by a combination of factors rather than by one dominating influence. Historians pay more attention to balance and proportion. They consider all elements: great men play a role in history but a mass society must be taken into consideration; not only political and economic but social and cultural factors are significant; and both national values and international influences are a part of the picture. The historian of today is more than ever aware of the labyrinths of history.

A problem in ideas: interpretations of the American Revolution

Ideas in the broader realm of general history are also reflected in the American experience by some of the more significant findings

[19] There is a particularly pertinent discussion of the question of progress in Carr, *op. cit.,* Ch. 5.

related to the American Revolution, the genesis of our own nation and the first of a series of such upheavals in modern times.

American involvement in war is a perennial subject of controversy. No conflict, and least of all the Revolution, has escaped the close scrutiny of the historian. The older patriotic or "Whig" interpretation derived mainly from the work of George Bancroft, author of the first multivolume history of the United States.[20] Writing in the years when the Civil War was transforming the federal Union into an American nation, Bancroft partook of the romantic nationalism characteristic of that period; and his history, in recalling the common revolutionary heritage, responded admirably to the demands of its own time. To his highly moral way of thinking, the course of history was part of a divine plan, and the Revolution was another great step in human progress. Most of the virtues lay on one side of the ocean. Here was an uprising of colonists who saw their freedom threatened by a foreign power ruled by George III, an evil tyrant working in collusion with a nest of reactionaries in Parliament. Long suffering under the burden of controls dictated by the principle that "the colonies exist for the good of the mother country," Americans after 1763 were deprived of the right of self-government, and their only recourse was to sever ties with the oppressor. The older school viewed the Revolution as arising mainly from political factors which centered around the question of taxation without representation.

It was an inspiring tradition and one which has colored popular thinking up to the present day. But later historians have raised grave doubts that the Revolution was simply a struggle between liberty and oppression, between people who wanted freedom and people who wanted hegemony. Twentieth-century writers are in general agreement that the subject is far more complex and are inclined to believe that the Revolution was the result of a combination of forces, but they have by no means reached a consensus upon the causes.

The motivation behind changing points of view is not always clear. That a more acute awareness of the complexity of human actions contributed is beyond doubt; that the increasing interest in a

---

[20] George Bancroft, *History of the United States from the Discovery of the Continent* (Boston: Little, Brown, 1834–74).

larger Anglo-Saxon civilization played a part seems likely; that the rapprochement between the United States and England during the forty years preceding World War I had some influence is possible. The perfection of critical methods of research was an important factor.

The "Imperial School" of historians lifted the Revolution out of the context of national history and placed it in the larger setting of a world struggle for empire. The pioneers in this widening of horizons were George Louis Beer and Charles M. Andrews. In the course of his four-volume history of the colonial period, Andrews insisted that the issue was colonial rather than national, and that a long, silent, and peaceful revolution preceded the Declaration of Independence. His student, Lawrence Henry Gipson, author of the monumental *British Empire before the Revolution,* maintained that the struggle followed logically from the British attempt to reorganize colonial government. Yet one cannot say that the various historians of this persuasion, whether British or American, are in agreement on all particulars.

Moreover, the appearance of the imperial version coincided with a conflicting interpretation. The great advance of the Industrial Revolution and the resulting acceleration of material progress were accompanied by a vogue in the economic interpretation of history, and it was only natural that the thesis was applied to the coming of the American Revolution. If not necessarily the progenitor of this line of thought, Charles A. Beard was certainly one of its outstanding exponents. In the first volume of his *The Rise of American Civilization,* Beard viewed the crisis as a clash of economic interests between the colonies and the mother country but also as rivalry between colonial and mercantile groups within the colonies. Beard's own times undoubtedly influenced his outlook. It was a period in which the Progressive Movement dominated by the middle class had followed hard upon the heels of agrarian populism in protest against the old order of the day. Of the same background was Arthur M. Schlesinger, Sr., for whom the Revolution, initiated by the colonial merchants, came to be dominated by the common man, that is, the town workers and the yeomanry. Amid these strong winds of economic determinism, Andrews protested that "it is too great a simplification of history to regard the events of the past as nothing but a struggle of classes, a clash of economic interests, for such an oversimplification of the problem leads inevitably to an oversimplified solution." [21]

With the passage of years, the open forum on the Revolution has come to resemble a New England town meeting in perpetual session. Though the representatives of the Imperial School continued to urge the logic of their position, Beard's general thesis came into such wide acceptance that it appeared supreme at the beginning of World War II. Nevertheless, it has had its adversaries both then and now. Among them are the biographers, who reacted against the discounting of contributions by Washington and other figures of the Great Generation and were at pains to re-establish the importance of individuals in the struggle with England. Others, elaborating on a Beardian premise no longer novel, regarded the Revolution as a dual process, an outer struggle with England and an inner struggle among Americans; not merely a question of home rule but a matter of who was to rule at home. The latter-day phase of the historic seesaw between conservative and liberal points of view has taken the form of a re-examination of the revolutionary mind: on one side, it is asserted that Americans were basically conservative; on the other, that they were fundamentally in favor of increased democracy.

This mélange of interpretations shows many of our larger ideas in action. In Bancroft, we see the wonder-working hand of divine providence; in the Imperial School, an emphasis upon the greater issue of a government for British civilization; in Beard, the role of economic causation; and in the biographers, a faint echo of the Great Man thesis. The excursion into the nuances of colonial thought is a reminder of John Adams' theory that the Revolution began in the hearts and minds of the people.

If modern interpreters more often see the struggle as the outcome of forces rather than the actions of men, it is intriguing to note that their more sophisticated approach does not altogether preclude a belief in human motivation. If Bancroft had his heroes and villians, so does Schlesinger, with his common men pitted against the merchants. Even George III, a hardy rascal since the Stamp Act, has undergone some rehabilitation at the hands of modern society, but

[21] Charles M. Andrews, *The Colonial Period of American History* (New Haven: Yale Univ. Press, 1938), Vol. IV, p. 427.

notably at British rather than American hands. The Tories, upon whose heads the Whig School heaped opprobrium, have traveled just as rocky a road but appear lately to be sharing the benefit of more enlightened viewpoints.[22] In the assertion of a recent scholar that opposition to the Stamp Act came spontaneously on grounds of principle, we glimpse a return to the older rationale of taxation without representation. Are we going from Bancroft to Bancroft? Not in the literal sense. It would be an exaggeration to say that history repeats itself or even that historians repeat each other; but these ever-changing views of the Revolution do give color to the idea that history is relative. They also suggest that myths die slowly if at all.

Bancroft remarked that "American independence, like the great rivers of the country, had many sources, but the headspring which colored all the stream was the Navigation Act."[23] It will be interesting to see whether the approaching bicentennial of the Revolution uncovers new tributaries or merely navigates old waters. Anticipation of this kind is one of the pleasures, if not necessarily uses, of history.

The uses of history

"Why should I study the dead past? I'm interested in what goes on now and what happens later," wrote a geology professor's son in contemplation of a mediocre examination paper. The teacher's reaction to this bit of myopia is not recorded. He might have said that without a sense of identity with the past the student's present would be chaos, his future even more a maze of uncertainty. The uses of history are legion.

History as Literature. One of such uses lies in "the pleasures of reading." In many of us there is a streak of imagination which history satisfies, enabling the reader to escape vicariously from the reality of the present to a romantic world of the past. But it is also important in the pursuit of knowledge for its own sake: it enriches the experience by fulfilling a natural human interest in names,

---

[22] See Carol Ann Furlong, "The American Tories in Fiction and History" (M.A. Thesis, Univ. of Tennessee, 1952).

[23] Bancroft, *op. cit.*, Vol. V, p. 159.

places, and traditions, whether one has a penchant for biography that may lead from Lincoln back to Plutarch's *Lives,* a hobby of military history that may allow him to speculate about Gettysburg or El Alamein, or a yen for pioneering that may induce him to share the vicissitudes of the great trek west.

The reading of history opens new horizons. It may be a springboard to an interest in the humanities or the other sciences, social and physical—areas for which history provides the larger setting. The literary heritage of the New England Brahmins is but dimly seen without an understanding of the historical forces that made New England the bellwether of early nineteenth-century American culture. Who can fathom the "gothic imagination" of Edgar Allan Poe without comprehending the Romantic Movement and its escape into the Middle Ages? The findings of the scientist Galileo led him to defend the Copernican system; but their revolutionary effect upon contemporary thought and the status quo drew the keen interest of the Inquisition to him.

Sir Walter Scott coined a term to describe dull historians—"Dryasdusts." The implication was plain: history is an art as well as a science. History told in a graphic way—the narrative of a Herodotus, the personalized touch of a Winston Churchill, or the interpretations of a Samuel Eliot Morison—makes the past live again. Listen to Vernon L. Parrington, as he introduces a young man destined to become a literary giant of the Old South: [24]

> From the background of old Charleston emerged, about the year 1825, the figure of Gilmore Simms, lately a drug clerk but now come to the dignity of admission to the bar; a tall, vigorous young fellow, with little formal schooling, no Latin or Greek, without land or slaves, but heavily involved in Byronic odes and like unprofitable investments; a social nobody soon to be married at the age of twenty to a girl of no better station than his own, who offered himself as candidate for the poet laureateship of the South.

Who can fail to be caught up in the drama of the approaching denouement as Allan Nevins summarizes the national reaction to the election of Lincoln: "Dreadfully clear now, to ears attuned to the

[24] Vernon Louis Parrington, *Main Currents in American Thought: An Interpretation of American Literature from the Beginnings to 1920* (New York: Harcourt, Brace & World, 1927–1930), Vol. II, p. 125.

future, sounded the drums and bugles." [25]   Yet history as a literary art has its dangers, when we remember that some of its partisans came to regard it as the handmaiden of belles lettres.   For Thomas Babington Macaulay, facts were but "the dross of history" and a graphic reconstruction of the past by a vivid imagination infinitely preferable.   Macaulay to the contrary, the historian's first loyalty is to truth.

History as a Functional Method.   But history has more pragmatic uses.   The value of historical method itself is so obvious that it is often overlooked.   As man faces a variety of problems in a complex society, he refers to the past, for he cannot make decisions without drawing on a store of generalizations from his own personal history. So this discipline, closest to ordinary life, has its advantages for all. It may be the First Citizen, like Harry Truman, who said "I trained myself to look back into history for precedents because instinctively I sought perspective . . . for the decisions I made." [26]   Or it may be Everyman,[27] who uses historical method as a tool for solving day-by-day problems.   He is arrested: at his disposal are legal recourses, the products of 1,000 years of history.   He is in an automobile wreck: immediately he begins to recapitulate the setting for the accident, he looks for witnesses, he avails himself of the other procedures which his knowledge of the past affords.   A physician treating a patient may experiment and thus create an innovation; but more often he relies on historical techniques.   A candidate for office is running "on his record."   Once more the voter brings historical method into play by an examination of that record; if he finds his facts, he is a historian.   Everyday life is an exercise in the use of historical method.

The study of history can provide a better understanding of the present through a systematic examination of the past; it can be "a lantern carried by the side of man."   Through history we under-

[25] Allan Nevins, *The Emergence of Lincoln* (New York: Charles Scribner's Sons, 1950), Vol. II, p. 317.   On this general theme, see Samuel Eliot Morison, "History as a Literary Art," in his *By Land and By Sea: Essays and Addresses* (New York: Alfred A. Knopf, 1954), Ch. 13.

[26] Cowherd, *op. cit.,* p. 145.

[27] For a delightful treatment of this theme, see Carl Becker, *Everyman His Own Historian* (New York: Appleton-Century-Crofts, 1935).

stand the evolution of government, of social and economic systems, of religion, of education, of the family, and of the individual. In short, we become familiar with the milieu in which we live.

History is a guide, providing a reservoir of ideas from which we can draw what we need. In this reservoir of ideas are "do's" and "don'ts." Indeed, one of the historian's main tasks is to keep minds free of unrealistic schemes for the present and future. Looking back into the American past, it would seem that we have learned that reform in morals should come primarily through education rather than through legislation. The ill-fated experiment of national prohibition is only one of a number of instances supporting this generalization. History cannot foretell the future, but it can give us an idea of what can and cannot be done.

History contributes to an enlightened patriotism, a state of mind which heightens respect for the individual, for able leadership, and for the nation. Not only can the lives of great leaders be an inspiration for our own; an analysis of the past in terms of cause and effect can show how leaders have been guides or impediments to progress. That history can be perverted to selfish ends is obvious. The voter should recognize the true nature of such campaign oratory as "we have reached a crisis as never before in history." [28] On another level are the writings of the "national schools" of historians, who contributed to the psychological preparation for World War I and other conflicts. It is interesting to see that since the Second World War an international campaign to remove or lessen bias in school textbooks has been launched—a worthy but gargantuan task.[29] That history can be made to serve the will of a particular regime was shown by Fascist Italy and Nazi Germany, whose propaganda minister Joseph Goebbels designed handsome uniforms for college professors. A writer of our own time voices a fear of "court historians" and concludes that in general there has been no historical writing since 1939 "which has substantially challenged or departed from the basic policy of the country of the writer." [30] Whether historians have indeed reached an "official consensus" remains a

[28] In this connection, see R. G. Cowherd, "The Political Use and Abuse of History," *Social Studies*, LIII (March), 94–98, 1962.
[29] These efforts are discussed briefly in E. H. Dance, *History the Betrayer: A Study in Bias* (London: Hutchinson of London, 1960).
[30] Barnes, *op. cit.*, pp. 397–398.

moot question but there is little doubt that the cold war provides an acid test for objectivity.

Changes of government have often been followed by a rewriting of history. The reaction in Russia against Stalinism and, more recently, against the policies of Khrushchev, is a case in point. If the Castro regime sustains itself, we can expect a revision of Cuban history, and particularly of that part which concerns the island's relationship with the United States. And our curiosity is piqued by the recently announced intention of Nasser's Egypt to study that country's history "along objective lines," with a view to "purging all the impurities deliberately introduced into it under imperialism and feudalism." [31] Only the *critical* study of history can cultivate a national patriotism based on reason and understanding.

Few qualities are more necessary than tolerance for other men and other societies. One of the causes of the Civil War was a lack of understanding: tragically, northerners and southerners did not know each other well enough, and each had gradually built up a hostile stereotype, a distorted image of the other. Nor, despite the shrinking world around them, did the generation of the early twentieth century share an adequate understanding. How ironic that two great forces, a large-scale campaign for peace and a deliberate preparation for war, paralleled each other down to the guns of August 1914. And how much more critical in our own times is the need for a knowledge of other civilizations and their viewpoints. Provincialism is a luxury that man can no longer afford. Speaking of the contradictions between the Old World and the New, a writer observes that "the resolution lies not in the submission of one hemisphere to another, but in the attainment of a higher level for Western civilization, in the use of all its resources to achieve a new unity of loyalties and values." [32] But it is not the fate of Western civilization alone that is at stake. Far too many courses and textbooks bearing the label of "Background of Modern Civilization" or some similar designation are in reality little more than the history and expansion of Europe. As Asia and Africa become increasingly significant in the international sphere, the necessity for a grasp of the essential features of these civilizations grows imperative. The

[31] San Francisco *Chronicle,* June 16, 1963.
[32] Philip Rahv, ed., *Discovery of Europe: The Story of American Experience in the Old World* (Garden City, N. Y.: Doubleday, 1960), p. xvi.

world is in the crucible; and history has incalculable possibilities as a key to international understanding.

Finally, history is identified with the mature mind. As a mental discipline, it develops intellectual honesty through the quest for truth, thus encouraging an enlightened skepticism. History deepens our understanding of human nature, showing it as a constant expressed in diverse ways. It explains how men have behaved and why they behaved that way, why they agree and disagree. In its multitude of uses, history is a synthesis of many things.

Some implications of history for other disciplines

A little more than a decade ago an economist complained that most texts used in economic history were written by historians. Only a few of these, he said, had the economics point of view. But he conceded that there was much history in his field: business history, history of business cycles, and history of economic thought. It is unnecessary to pursue this particular matter; after all, complaints about the intrusions of neighbors are hardly novel. Yet it reminds us that the barriers between history and the other social sciences are largely artificial. A small volume could be written on interrelationships; here we are interested only in some general contributions made by history.

The work of Herodotus, the "father of history," contains elements of anthropology, archaeology, economics, geography, political science, psychology, and sociology. In one sense of the word, the historian is a "father," for it is his role to define the setting for the other disciplines. Before he begins his experiment, the scientist must understand what conditions led up to it; before he begins his analysis of social behavior, the sociologist must await the accumulation of a number of historical facts. Even the novel rests on a background of authentic social data which can be called history. In other words, history meets the problem of genesis by explaining how a particular situation came to be. "We want [students] to have respect for good, hard, empirical facts," says a psychologist.[33] This groundwork is laid by history.

But the setting is not enough; man and his institutions do not

[33] W. J. McKeachie, "Psychology," in *The Social Studies and the Social Sciences* (New York: Harcourt, Brace & World, 1962), 175–176.

remain static. And here we recall that one of the functions of history is the analysis of change over periods of time. Though many social science investigations do not involve any time element, inquiry into human affairs must be essentially historical in character. History not only provides concrete information regarding a particular society at a particular time but it shows the evolution of that society and indeed of all societies. As a necessary accompaniment to its evaluation of change, history adds the framework of chronology.

Without laboring the touchy question of family relationships, we can point out that most of the social sciences arose out of historical investigation. All employ a process similar to historical method: the posing of hypotheses, the accumulation of data, the criticism of facts, the drawing of conclusions, and the presentation of the results. Methods in the social sciences vary in their details but their general procedure is the same.

It is impossible to devote more than a passing glance to history's specific contributions. To mention a few, it gives to the economist examples of the relationship between economic institutions and other types of institutions; to the geographer, a sense of time to add to his sense of space; to the political scientist, a record of the evolution of governing agencies; and to the psychologist, case studies of virtually every character type. To all, historical research contributes the setting, the facts, the time sense, and the method.

The Organization of History

In his engaging *History: Its Purpose and Method,* G. J. Renier asks philosophically: "Is life one, or is it manifold? This is a question for the metaphysician." And he adds that the human past, the area of the historian's labors, seems to invite a similar question.[34] But historians have long since burst metaphysical barriers in organizing their subject.

The question itself suggests a partial answer. Time is the most obvious division of history; for history is a science of time and therefore its organization must be chronological. Of course, we are

[34] G. J. Renier, *History: Its Purpose and Method* (Boston: Beacon Press, 1950), p. 54.

aware of the continuity of events and know that arbitrary divisions are to a degree artificial, indeed something of an abstraction. There is no sharp line between ancient, medieval, and modern history; such breaks are in reality sequences of time, concepts established by historians. There was much that was medieval about the western Roman Empire long before its "fall" in 476. Though the men of the Renaissance scorned the Middle Ages, we know that the Renaissance was a transition period with elements of both the medieval and the modern. Yet such divisions, epochs, eras, and periods have some logic. Not only is a straight time-line impossibly unwieldy: the Middle Ages, to consider a span of several centuries, and the Age of Jackson, to consider some three decades, each had common characteristics which allow an approximate chronological division. Perhaps one might say that history is composed of a series of pieces joined end to end, each retaining an essential unity yet each fitting into the larger whole.

Thus the chronological scheme of history is horizontal; but if history is a broad stream it has a number of channels, and an analysis in depth suggests further division according to subject. Our second departure in organization, therefore, is topical. In discussing college courses, we pointed out some varieties of history, such as political, social, constitutional, and economic. This approach affords the opportunity for a more intensive examination of types of history and hence a better understanding of its essentials. Within his chronological and topical divisions the historian looks for cause and effect.

The reduction of emphasis upon formal history after 1920 brought with it greater awareness of general social problems and hence promoted the crossing of interdisciplinary lines. Other fields now seemed much closer; there was history in geography, economics, psychology, sociology. There was a philosophy of history but also a history of philosophy. Again, college history courses reflect this development.

At about the same time, the growing interdependence of the world and the increasing knowledge of its peoples prompted still other ways of organization. There were divisions according to place: continents, hemispheres, regions, states, even cities. There was a heightened interest in civilizations: their origins, their growth, and their decline. The "New History" of this century takes as its subject matter, and hence as bases of organization, not only nations and eras but social groups, economic classes, religious denominations, institutions, and even abstract ideas or forces, such as conservativism, democracy, communism, and mercantilism.

Yet such compartmentalization remains relative. Conventional labels tend to become outmoded by the increase of knowledge and increasingly we think of the evolution of civilizations, with less emphasis upon sharp breaks and more emphasis upon continuous development.

The Process of Historical Investigation

Scattered throughout the discussion thus far are statements about the nature of historical method. We have seen that the processes of research resemble those in other sciences and that among the goals of the historian are the search for truth (though precise truth is not possible) and the ideal of objectivity (though the mind is not a *tabula rasa*). Speaking of a state of mind, this is the place to summarize some qualities of the researcher.

A "desirable" state of mind

As part of his inherent loyalty to truth, the historian should possess intellectual honesty. In the Andrew Johnson Papers are letters in which the plebeian (a favorite word of his) expresses himself in language so picturesque as to leave doubt about its publication. Yet if it illuminates the man and the times, it must be published; to fail to do so would be a species of dishonesty. A high regard for accuracy is in order, with due care for names, dates, and other information. Van Wyck Brooks writes of Bonaventure Cemetery in Savannah: "Who could forget an alley there, flanked by ancient live-oak trees, with streamers of grey moss overhanging the path, leading down to the moss-covered tomb of a long-dead senator and his daughter, with the waves of the sounding sea breaking behind it?" [35] Alas! The waves of the sounding sea break many miles away, for Bonaventure is on the Wilmington River. The historian should have a healthy

[35] Van Wyck Brooks, *The World of Washington Irving* (Cleveland: The World Publishing Company, 1944), p. 273 *n*.

51

skepticism which makes him question every unproven statement. He needs judgment and perspective; and here the old cliché of the woods and the trees comes to mind. Though he cannot extinguish the self, modesty and humility should persuade him to entertain a decent respect for the opinions of mankind. He should have a historical imagination. And he needs a sense of responsibility to himself, to his readers, and indeed to history.

Some working bases

Once the problem is set and the background reading done, the historian may draw from his own experience and from the other social sciences techniques that provide bases for investigation and experiment. He may operate on the *hypothesis* that the American Revolution was a democratic movement or that the aristocracy of the Old South was an essentially flexible one. He may pose leading *questions*. In a consideration of ante-bellum southern culture, he may ask why the South led the nation in the establishment of state universities. Or he may look at the *structure* of the situation in which events take place—a business firm, a political party, or a revolution—in order to build a theoretical bridge between events and the environment in which action is taken. He may evaluate occurrences in terms of *process,* changes in structure which follow definite patterns over a period of time; for example, "the process of industrialization." Such aids to research may come simultaneously with the accumulation of data.

Gathering and interpreting information

With the problem outlined and the working bases established, the historian turns to the search for data. He begins with statements, not facts; and he must be skeptical of them until they are tested. At this point he applies some common-sense rules of historical criticism. First, he tries to obtain all possible information about the material: the author, the date of writing, and the authenticity of the document. Second, he tries to determine the meaning and dependability of statements within the document: literal and real meanings, trustworthiness of witnesses, the element of bias, and other things.

Elsewhere it has been suggested that recapturing the past in a literal sense is impossible. Facts do not speak for themselves; they speak only as they are collected and arranged in order. Seldom a witness to the subject of his inquiry, the historian cannot have access to all the records and in many cases must depend upon dubious data. The truth is possible only on limited and precise subjects. We know when the American Iliad became a "shooting war," but we have many interpretations of its causes. We know when Lincoln became President, and even the exact moment of his assassination; but Lincoln as a man still remains something of an enigma. However, a great deal of the past can be recovered. If the underlying causes of the Spanish-American War remain debatable, we have many facts about that conflict. We know that there was trouble in Cuba, American humanitarian sentiment was aroused in behalf of the Cubans, Dupuy de Lôme's bumbling letter about McKinley fell into the hands of the Hearst Press, the *Maine* was sunk in Havana Harbor, Dewey won the Battle of Manila Bay, and Theodore Roosevelt (according to his own account and those of others) charged up San Juan Hill. So there are many facts from the past—indeed far too many for the historian to cope with.

The evaluation of evidence is the central problem of historical research, and the selection of facts one of the most critical elements in that problem. Obviously, the historian must interpret his information. But what facts should he select? Those that are significant. How is this to be determined? Though there is no hard-and-fast rule, a number of guidelines may be followed. That which has exercised greater or more lasting influence must loom most prominently. One fact or a group of facts is more important than another if it affects more people in particularly intensive fashion or for a longer period of time. Information which has a bearing on the present is significant; but so is information which illuminates the viewpoints of other ages. Inevitably the historian will select according to his own subjectivity: his background, his training, his interests, and the assumptions of his age. And finally, as he draws his conclusions, he is bound to make no generalization unless all the available evidence has been examined.

The contributions of other sciences to historical method

Despite the intricacies of historical method, research has become so complex that the historian of necessity draws upon the techniques of related fields. Some of these are known as auxiliary sciences, disciplines which grew out of history and are concerned with historical phenomena. Among them are archaeology, the analysis of civilizations through examination of their remains; epigraphy, the study of inscriptions; paleography, the science of ancient handwriting; numismatics, concerned with coins, medals, and medallions; genealogy, the investigation of family pedigrees; and diplomatics, the study of official documents.

Moreover, the purview of history is broadened by a reciprocal process with the other sciences. Significant here are the anthropologist's techniques of interpreting the evolution of human culture and of explaining its similarities and parallels as well as its variations and contrasts. From economics the historian gains a greater understanding of the creation and use of material wealth, and uses such concepts as "the business cycle" and the "law of diminishing returns." Geography has expanded history in space, both in terms of a broader view of man's environment and of intensive studies of natural geographic regions. The link between these disciplines is reflected in such works as Frederick Jackson Turner's *The Frontier in American History* and Walter Prescott Webb's *The Great Plains*. Psychology has brought new concepts of great leaders and has thrown much light upon mass thinking and mass motivation. A president of the American Historical Association recently devoted his entire address to pointing out the possibilities in the use of retroactive psychoanalysis.[36] Sociology, a study of the life of men in groups, contributes an overall view of the whole social process and as such furnishes provocative generalizations for history. And the historian studying the evolution of political institutions would be naive indeed without a grasp of the fundamental principles and the basic forms of these institutions, an understanding derived from political science. A number of these fields add significantly to history in the compilation and scientific use of statistics. In sum, the historian must possess an elementary knowledge of the other social sciences and their methods. How incongruous, as Harry Elmer Barnes remarks, is the historian's insistence "upon intensive training in paleography, diplomatics, lexicography and the principles of internal and external criticism . . . and the co-existent ignoring of

[36] William L. Langer, "The Next Assignment," *American Historical Review*, LXIII (January), 283–304, 1958.

adequate training in the only group of studies which can make it possible . . . intelligently to organize and interpret his materials." [37]

A problem in historical method:
the Boston Massacre

Since we have already chosen the American Revolution as an illustration of the role of ideas, let us select as a problem in historical method one of its most famous episodes. On the evening of March 5, 1770, a squad of British soldiers, sorely beset by a large crowd of townspeople, fired upon them and killed and wounded several colonists. This was the Boston Massacre, one of the most controversial twenty-minute periods in American history. For all its fascination, there is no single, detailed treatment.[38] In the course of our investigation, we shall consider (1) the setting, (2) the affair, (3) the materials available, and (4) some leading interpretations. Because of limitations of space we shall make no great effort to assess the significance of the massacre.

An exploration of the background shows that England's tightening of the strings of colonial policy after 1763 had several objectives, one of which was the raising of additional revenue. To that end Parliament passed a series of measures including the Sugar Act, the Stamp Act, and the Townshend Acts. Colonial reaction to these and other pieces of legislation took various forms: protests against taxation without representation, nonimportation agreements, and even physical resistance. The situation seemed especially critical in Boston; and beginning in 1768, British troops were dispatched to that area. Their mere presence fanned the flames of discontent, and the taunts directed at the "bloody backs" and "lobsters" were given real meaning by the activities of mobs, which were often used by radical political leaders such as Samuel Adams. On the other hand, the town had its conservatives, whether patriots or Tories. Thus we have the setting, a tug of war between colonies and mother country and a miniature powder keg in Boston.

History has demonstrated that provocative incidents occur in situations of this kind. In the late evening of March 5, with a large

---

[37] Barnes, *op. cit.,* p. 361.
[38] This section is based upon Robert Verle Bogle, "The Boston Massacre: Fact, Myth and Historiography" (M. A. Thesis, Univ. of Tennessee, 1962).

number of men and boys roaming the streets, a series of incidents occurred almost simultaneously: a barracks guard was pelted with snowballs; a Customhouse sentry who had knocked down a boy was in turn set upon by a crowd; his shouts for aid brought a Captain Preston and a squad of seven soldiers; the town firebells were rung; and from Dock Square to King Street came a great mass of towns-people who had been harangued by "a tall gentleman in a red coat and a white wig." The mob now facing the Redcoats punctuated its invectives with clubs, oyster shells, and jagged chunks of ice. The climax came when a soldier fired into the crowd. His com-panions followed suit and—these numbers have long been the bane of later writers—three citizens were killed outright, two fatally wounded, and six others seriously injured. As additional soldiers and civilians rushed to the scene, there followed a massive confron-tation in which several hundred troops faced thousands of colonials. The aftermath was featured by the removal of the troops from Boston, by a series of trials in which most of the accused were exonerated,[39] and by a wave of American indignation.

At once a number of questions come to mind, questions that provide us with a working basis for research. Who was the pictur-esque orator in the red cloak? Did the customs commissioners have anything to do with the massacre? Why were the firebells rung beforehand and who rang them? Did Preston really give an order to fire? Some hypotheses may also be offered. One is that Samuel Adams and the radicals had much to gain from a *cause célèbre*. But, conversely, mob violence might well alienate some of the more con-servative Bostonians in a climate of public opinion that had by no means jelled. The vacillating British government had thus far shown no taste for drastic action; so it is possible that the first shot was unpremeditated and the result of excitement. It might even have been suggested by the firebells and the cry of "Fire."

Having posed some leading questions, our next step is to ac-cumulate materials for a study of the massacre, its sequel, and later interpretations. Investigation discloses various primary sources. In 1770 the Boston Town Committee circulated its version, resting on

---

[39] Of the three separate trials involving Preston, the soldiers, and some armed men who had been in the Customhouse, two soldiers were found guilty of manslaughter, pleaded benefit of clergy, were each branded on the thumb with a hot iron, and then released.

the deposition of ninety-six witnesses, and entitled *A Short Narrative of the Horrid Massacre in Boston, Perpetrated . . . by Soldiers of the XXIX Regiment*.[40]   There are the proceedings of the trials, all with the exception of Preston's eventually printed in full.   Apparently not discovered until 1930 was correspondence between British military personnel in Boston and New York.   There are memoirs and papers of John Adams and Josiah Quincy (lawyers for the accused soldiers), as well as letters, diaries, and other fragments of the time.   Finally, there are several newspapers, of which the Boston *Gazette* is a sample.   No single primary source deals with all aspects of the episode.   And adherence to the canons of scholarship requires us to examine the work of later interpreters to see what information it contains or what ideas they may offer.   These secondary references include general and specialized histories, biographies, pamphlets, and periodical articles.

But the investigation must first proceed with a criticism of primary materials.   Just how reliable is this evidence?   The Committee made clear its position: the soldiers "fired upon the inhabitants, promiscuously, in King Street, without the least warning of their intention."   George Bancroft, who depended upon the *Narrative,* insisted that "the Depositions were taken openly and in the presence of persons representing all parties." [41]   Yet the testimony of some of these witnesses seems contradictory; and a British account of the same year included the ninety-six affidavits but appended twenty-six others which the British believed tended to exonerate the soldiers.   Even the reports of the trials leave much room for doubt.   The witnesses disagreed on the number present at the scene of the massacre, the identity of the Customhouse sentry, and as to whether or not the soldier had been knocked down before he fired the opening shot.   Two witnesses insisted that there had been firing from the Customhouse but Lieutenant Governor Thomas Hutchinson later wrote that it was incredible that only two out of hundreds saw this action and that one of these had an infamous character and

[40] The Boston Customs Commissioners printed their own version, which appears to have differed markedly from the *Narrative* and which is no longer available.

[41] According to the Committee report, ninety-four witnesses placed the entire blame on the soldiers, one deposition was that of the doctor who examined the body of Crispus Attucks, a mulatto, and the other that of a notorious liar and friend of the Crown.

the other was an idiot. Hutchinson obviously had an axe to grind and so one must be skeptical of his statement. Patrick Carr, one of the victims, made a deathbed confession in which he called the townsmen aggressors and declared that the soldiers fired in self-defense. In rebuttal, Sam Adams pointed out that Carr was an Irish "papist," implying that he hoped to die in the odor of sanctity. Not the least interesting angle was the fact that Adams persuaded his cousin John Adams to take the case. Subsequent writers have reasoned that a patriot lawyer would not cross-examine the town's witnesses as closely as would a Crown lawyer, and the latter might implicate Bostonians in the planning of the affair on King Street. But there is no evidence to support this idea. Another Whig version, not offered at the trial, maintained that the Customs Commissioners deliberately planned the massacre; but the commissioners proved that they were miles away at the time. The British military correspondence tends to absolve that side from blame. Most of the newspapers followed the *Narrative* and the papers of Adams and others shed little light. Amid confusing primary evidence, the historian must rely to a greater extent on the trials than on the other sources. But subsequent writers may provide a clue to further search and certainly will contribute interpretation.

"First impressions are apt to be the most lasting," observed one of the investigators of the Boston Massacre. Here at least he was correct, for attitudes remind us that even historians have difficulty in ridding themselves of myth and tradition. After earlier writers contented themselves with cursory accounts or with publishing one source version or another, George Bancroft took up the cudgels for the patriots. Insisting that the townspeople were on the defensive, he accepted the *Narrative* and the "uncontroverted reasoning of Samuel Adams." Though his chapter is the first detailed treatment by a historian of stature, it adds little to the story and tells much more about the viewpoint of George Bancroft. The popular historian John Fiske demonstrated that the Whig version still remained authoritative in the late nineteenth century when he wrote that the death of these men "conveyed as much meaning as a St. Bartholomew massacre would have conveyed to the minds of men in a lower stage of political development."

But times and attitudes change, and if twentieth-century historians have been neither particularly accurate in their details of the massacre nor overly solicitous about offering judgments on its significance, they have as a whole a more balanced point of view than their predecessors. One placed the affair in a larger setting, comparing it with similar incidents in the history of other nations. Another issued a declaration of historical relativity by saying that the question of blame led "ultimately to ethical questions of right and wrong upon which none may speak with finality." Recent biographers of both the Adamses stress the role of radical leaders in fomenting disorder in Boston and stirring up sympathy in surrounding areas. On the other hand, a recent historian relies partly on the science of ballistics and partly on the testimony of witnesses to raise a provocative question about the role of the Customs Commissioners.[42] Some day we may be able to establish more definitely Paul Revere's connection with the affair, for he made both a diagram and a famous engraving and may have been either a participant or a spectator.

Having exercised our historical method on a detective story whose diverse threads have not yet been put together, we must leave things as they stand. Perhaps posterity will accomplish what nearly two centuries of endeavor have failed to do.

Some Major Theories of History

There is nothing novel about trying to "make sense of history" by formulating some larger theme out of the mass of facts at the historian's disposal. Nor are such syntheses without practical value; the deeds of mankind must be understood and evaluated if they are to have any significance. More than at any time in the past the historian is in a position to take advantage of knowledge denied his predecessors. More than ever before, it is incumbent upon him to preserve man's sense of freedom.

In the realm of ideas one must cope with the difficult distinc-

[42] The reader may be interested in the following recent works: Catherine Drinker Bowen, *John Adams and the American Revolution* (New York: Grosset and Dunlap, 1950); John C. Miller, *Sam Adams: Pioneer in Propaganda* (Boston: Little, Brown, 1936); Esther Forbes, *Paul Revere and the World He Lived In* (Boston: Houghton Mifflin, 1942); and Oliver M. Dickerson, "The Commissioners of the Customs and the 'Boston Massacre,'" in *New England Quarterly*, XXVII (September), 307–325, 1954.

tion between "philosophies" and "theories" of history. A philosophy of history tries to explain the historical process as a whole, conforming to a single ordered pattern. A theory of history also tries to explain the process in general terms, but insists that a number of constant factors govern historical change. The former usually rests less upon the accumulation of evidence than upon pure reason, and is therefore less subject to pragmatic test; the latter is based to a greater degree upon evidence and can be more easily tested. The philosophy of history is directed toward some final goal; the theory of history makes no such pretensions. Yet the two are not mutually exclusive, for each has elements of the other. There have been many philosophers of history: St. Augustine, Hegel, Marx, and Toynbee, to name a few.

According to the Christian philosophy (or providential interpretation) of history, God contrived a world plan when He created the heavens and the earth. The birth of Christ was the decisive event in human history. This idea originated in the early Christian era and gained popularity with the diffusion of Christianity in western Europe. A corollary, the "interventionist" thesis, asserts that the Creator did not plan human history totally in advance but intervenes in emergencies, sometimes because of His own decision and sometimes in answer to man's supplications. These interventions are proof of God's inscrutable purpose. Dominant when Christianity was the central pattern of Western civilization, these doctrines lost authority in an increasingly secularized world which no longer demanded religious sanctions. Yet they have by no means been abandoned.

Of all theories of economic causation, the Marxian philosophy of history has been the most fateful for our own day. According to Karl Marx, a nineteenth-century German of middle-class origins, the *prevailing mode* of economic production in life determines the nature and operation of existing institutions. "The final causes of all social changes and political revolutions are to be sought . . . not in the philosophy, but the economics of each particular epoch," said Marx's colleague Friedrich Engels.[43] Thus the rationale does not exclude noneconomic factors, but considers them purely secondary.

[43] Quoted by Herbert Heaton, "The Economic Impact on History," in Strayer, *op. cit.*, pp. 91–92.

Historical accident, say the Marxists, is always governed by hidden laws beyond man's comprehension. Admitting that every society needs its great men, they discount the individual in favor of classes and forces. An article of faith in Marxist historical thought is the doctrine of the perennial class struggle, between freeman and slave in antiquity, lord and serf in the Middle Ages, capitalist and proletarian in modern times. Marx saw the American Civil War as basically a struggle between the reactionary southern landed aristocracy and the northern masters of capital. The final goal of the Marxists, a classless society, has yet to be realized.

Oswald Spengler's *The Decline of the West* and Arnold Toynbee's *A Study of History* illustrate both the persistence of unitary ideas of history and the increasing preoccupation with the study of whole civilizations.[44] These works stand out sharply against the background of a world of uncertainty. It is no mere coincidence that their theme, the collapse of civilizations, and their timing, the one appearing just after World War I and the other begun before the Second World War and still in progress, have appealed to a vast audience. Spengler and Toynbee are cyclical historians, sharing a belief in civilizations fated to rise, flourish, and decay, a state of mind which E. H. Carr calls "the characteristic ideology of a society in decline."[45] Both reject the optimistic nineteenth-century doctrine of inevitable progress.

A German mathematician with a knowledge of science, Spengler draws an analogy between the life of civilizations and that of plant and animal organisms. In lyrical prose he predicates four seasonal phases of the historical cycle, phases comparable to the ages of man, through which all cultures pass. As he speaks of "the approaching end, the falling leaf," he seems to echo the poet's "the melancholy days are come, the saddest of the year." For the West is in its winter of decay, to be followed by a period of Asiatic rule. Spengler's very phrases carry an air of inevitability: "pre-ordained" and "the unalterable necessity of destiny." But he takes undue

---

[44] Oswald Spengler, *The Decline of the West,* ed. Helmut Werner (1st Am. ed.) (New York: Alfred A. Knopf, 1962); Arnold Joseph Toynbee, *A Study of History,* abridged by D. C. Somervell (2 vols.) (New York: Oxford Univ. Press, 1947–1957).

[45] Carr, *op. cit.,* p. 52.

liberties with history, his analogy of civilization and biology is dubious, and his "seasons" of a civilization unproven. By its very exaggeration, Spengler's is a romantic view of history.

Arnold Toynbee's *A Study of History* is an Olympus of scholarship and learning. Contending that history is enacted within civilizations rather than nations, he surveys more than a score of cultures, some of which have completed their span and are dead and dying. Civilizations break down from both external and internal factors. The West, he maintains, has such symptoms of decay as reactionary nationalism. But decline comes also from such internal causes as "failures of nerve and brain." Lessons of history abound in Toynbee's pages. According to his doctrine of challenge and response, the best qualities in man are brought out by adversity rather than by ease. He insists that the evolution of Christianity and the other great religions has given humanity its hope for the future. Toynbee's grand scheme of history has provoked endless controversy. His critics charge that his case studies are arbitrarily selected, that his use of evidence is inconsistent, and that he is deterministic and even dogmatic.

Yet in pondering the rise and decline of civilizations, Toynbee and others invoke a subject of universal interest. Why do civilizations decay? A combination of factors: perhaps urbanization carried to an undesirable degree, producing crime, disease, corruption, and poverty; undoubtedly war, with its loss of life, destruction of property, and upsetting of the human balance. Both philosophies and theories of history, the latter occupying a lower rung on the ladder of abstraction, afford new insights into history in general.

To the votaries of the Great Man theory, the outstanding personalities of history are the main factors in historical development. "Universal History . . . is at bottom the History of the Great Men who have worked here," wrote Thomas Carlyle.[46] Speculations about the "man of the year" or of the century remind us of this thesis. No one can quarrel with the humanizing of history or believe that man is a mere pawn of the cosmos; the decisions of individuals are of utmost importance. Yet the biographical approach represents an oversimplification, emphasizing the men to the neglect of their times,

[46] Thomas Carlyle, "On Heroes, Hero-Worship, and the Heroic in History," in Fritz Stern, ed., *The Varieties of History from Voltaire to the Present* (New York: Meridian Books, 1957), p. 101.

stressing politics while playing down economics, and offering little understanding of social evolution. Many scholars believe that the general tendencies of a society furnish the framework within which decisions are made and that great men simply do what they·have to do in certain situations. No one can gainsay Theodore Roosevelt's dramatic role in the Progressive Movement; but he did not originate it and he was only one of a number of types of reform leaders. Once in power, Adolf Hitler exerted a dynamic influence upon his own times but the times created Hitler. Perhaps great men often symbolize their eras.

The contribution of other social sciences to historical thinking is reflected in theories emphasizing the role of geography, economics, and sociology. The geographical interpretation of history, a natural accompaniment of our widening knowledge of the world at large, contends that the degree of a people's civilization is determined chiefly by physical surroundings and climatic influences. "Geography is the basis of History," wrote Herder, and "History is nothing but the Geography of times and peoples set into motion." [47] One of the favorite tenets of the geographical school is that great civilizations rise in a few favored areas, such as western Europe or eastern North America, and that at their height all the successive centers of civilization had about the same climate. To the eternal debate about the decline and fall of the Roman Empire, Ellsworth Huntington contributed the idea that it was due to a lessening in rainfall in the Mediterranean world during the fourth, fifth, and sixth centuries of the Christian era.[48] Intriguing as such theories of the role of nature are, it is more likely that the decay of a great civilization arose from a multiplicity of factors. One can concede the significance of geography in molding the course of history but the advance of technology often modifies or even revolutionizes geographic controls, for example, the effect of air conditioning upon the South, and in any case the environment is composed of both human and nonhuman factors.

The Marxist thesis is only one of a variety of economic inter-

[47] Johann Gottfried Herder, *Sämmtliche Werke* (Berlin, Weidmannische Buchhandlung, 1877–), Vol. XXX, p. 102.
[48] N. H. Baynes, "The Decline of the Roman Empire in Western Europe: Some Modern Explanations," in *Decline and Fall of the Roman Empire: Why Did It Collapse?*, ed. Donald Kagan (Boston: D. C. Heath, 1962), p. 80.

pretations of history. These center in the proposition that "the existence of man depends upon his ability to sustain himself; the economic life is therefore the fundamental condition of all life." [49] Basic economic forces, underlying other human institutions, are the driving forces of history. No one can doubt seriously that the economic theory of history is a valuable antidote to the older interpretations based on religion and politics. It has rounded out our knowledge of the life of man. It has clarified human relationships by bringing other types of history into sharper focus. It is a valuable vehicle for explaining broad movements. The theory remains popular even among many historians who are not Marxists, but it has the usual handicap of the one-dominant-factor approach.

For those who advocate a sociological view of history, the past is primarily a record of social evolution whose central feature is the basic conflict between the interests of the self-assertive individual and those of the social organism. This individual must obey immutable sociological law, a corpus which is as yet undetermined. The great man is largely dependent upon his environment and geniuses represent deviations from the normal sociological variations. It is likely that the historian of the future, while emphasizing social trends over the role of the individual, will continue to try to strike a balance between the two.

There are other theories of history but enough has been said to indicate the nature of a few outstanding ones. As is true with great ideas, most present-day historians look askance at single causation. But there is no doubt that these philosophies and theories have given new directions to thought, pointed out new areas of research, and enriched history in general.

History in the Schools

This discussion is focused on selected issues and problems rather than on a detailed treatment of history in the social studies program. It does not include specific suggestions for each grade, nor does it offer a rounded program of courses and methods. It contains some sug-

---

[49] Edwin R. A. Seligman, *The Economic Interpretation of History,* 2d ed. (New York: Columbia Univ. Press, 1961), p. 3.

gestions about (1) the material to be covered, (2) the question of organization, (3) the role of biography, and (4) the development of critical thinking.

What should be covered?

In general, the elementary and junior high school teacher should introduce the student to his own country and his own age through an emphasis on local, state, and national history. Local history should be taught not only for its own sake but as a microcosm of the larger story. The community can serve as a laboratory for progression from the near to the remote, the known to the unknown, and from locality to state and nation. Familiar landmarks in the vicinity—monuments, old houses, street names, highway markers—can be a link with the past. During a recent trip to New England the writer took the route followed by the British as they left Boston, paused at Lexington, and headed for Concord on that fateful April 18, 1775. At Concord he stood, like the embattled farmers, "by the rude bridge that arched the flood"; he visited Sleepy Hollow Cemetery and the graves of Emerson, Hawthorne, and Thoreau; he drove past Walden Pond, where Thoreau communed with nature; and he spent the night at the Colonial Inn, a structure dating from the early eighteenth century. Thus in a twentieth-century setting he caught a glimpse of the colonial period, the Revolution, and the nineteenth century. But the neighborhood of Concord is not the only locale steeped in history.

An understanding of national history is essential to an intelligent understanding of the present. Experience in the elementary grades seems to indicate that much can be done with the earlier period: the background of discovery and exploration, the colonial era, and the life of the nation to 1865. Though the later periods might be considered, it is perhaps better to leave them to the higher grades. And history at this level must be general rather than political, economic, or cultural.

Yet today's student has a much broader acquaintance with the world at large and so American history can be viewed as a part of the larger setting. We have never been strictly isolated from other peoples. The New World was a main objective of European imperialism; but so eventually were Africa, Asia, and indeed much of the seven seas. The Civil War, culminating in national unity, was one aspect of a larger process of nationalism which saw the unification of Italy and Germany, the defeat of federalism in Argentina, and the ascendancy of Canada to dominion status. The industrialization of the United States was part of a larger Industrial Revolution that spread through most of the Western world and even to areas beyond. If the elementary and junior high schools must concentrate upon American history, they can also point out our relationship to the world.

How should courses be organized?

They should follow mainly the familiar chronological and topical arrangement characteristic of history courses in general. "To make sense of our lives," says Joseph Grannis, "we must survey the stream of events that courses through them out of the past." [50] Instead of a general chronology, it would be preferable to use a series of shorter time spans involving a frame of reference of some kind, such as the European background, the winning of independence, or the westward movement. Ideally, for the student of these ages, the course should begin with the present; current events are an effective springboard to the past. At any rate, the bearing of past upon present should be made clear. Most programs appear to utilize the "here and now" approach, moving from the familiar to the strange, and from the present to past; in other words, from the child's immediate environment to the locality, the state, and the nation, and then to other civilizations.[51]

Beginning in the lower grades with an informal, storylike approach characterized by stress upon biography and important events, the history course should progress to increasing emphasis upon chronological and topical history, and in the higher grades to cause and effect relationships, so that students can look for the reasons behind historical occurrences. It must highlight the element of change and progress, so as to provide a fundamental understanding of social evolution.

For example, in the period up to the close of the Civil War, a

[50] Joseph C. Grannis, "The Framework of the Social Studies Curriculum," *The National Elementary Principal,* XLII (April), 20, 1963.

[51] John U. Michaelis, *Social Studies for Children in a Democracy,* 2d ed. (Englewood Cliffs, N.J.: Prentice-Hall, 1956), p. 6.

number of major topics can be developed with a concentration upon stories of famous people and significant events:

1. The Era of Discovery and Exploration: general factors in the broadening of the European horizon; motives for exploration; the New World setting; areas explored by various nations.
2. The Colonies: reasons for migration; contributions of national groups; study of representative colonies; evolution of the concept of democracy; the story of a basically rural society.
3. The Winning of Independence: the two sides to the dispute; outstanding people and events; stories associated with the Declaration of Independence and other historical documents.
4. Establishment of a Permanent Government: lives of selected Founding Fathers; difficulties faced by the governments; stories connected with the Constitution and the Bill of Rights; the nation in 1800.
5. The Splendid Wayfaring: reasons for migration west; modes of transportation; life on the frontier; what the frontier meant to America.
6. Division and Reunion: the nature of the quarrel between North and South; issues at stake; the role of individuals such as Lincoln and Davis; the war and its results.

These sections can be of absorbing interest. In the first, technology and geography can be linked with history. Much can be made of advances in the sailing of the seas (increase in size of ships and the use of instruments of navigation) and of the achievements of Henry the Navigator. Columbus' success in reaching the New World was due both to his ability and to a series of accidents. He miscalculated by several thousand miles the distance to the Far East; he altered his course by following the flights of birds and so reached the Caribbean islands rather than the North American mainland; and he was exceedingly lucky, considering the fact that he sailed during the hurricane season. In one sense, his voyage is a vivid illustration of the fortuitous in history. In evaluating the contribution of other nations to the larger American heritage, a unit on New England might begin with a comparison and contrast of the life of that region with Quebec, the predominantly French province to the north, and then proceed with the French colonial story. Students living in the southwestern United States would profit from a similar experiment with present-day Mexico. It is better to sample the colonies: Virginia, the pioneer and in many ways the prototype of the southern colonies; Massachusetts Bay, the hub of New England; and Pennsylvania, unique in its Quaker heritage but in other ways representative of the Middle Colonies. In the American Revolution, the teacher should be careful to discuss both sides and to devote considerable attention to the Decalaration of Independence. Is it not of human interest that two members of the drafting committee, John Adams and Thomas Jefferson, died within a few hours of each other on July 4, 1826, fifty years to the day of the signing? The framing of the Constitution and the establishment of a new government can readily be traced through the lives of such men as Washington, Hamilton, and Jefferson. Stories of pioneer life in the westward movement are always absorbing. During the past summer, the writer was at Fort Defiance Park in Illinois, where the Ohio and the Mississippi Rivers meet, and thought of the variety of queer craft used for transportation on the great rivers—vivid examples of American pioneer ingenuity. The West is interesting in many ways: deep woods in the Middle West but treeless plains in trans-Mississippi regions; in the one, flights of passenger pigeons that darkened the sky for hours, and in the other, buffalo herds so immense that they literally covered the horizon. The slaughter of the pigeon and the near extinction of the buffalo provide a melancholy object lesson in the conservation of natural resources. The Civil War Centennial has added to the already immense store of information about that era. Of course, the teacher must emphasize the larger and more significant historical facts; our point here is that incidental information can also be very useful.

The role of biography

If biography is not necessarily the basis of organization for the history course in the lower schools, it has, nevertheless, a number of advantages. Children at this level, as Ralph Adams Brown points out, often do not understand the more intricate movements such as industrialization; but the biographies of leaders who symbolize these larger trends increase their comprehension and their interest. The biographical approach is also valuable for training in the evaluation of current leadership as the child looks at the strengths and weaknesses of leadership in the past. Not the least significant contribution is the power to enrich the student's personality and contribute to his adjustment through identification with some great figure of the past.[52]   It is true that the child has difficulty in visualizing these personages as human beings who faced many of the same problems that people of today face.   Though the findings of psychologists seem to indicate that the years between one and fifteen are the most important period of personality development, biographers generally underplay these years and stress adulthood.[53] This is the point at which to humanize instruction.   Certainly George Washington was a highly dignified and at times even austere individual.   However, Washington assumes another dimension when we remember his great fondness for iced cream; and the fact that a contemporary traveler, visiting the headquarters of the Continental Army, could report that "apples and a great quantity of nuts were served, which General Washington continues eating for two hours, 'toasting' and conversing all the time." [54]   This is reminiscent of Franklin's two loaves of bread, Lincoln's rail splitting, and Theodore Roosevelt's children bursting into a cabinet meeting to announce the birth of a family of guinea pigs.

Developing critical thinking

In all grades, much attention should be given to the development of critical thinking.   One approach is by problem-solving through the use of historical method.   The rudiments of research can be taught: the collection of information, the establishment of facts, the distinction between primary and secondary materials, and the organization of a final report.   Problem-solving in this manner stresses training in a *process*: not the mere accumulation of facts but training in independent or original work, in the weighing of evidence, and in the systematic presentation of results.   Out of it the student gains an appreciation of the value of free inquiry and learns to

[52] For a convenient summary of values in the biographical approach, see Ralph Adams Brown, "Biography in the Social Studies," in *Social Studies in Elementary Schools,* ed. John U. Michaelis (Washington: National Council for the Social Studies, 1962), pp. 243–252.

[53] John C. Appel, "The Treatment of Childhood Years in American Biography," *Social Studies,* LI (November), 215–216, 1960.

[54] Marquis de Chastellux, *Travels in North America in the Years 1780, 1781 and 1782,* trans. Howard C. Rice, Jr. (Chapel Hill: Univ. of North Carolina Press, 1963), Vol. I, p. 109.

make intelligent judgments on many of the problems with which he will be faced. If man makes abundant use of the historical method in everyday life, the elementary grades are the place to begin. Here is preparation for the future.

When one says that the essential historical facts are those which furnish a clearer understanding of the present and a deeper insight into the forces which have produced present civilization, he touches on another necessity for critical thinking: students must go beyond facts to ideas. They can be taught the simpler concepts concerning geography in history, such as mountains, plains, and rivers. With difficulty, they can be introduced to more intangible concepts, such as democracy and cooperation. Through problem-solving they can grasp the relationship between concepts and thus reach generalizations such as "man adjusts to his environment" or "historical events nowadays affect people and places far beyond the limits of the place of their origin." [55] A writer suggests that the historical method can be used in the schools through the various theories of history that we have just discussed. The biographical interpretation develops an understanding of the continuity of history through illustration of the interdependence of great men; the spiritual thesis shows the persistence of an idea, such as the quest for freedom; the economic theory shows the transition from an agricultural to an industrial society; and the geographical interpretation shows historical change through a geographical structure.[56] This is at once an exercise in the use of historical method and an introduction to larger ideas.

Some final words about critical thinking are concerned with truth and controversy. Is the one to be distorted and the other to be avoided in teaching children and youth? Though the teacher must present the historical truth as established by fact, history is not to be regarded as a precise body of knowledge proven beyond all doubt. We have seen that historical truth is at times well established but that at other times it is relative. Myths and legends should be recognized as such. Yet if Parson Weems's story of Washington and the cherry tree represents the product of a fertile

[55] For a summary of some larger ideas and generalizations, see Vincent R. Rogers, "History for the Elementary School Child," *Kappan* (December), 132–135, 1952.

[56] J. D. McAulay, "Using the Historical Method in the Elementary School," *Social Education*, XXV (May), 247–249, 1961.

imagination, it also symbolizes honesty, at least on Washington's part.

The history course must include controversial issues. Naturally there are determinants such as degree of importance, availability of information, and suitability to age level. Obviously, elementary school children will not be debating the admission of Red China to the United Nations. But they should understand that complex situations arising from a multiplicity of causes admit of no simple solutions. There are many problems that history cannot solve. In such cases, a desirable attitude might be expressed as "yes, but—" or "no, but—." And above all, the fundamental principle of the right of dissenting opinion must be recognized and practiced.[57]

Should the history course be an indoctrination in democracy? It would be virtually impossible to avoid perpetuating the social order that created the system. And why not? If there are flaws in democracy, a way of life which requires a considerable degree of sophistication, it has worked well for Americans. Still, democracy should not be taught as something that is beyond question. That it allows for self-criticism is one of the great strengths of the democratic process.

In this excursion into history, we have elaborated on its meaning, discussed and applied some of its main ideas, and touched briefly on its organization of knowledge. After a general commentary on the nature of historical method, we have illustrated the process through the examination of a specific research problem. We have looked at some philosophies and theories of history and at intervals we have pointed out the connection between history and other sciences. Finally, we have offered a few suggestions as to the role of this discipline in the schools. These are some of Clio's many faces.

SUGGESTED READINGS

This sampling represents primarily the ideas, goals, methods, and materials of history rather than its facts. Some works are oriented

[57] For an excellent discussion on this subject, see Robert L. Brackenbury, "Case for Controversy," *The National Elementary Principal*, XLII (April), 14–19, 1963.

toward the layman, the amateur, and the student (though the teacher can read them with profit), and have as their theme a general understanding of history. Others are more technical manuals of historical method, and a few are histories of historiography. A number, anthologies or otherwise, reflect theories, "schools," or philosophies of history. In one way or another, all are concerned with the meaning of history.

INTRODUCTIONS TO HISTORY

GUSTAVSON, CARL G., *A Preface to History* (New York: McGraw-Hill, 1955). An outline of the nature of historical-mindedness on a level elementary enough for first-year college students. Thoughtful discussions of the nature of history and the relevancy of the past to the present.

NEVINS, ALLAN, *The Gateway to History* (Garden City, N.Y.: Doubleday, 1962). A delightful off-the-record book, written by a distinguished historian who insists on calling himself "an amateur of history," and who hopes that it may assist other amateurs.

ROWSE, A. L., *The Use of History* (New York: Macmillan, 1948). Chatty, informal discussion by a British historian who is particularly concerned with the values of history.

MANUALS

GARRAGHAN, GILBERT J., *A Guide to Historical Method,* ed. Jean Delanglez (New York: Fordham Univ. Press, 1946). More involved with ideas and with general history than the other manuals. One interesting feature is the multitude of excerpts from historians and other writers.

GOTTSCHALK, LOUIS, *Understanding History: A Primer of Historical Method* (New York: Alfred A. Knopf, 1950). Deals not only with method but with theories and philosophies of history and with the relationship of history to various sciences.

GRAY, WOOD, and others, *Historian's Handbook: A Key to the Study and Writing of History* (Boston: Houghton Mifflin, 1959). Right to the point, and the briefest treatment of the subject.

HOCKETT, HOMER CARY, *The Critical Method in Historical Research and Writing* (New York: Macmillan, 1955). An old standby for the teacher and student, with extensive bibliography. Restricted mostly to American history.

HISTORIES OF HISTORIOGRAPHY

BARNES, HARRY ELMER, *A History of Historical Writing* (New York: Dover Publications, 1962). A compendium of the development of historical writing from ancient times to the present.

———, "History," in *Encyclopaedia Britannica* (1963), Vol. XIV, pp.

205–264. A more concise history of historiography, and particularly good on trends in the theory and philosophy of history.

FITZSIMMONS, MATTHEW, and others, eds., *The Development of Historiography* (Harrisburg, Pa.: The Stackpole Company, 1954). Presents an account of the evolution of historical writing from its beginnings to contemporary times. Includes a brief introduction which discusses the nature of the historian's task.

HISTORY, THE ARTS, AND THE SCIENCES

HULME, EDWARD MASLIN, *History and Its Neighbors* (London: Oxford Univ. Press, 1942). An interesting and well-written discussion of anthropology, literature, economics, statistics, and other neighbors of history.

NEFF, EMERY, *The Poetry of History: The Contribution of Literature and Literary Scholarship to the Writing of History Since Voltaire* (New York: Columbia Univ. Press, 1961). One volume in a series designed to illustrate the interdependence between arts and science.

SHERA, JESSE HAUK, *Historians, Books, and Libraries: A Survey of Historical Scholarship in Relation to Library Resources, Organization and Services* (Cleveland: The Press of Western Reserve Univ., 1953). Keyed to the librarian but has good summary sections on history in general and the materials of history.

SALMON, LUCY MARNARD, *Historical Material* (New York: Oxford Univ. Press, 1933). In addition to chapters dealing with the records of nature, myth, language, and other sources, has two entertaining and illuminating sections on local history.

IDEAS AND INTERPRETATIONS

CARR, EDWARD HALLETT, *What Is History?* (New York: Alfred A. Knopf, 1962). Not detailed but one of the most stimulating discussions of the subject.

COHEN, MORRIS R., *The Meaning of Human History* (La Salle, Ill.: The Open Court Publishing Company, 1947). One of the best books on the interpretation of history.

GARDINER, PATRICK, ed., *Theories of History* (New York: The Free Press of Glencoe, 1959). An anthology which includes both theories and philosophies of history, as well as a section dealing with history and the social sciences.

HIGHET, GILBERT, *The Migration of Ideas* (New York: Oxford Univ. Press, 1954). Interesting brief and simplified discussion of the transit of ideas from one civilization to another.

MEYERHOFF, HANS, ed., *The Philosophy of History in Our Time: An Anthology* (Garden City, N.Y.: Doubleday, 1959). A good editorial introduction, followed by a selection of writings "contemporary" in their application to the present.

RENIER, G. J., *History: Its Purpose and Method* (Boston: Beacon Press,

1950). Deals with history and its methods but to a great extent with ideas as well.

SELIGMAN, EDWIN R. A., *The Economic Interpretation of History* (New York: Columbia Univ. Press, 1961). A classic statement of a point of view by one of its pioneers.

STERN, FRITZ, ed., *The Varieties of History from Voltaire to the Present* (New York: Meridian Books, 1957). An anthology, with a good editorial introduction, which presents views of "practicing" western historians on historical problems, as well as the major movements in historiography since 1750.

STRAYER, JOSEPH R., ed., *The Interpretation of History* (New York: Peter Smith, 1950). Strayer's thoughtful introduction on the nature and use of history is followed by provocative chapters on popular and unpopular history, the place of biography, the science and theology of history, and the economic impact on history.

3   Geography

Lillian W. Stimson
Department of Geography
University of Tennessee

THE PAST QUARTER OF A CENTURY HAS SEEN A MARKED REVIVAL OF
interest in geography at all levels. Geography is a subject that is
most intimately connected with daily life. Signs of man's use and
occupancy of the environment in many kinds of interlocking relationships are evident everywhere. Instruction in geography helps
students to understand changes in their environment, man's use of
resources, the variety of human settlements on the earth, and the
interactions of people, physical forces, and animal and plant life.
As Hill has stated: "The study of geography involves locations and
distributions as deep into the earth and as far above the earth as
man goes. Knowledge and skills acquired from thinking geographically enhance the learner's sense of value as a citizen in his community, state, nation and world." [1]

Geography encourages exploration, stresses location and spatial
interaction, involves measurement, and draws ideas from other disciplines. Like other sciences, geography applies definite methods
of study to certain groups of systematically collected facts in an at-

---

[1] Wilhelmina Hill, ed., *Curriculum Guide For Geographic Education,*
Geographic Education Series (Normal, Ill.: National Council For Geographic
Education, Illinois State Normal Univ., 1963), p. v.

tempt to describe, explain, and predict relationships. It attempts to define and focus on the action of fundamental recurring elements or forces at work in the physical and cultural environments of mankind. Geography finds its unity and distinction as a field of knowledge in studying the character of areas in different regions on the earth surface.

Geography is both an art and a science. As an art, geography presents descriptions of regions that portray selected features which are a representation of reality, but which like a painting do not reveal all of the details. As a science, geography presents concepts and theories that are useful in explaining spatial relations among physical, cultural, and biologic elements.

Backgrounds

Geography was a concern of the early civilizations inhabiting the Nile and Tigris-Euphrates valleys, and later of the peoples around the Aegean Sea. Early scholars were interested in geographic information pertaining to three areas: (1) facts concerning the inhabited world, (2) beliefs as to the shape of the earth and its place in the universe, and (3) measurement.[2] About 520 B.C., Hecateus wrote *Description of the Earth,* which included accounts of coastal areas, inland tribes, and the Persian Empire. In the fifth century B.C., Herodotus wrote comparative descriptions of peoples living in different environments in Greece and Persia. Another historian-geographer was Thucydides, who included geographic facts in his account of the Peloponnesian War. About 300 years later, Polybius wrote a volume that dealt with geography in relation to history. A member of the Pythagorean school of philosophers appears to have been the first to advance the concept of a spherical earth.[3] Eratosthenes (276–194 B.C.) wrote a critical history of geography beginning with the Homeric period, mapped his world, and calculated the circumference of the earth to be 25,000 miles.[4] Hipparchus, in about 140 B.C., was the first to map with any degree of accuracy the

---

[2] R. E. Dickinson and O. J. R. Howarth, *The Making of Geography* (London: Oxford Univ. Press), 1933, p. 2.

[3] *Ibid.,* p. 10.

[4] *Ibid.,* p. 24.

known world using points of latitude and longitude. He divided the great circle into 360 degrees and introduced a system of climatic zones based on latitude.[5]   Strabo, who lived at the time of the birth of Christ, wrote seventeen volumes on the geography of Europe, Asia, and Africa, describing these continents in more detail than was done previously and establishing the method which was followed later during the Renaissance revival. These great scholars were followed by Seneca the younger, who added much to existing physical geographic knowledge, and Ptolemy, who toward the end of the classical period compiled geographic reports that were not surpassed for centuries to come.   Ptolemy was the first to use the still standard geographical conception of the network of meridians and parallels; he placed mathematical geography on a firm foundation.[6]

From earliest times, some aspects of geography have been much the same: the study of the arrangement of things on the face of the earth and the reasons for the differences from place to place. All persons who face problems involving location, or who examine the conditions peculiar to specific locations are concerned with geography.   No doubt geography was understood and spoken of long before it was written.   Today, geographic writing is directed to many audiences.   Much of the literature is descriptive, popularly written and intended for the layman; some of it is highly theoretical and intended primarily for the student of geography; some of it is practical and intended for the immediate use of persons in such fields as planning, transportation, and industry.

Early geographers were concerned primarily with the identification of phenomena which gave distinction to areas; they described what they saw and made the first attempts to find ways to measure things and to transfer data to maps.   Until the nineteenth century, geography was considered to be a description of the earth and as such had three distinct aspects: (1) the earth as a member of the universe, (2) the earth, its shape, size, latitude, and longitude, and (3) the detailed description of its several parts based on political divisions.   Ptolemy gave to these aspects the titles of cosmography, geography and chorography; he thought of them as three separate subjects, dealing with different groups of related facts.[7]   During the

---

[5] *Ibid.,* p. 26.
[6] *Ibid.,* p. 35.
[7] *Ibid.,* p. 246.

Dark Ages in Europe, little was added to geographic knowledge, but with the voyages of exploration and discovery all known methods and techniques were brought into use in an attempt to map and record data pertaining to the new lands. Advances were made in cartography using the method of triangulation with the compass and plane-table for making detailed surveys.[8]

Geography as we know it today is new, its foundation having been laid by Humboldt and Ritter, nineteenth-century German scholars. Humboldt is acclaimed for his research and writing on the character and interrelationships of physical phenomena, while Ritter is recognized for his understanding of the interdependence of man and nature. Humboldt was primarily a physical geographer who attempted not only to coordinate facts but to establish laws to explain their character and distribution. Ritter's interest in geography lay in showing the dependence of the history of man on the environment, thus laying the foundations of modern human and regional geography.[9] Ratzel (1844–1904) promoted human geography through his works on anthropogeography and political geography. His views were brought to the attention of American geographers by Ellen Churchill Semple in her works on *American History and Its Geographic Conditions*[10] and *Influences of Geographic Environment on the Basis of Ratzel's System of Anthropogeography.*[11]

Two French geographers, Paul Vidal de la Blache (d. 1918) and Jean Brunhes (d. 1930) advanced the modern concept of geography, labeled as *Possibilism,* as contrasted with Ratzelian *Determinism.* La Blache recognized the necessity for more detailed synthetic studies in geography, and through his efforts several regional monographs were published. He was interested in the study of cause and effect and in establishing general principles through the comparative study of different parts of the globe.[12] Brunhes introduced order, a principle of classification, and a method of treatment to the facts of human occupation of the earth, thus encompassing

[8] *Ibid.,* p. 247.
[9] *Ibid.,* pp. 142–143.
[10] Ellen Churchill Semple, *American History and Its Geographic Conditions* (New York: Henry Holt & Co., 1903).
[11] Ellen Churchill Semple, *Influences of Geographic Environment* (New York: Henry Holt & Co., 1911).
[12] *Ibid.,* p. 207.

the field of economic, political, and social geography.[13]   Alfred Hettner, a German scholar, was to advance both the regional concept and geographic method in his writings based on field studies made in South America and in his own country.   While concerned with the same phenomena, geography has been enriched by the growth of science and by the background of systematic knowledge provided by other disciplines.   Today's geographer looks at particular places with a view to understanding how physical, cultural, and biotic processes operate in different regions of the earth.   He is concerned increasingly with the application of "mathematical formulas from the field of physics to the description of the volume and velocity of movements in relation to the factors of location and distance." [14]

During the past two centuries a number of deviations from the mainstream of geographic thought have appeared.   Some of these disappeared quickly; others persisted for a longer time.   In the nineteenth century, the concepts of causal relationship led some geographers to overemphasize physical and biologic phenomena at the expense of human relationships.   This was notably true of the work of William Morris Davis in his studies of physical geography dealing with the cycle of youth, maturity, and old age in landforms. Many of Ratzel's disciples, who were not as careful observers as he had hoped, insisted that geographic analysis must show relationships which cross the border between physical and human phenomena, overlooking the relationships on the same side of the border.   Many geographers who were trained in physical geography deliberately sought examples of environmental influence and refused to recognize other evidence.   Today, geography cannot be divided into just physical and human; the geographer must recognize any factor of location or areal association which is pertinent to his problem and treat it in a geographic manner.[15]

According to Preston James, geography has three distinctive contributions to make to the advancement of knowledge:

(1) it contributes toward a better understanding of the earth as the habitat of man by extending the findings of the other sciences; (2) it pro-

[13] *Ibid.*, p. 210.
[14] Preston E. James, ed., *New Viewpoints In Geography,* Twenty-ninth Yearbook (Washington: National Council for the Social Studies, 1959), p. 13.
[15] *Ibid.*, pp. 13–16.

vides a means of testing the validity of certain concepts developed by the other sciences by applying them in particular places; and (3) it offers its own peculiar perspective to the clarification of the issues involved in problems of public or private policy.[16]

Three excellent books have been published in the United States which discuss the field of geography. Richard Hartshorne's *The Nature of Geography* [17] is a historical study which traces the mainstream of geographic thought and the important deviations. Hartshorne presents the many points of view held by geographers over the centuries regarding the systematic description and analysis of regions. The second book, *American Geography: Inventory and Prospect,* previously cited, involved the efforts of many professional geographers and was edited by Preston E. James and Clarence F. Jones. This study brought together the experience of several decades in the formulation of geographic concepts and in the development of procedures for carrying on geographic research. The third, by Richard Hartshorne, *Perspective on the Nature of Geography* (1959) [18] deals with selected issues and problems in geography as a field of study. In this volume Hartshorne discusses definitions of geography, meaning of the "earth surface," integration of ideas, human and natural factors, systematic and regional geography, and other concerns of modern geographers.

James [19] explains and identifies geography as follows:

Geography is that field of learning in which the characteristics of particular places on the earth's surface are examined. It is concerned with the arrangement of things and with the associations of things that distinguish one area from another. It is concerned with the connections and movements between areas. The face of the earth is made up of many different kinds of features each the momentary result of an ongoing process . . . the face of the earth is marked off into distinctive areas; geography seeks to interpret the significance of likenesses and differences among places in terms of causes and consequences.

[16] Preston E. James and Clarence F. Jones, eds., *American Geography: Inventory and Prospect,* Association of American Geographers (Syracuse, N.Y.: Syracuse Univ. Press, 1954), p. 6.

[17] Richard Hartshorne, *The Nature of Geography* (Lancaster, Pa.: Association of American Geographers, 1939; Edwards Brothers, Inc., reprinted with corrections, 1961).

[18] Richard Hartshorne, *Perspective on the Nature of Geography* (Chicago: Rand McNally, 1959).

[19] James, *op. cit.,* p. 10.

UNESCO offers the following definition of geography: "Geography consists in locating, describing, explaining and comparing scenery and human activities on the globe," [20] thus placing man in his geographic environment and studying his relations to it. Hartshorne put it very concisely when he said, "Geography . . . studies phenomena of unlimited variety in interrelationships of the greatest variety." [21]

The determination of the nature, scope, and purposes of geography is largely a problem in empirical research. Because of its long historical development, geography possesses a rich literature, both methodological and substantive; it is what geographers have made it. The scientific approach fosters new ideas about geography so that the scholar need not feel that he must continue to work with the same concepts which guided earlier students in the field. Hartshorne feels that "New conceptual approaches and techniques will result only from intensive substantive work in particular branches or aspects of the field." [22]

To the extent that geography deals with human groupings in their activities around the globe, and to the degree that it helps to meet the behavioral needs of people living in a free society, geography is a behavioral science. The geographer is concerned with values, knowledge, and skills just as other social scientists are.

Subdivisions of Geography

Although most geographers agree on the essential unity of the field, various forms of duality have appeared in the past which have cast a shadow over the field. Geography is not physical versus human or regional versus topical; it is all of these and more if it is to lead to an understanding of the integration of phenomena distributed over areas of the earth. Man studies landforms in order that he may be aware of the various ways in which he may influence his activities on the earth, just as he studies crops and cropping systems so that he may understand his relationship to soils and productivity

[20] UNESCO, *Some Suggestions on the Teaching of Geography: Towards World Understanding* (Paris: UNESCO, 1949), VII, p. 9.
[21] Richard Hartshorne, *Perspective on the Nature of Geography*, p. 34.
[22] *Ibid.*, p. 9.

and their contribution to the satisfaction of his needs or wants. Because some features of the environment are largely independent of man while others are primarily the results of his work, it is feasible to specialize in the study of both areas and topics. Such specialization will be more fruitful when based on phenomena which are usually found in close interrelationships, such as rural areas where man uses the land primarily for crop production, or urban areas where he has modified the entire landscape to make it fit for such functions as manufacturing, commerce, and transportation.

Hartshorne feels that it is unfortunate, from the point of view of sound development in geography and of the student's comprehension of his world, that college faculties and course requirements are divided between the "natural" and the "social" sciences and that each of these is further subdivided. He feels that "To establish our proper place in the over-all education function, we need to impress on our faculties and administrators the distinctive value which, as Hettner and Schütter observed, geography can offer in reuniting our cultural life, which now tends to fall apart in diverging directions." [23]

The committee of the Association of American Geographers which prepared *American Geography: Inventory and Prospect* listed the following subdivisions of geography as parts of the whole in which geographers in the United States have been actively at work for more than half a century or believe it essential that geographers should work: [24]

Regional Geography	Medical Geography
Historical Geography	The Geography of Resources
Population Geography	Economic Geography
Settlement Geography	Marketing Geography
Urban Geography	Recreational Geography
Political Geography	Agricultural Geography
Climatology	The Geography of Mineral Production
Physiological Climatology	
Geomorphology	The Geography of Manufacturing
The Geography of Water Resources	Transportation Geography
	Military Geography
Plant Geography	Field Techniques
Animal Geography	Photogrammetry
Soils Geography	Cartography

[23] *Ibid.*, p. 80.
[24] James and Jones, *op. cit.*, pp. x–xi.

It is apparent from the foregoing list that many other disciplines are germane to the work of geographers. In the interpretation of environmental relationships, facts must be drawn from the physical and the social sciences. For example, climatology is based on meteorology, physical geography or geology, mathematical geography in part on astronomy, and biogeography on botany and zoology; while on the social side, economic geography is dependent upon economics, human geography on sociology, political and historical geography on history, and racial geography on anthropology and psychology. It is the nature of geography to be an integrating science, and it is in regional geography that one sees the synthesis of human and physical elements crystallized. Many persons think of geography as a bridge between the physical and social sciences, probably more used by students of the social sciences, but of importance to both in understanding world problems.

Four Traditions

The work of American geographers has shown broad consistency, and this essential unity may be attributed to four distinct but related traditions operating as binders in the minds of members of the profession: (1) a spatial tradition, (2) an area studies tradition, (3) a man-land tradition, and (4) an earth science tradition.[25]

From the beginning, American geographers have been concerned with the significance of *spatial analysis,* that is, abstracting from the happenings of experience certain aspects of reality such as distance, form, direction, and position. Thus, the elementary school teacher who uses the most simple instruction in directions and mapping may feel himself identified with the contemporary research geographer struggling to portray more accurately shore lines or to interpret Antarctica.

The *area studies* tradition, distinguished as it is by a point of view, is quite as important today as it was in Strabo's world. Geographers have long been concerned with the nature of places, their similarities and differences. Teachers are accustomed to us-

[25] William D. Pattison, "The Four Traditions of Geography," *Journal of Geography,* 63 (May), 211–216, 1964.

ing area studies as a method of presentation, and citizens of the United States today should understand the term since it is commonly used with reference not only to a variety of internal studies but to numerous activities of this nation in its relations with other countries. A current problem in America today is our inability to understand how the South Vietnamese expect to stop the Communist threat; our knowledge of the physical environment is sparse but our lack of knowledge and understanding relative to different cultural and religious philosophies is far greater.

That people generally are beginning to be concerned about the *man-land* tradition which dwells upon relationships is evidenced by the widespread interest in the publication of a collection of papers edited by William L. Thomas and titled *Man's Role in Changing the Face of the Earth*.[26] There is a definite concern for the way in which man has used the environment, and especially for the problems relating to a rapidly expanding population in terms of the available food supply. Interest in such matters immediately centers on use of resources and conservation. In Formosa in 1951 there were 667 persons per square mile as compared to 586 in Japan, 150 in Communist China and 51 in the United States. These figures are alarming enough but when viewed against the amount of arable land available they become a challenge to the population expert and to the agricultural scientist: Formosa has 2,864 persons per square mile of cultivable land, Japan has 3,534, Red China, 1,485, and the United States, 188.

For many years the *earth science* tradition received the primary emphasis in geography; it comprises a study of the earth, its waters, its atmosphere, and earth-sun relations. This tradition is recognizable through concrete objects, so social scientists as well as other scholars readily accept help from this part of geography. Social scientists view earth science as something physically associated with their discipline, yet not within their area of competence; herein lies the strength for geography in the earth science curriculum. This concept emphasizes the earth from the standpoint of the physical sciences. Emphasis is placed on the earth as a sphere, the lands of the earth, the waters of the earth, climate and the seasons, plant

[26] William L. Thomas, *Man's Role In Changing the Face of the Earth* (Chicago: Wenner-Gren Foundation, Univ. of Chicago Press, 1956).

and animal life, and rocks and minerals. It is in this realm also that the conservation-minded person of today feels great concern, for he recognizes the fixed quantities and lowered quality of many of these items. He recognizes, for example, the need for improved technology in petroleum, ranging from surveys of deposits to the final instrument in usage, whether it be in a jet plane or an oil-burning furnace in the home.

The four traditions, while distinct, are joined in action; geography currently pursues all of the traditions; and from scrutinizing them one sees the explanations for the customary divisions of geography into the human, physical, systematic, regional, urban, and industrial. There is a place for each tradition in the schools. The teacher of geography and the social studies must recognize this and prepare himself to introduce his pupils to the many nations of the world in their current role as close neighbors. Children and youth must understand that man's activities depend not only on the physical properties of the land but also on people's attitudes toward the land and the skill they manifest in using it.

Primary Elements of the Physical and Cultural Environment

In considering concepts and generalizations from geography, it is helpful to start with key elements of the physical and cultural environment. Although writers disagree on the specifics to emphasize, there is general agreement on at least five categories for the elementary school: (1) the earth as a planet, (2) the many different ways of making a living, (3) the variety of natural regions, (4) the importance of regions to man, and (5) the significance of location to those who want to understand world affairs.[27]

Most geographers agree that geography is a study of the description and interpretation of the physical and cultural environments with an emphasis placed on the interplay among the elements

[27] Gertrude Whipple, "Geography in the Elementary Social Studies Program: Concepts, Generalizations, and Skills to Be Developed," in James, *op. cit.*, pp. 115–116.

of each environment and between the two environments. Geographic concepts, techniques of study, and skills should be included in the social studies so that students will learn to "think geographically" and to describe and interpret the environments as geographers do. Attention should be given to both environments and to the interaction between them.

A first step in planning the curriculum in the schools is to identify the primary elements in both the physical and cultural environments. The primary elements of the physical environment are: earth and universe, land and landforms, minerals and rocks, soil, water and water bodies, weather and climate, plant life, animal life, and locational and spatial relationships. The primary geographic elements of the cultural environment are: amount and distribution of population, houses and settlements, production and distribution, transportation and communication, conservation, and recreation. These elements can be made a part of units of study at all levels of instruction.

Having established the two primary concepts of geography as, first, having to do with the make-up of regions and, second, dealing with causal relationships, it is now desirable to see how these may be applied to programs of instruction, grades K–12. Since geography is a definite concern of those working with it as a discipline, they desire that this field of study be implemented in the social studies curricula of the public schools.

It is not enough simply to list the elements in the physical and cultural environments; each needs to be elaborated to reveal teachable concepts and generalizations that can be incorporated in the instructional program. One approach is to state generalizations that may be used as strands that run through the program and are given appropriate attention at each level of instruction. A good example of this approach is presented in the Appendix. Notice that the elements presented above are included in the generalizations drawn from physical and cultural geography. School personnel are urged to review each generalization systematically in order to identify points in the curriculum at which related content can be used to sharpen students' comprehension of geographic elements and to improve their ability in formulating generalizations.

Another approach is to identify fundamental concepts and to indicate ways in which they can be made a part of the instructional program in both elementary and secondary schools. Recently the National Council for Geographic Education published a report, *Curriculum Guide for Geographic Education,* in which Henry J. Warman outlined nine fundamental concepts and discussed each one in detail.[28]

Globalism

The earth's sphericity is a concept that can be used to develop understandings about location, distance, and periods of daylight and darkness. Understanding of the latter calls for a study of earth-sun relationships, the earth's rotation and revolution, and the inclination and the parallelism of the axis, which are also basic to an understanding of the seasonal distribution of heat on the earth. From an understanding of the global shape of the earth, one is able to see where the greatest heat from the sun is received and how it is distributed throughout the year over the curved surface of the earth. This provides a basis for the description of climatic patterns, vegetation zones, and the seasonal activities of mankind.

The round earth on flat paper

This concept suggests both ideas and problems in the portrayal of the curved surface of the earth on a plane. Mathematics is required if one is to understand the construction of a projection. One must use horizontal and vertical distances, and the cardinal directions (north-south, east-west) as well as up and down in the development of essential understandings.

The principal phases of cartography are related to the uses to which the map or maps are to be put. Is one constructing a map which shows true shape, or is he interested in one which has "equal area" characteristics? If neither is entirely desirable, what compromises are best? When decisions have been made and the map completed, the symbols used will have been adjusted and adapted to the projection and the scale. The symbols may be of physical or

[28] Henry J. Warman, "Major Concepts in Geography," in Hill, *op. cit.,* pp. 9–27.

cultural geographic phenomena, but all have been fitted onto a plane surface representing all or a part of the "round earth on paper."

The life-layer

Perhaps the most important function of the continents is that they provide living space for people. On each continent there are certain areas which are preferred over others for the desirability of a place for habitation, which concept is understood primarily in terms of three significant elements: soil, air, and water. People, plants, and animals tend to live in the greatest numbers where soil, air, and water are found in the most desirable combinations and where sustenance may be obtained not only from each other but from inanimate factors around them.

Areal distinction, differences, and likenesses

This concept follows that of the life-layer but it could just as well be considered under that of *the region,* which is discussed next. The understandings essential to its realization are based on two simple assertions: people differ from place to place, and environment differs from place to place. Students should search for the arrangement of people and things and how distinctive associations and interactions exist in selected areas; the comparison of areas calls for the imaginative use of geographic data and should lead to clearer understanding of the unity and diversity of both the physical and cultural elements in man's environment.

The region and regionalizing

This is a key concept of geography. To build this concept one must know how to identify regions and how to develop and use the techniques of regionalizing: one cannot draw lines around an area and call it a region. Geographers seek to recognize and identify meaningful nucleations of phenomena in space; they may try to show certain physical elements of an environment in their varied interlocking relations; or they may attempt to present patterns of man-made phenomena. Inherent in the development of the regional concept is the choice of significant criteria. Such criteria may be mapped individually, but the real challenge comes in trying to portray the functionally interrelated complexes. At the primary level, seasonal changes in terms of plant and animal behavior are often studied; while at the intermediate level the pupils are ready to talk about areas in terms of how people residing in them meet the basic needs of living, and the tools and skills required for meeting these needs.

In the junior high school, students are ready for an analysis of the elements of geography and are ready to begin regionalizing about such things as climate, natural vegetation, certain crops, and the distribution of man; while at the senior high level, the student should be ready to look at the globe in terms of resources, ways of making a living, and "tension spots." This type of selection and analysis calls for the use of scale and measurement as well as criteria for defining a region.

The geographer may be confronted with a variety of kinds of regions—the physical, cultural, systematic, economic, the one-element, and the multi-element, or one which may be easy to delineate, such as the nation-state. In addition, it must be recognized that areal differences are in process of changing. One must be constantly aware of the need for observation, appraisal, and synthesis if he is to present clearly the many functionally related and interlocking phenomena which exist in a region.

Resources culturally defined

Man's concern today is with the use of such physical resources as soil, water, minerals and metals, fish and wildlife, and plants to meet bodily and esthetic needs. From these he derives other materials to be used in the creation of a vast array of items which are either useful or decorative and ornamental. In this concept are implicit man-land generalizations of many kinds, as well as an emphasis upon people as resources, a phenomenon often overlooked.

Man the chooser

In any environment it is man, individually or in groups, who makes decisions about how to use the environment, and whether for exploitative or continuing developmental purposes. He has organized various spatial systems which appeared rational at the time in his particular cultural milieu.

Spatial interaction

Movement within and between regions is facilitated by transport and communications routes; the goods carried and the particular mode of transportation used are some of the facts needed to develop an understanding of the concept. There is constant interplay and interdependence in the vegetative and animal life of the earth. Large regions of the world today interact in a variety of economic and political ways, e.g., the Common Market and the United Nations call for a certain degree of unity which may be achieved only by considering problems and differences among nations.

Perpetual transformation

Inherent in this concept are open-mindedness, and the knowledge and understanding that change is continuous, that regions once considered well developed now may be ill-developed in terms of meeting the demands of the technological age. The cultural environment is undergoing perpetual change, and so also is the physical world through the processes of tectonic change, and of aggradation and degradation. Thus there are no final answers in geography teaching; there is a geography for any and every time.

The concepts listed previously will seldom if ever be taught per se. Rather, they will be embedded in units of study and used repeatedly as foci for the organization of content. Each concept may well be viewed as a strand running through the K–12 program of instruction, with teachers in each grade guiding students to develop deeper and broader understandings. The concepts can also be used to generate questions and hypotheses about regions, use of resources, ways of living, and changes that are taking place in different areas. Viewed as core ideas of geography that should be stressed in the schools, the nine basic concepts may be coupled with methods of inquiry to give students deeper appreciation for the styles of thought so important in geography.

Methods of Inquiry

Geography is a discipline recognized by its point of view and its methods of investigation as well as by its subject matter. Its point of view is identified in terms of the regional concept; its method is the regional method. Geographers see the region as a device for selecting and studying the areal distributions of the vast array of phenomena found on the earth. If a portion of the earth's surface is found to be homogeneous in terms of an areal distribution, it may be studied as a region. Viewed in this manner, a region is not an object, but rather an intellectual concept. This interpretation of a region stemmed from experience in detailed field studies. Regional study which is basic to all phases of geography is neither fixed nor standardized. The late Derwent Whittlesey [29] said, "A student of regions is still forced to think for himself, to develop his own competence in making value judgments, and to bring to bear upon both accepted routines and untried possibilities the freshness of his own imagination."

Geography begins with the understandings provided by other systematic sciences (physics, geology, economics, etc.), and the student of geography searches for those areal variations on the earth's surface which have resulted from the operation of the processes of change. Anything which is irregularly distributed over the earth's surface may be studied to advantage by geographic methods which include mapping, census taking, graphing, observation, photography, and analyzing documents. The regions which a geographer identifies and views are plotted on maps. Utilizing modern methods of field observation, including areal photos, and modern statistical methods of defining and measuring areal relations, geographers can now achieve a degree of exactness and objectivity impossible earlier. Once a homogeneous area has been identified and plotted on a map, its outline may be matched against the outlines of other types of phenomena. Each phenomenon bears some kind of areal relationship to all other phenomena: some relationships are

[29] D. Whittlesey, "The Regional Concept and the Regional Method," in James and Jones, *op. cit.*, p. 65.

accordant and some are discordant. James says, "Accordant areal relations are found by matching maps and noting where regional outlines coincide or correspond. This is the regional method." [30]

Application of geographic procedures leads to the development of two kinds of concepts, one having to do with the make-up of regions, and the second dealing with causal relationships, explained by James as: "A casual connection can be demonstrated only by tracing the operation of a process through time. Coincident areal relations may indicate a probability of some kind of causal connection; but to prove that such a connection exists the nature of the process or processes that have produced the observed phenomena must be described." [31] Through the use of statistical techniques it is now possible to distinguish cause and effect relationships among areally associated phenomena and to eliminate such associations as may be the result of chance. Geographers continue to search for ways to describe more accurately and with greater proficiency the arrangement and association of phenomena on the earth. According to James [32] geographic study makes three kinds of contributions to understanding:

(1) it extends the findings of the systematic sciences by observing the differences between the theoretical operation of a process in isolation and the actual operation as modified by the conditions of the total environment of a particular place; (2) it provides a method of testing the validity of concepts developed by the systematic sciences; and (3) it provides a realistic analysis of the conditions of particular places and so aids in the clarification of the issues involved in all kinds of policy decisions.

Geographic study must be approached historically if it is to be complete. Hence, the methods of investigation discussed in Chapter 2 are used in historical geography. Geographers who are specialists in political, economic, or population geography (or others listed earlier) employ methods of study drawn from the related discipline. Thus, methods employed by political scientists, economists, sociologists, and anthropologists are used in different branches of geography. What is unique about their use in geography is the way in which

[30] Preston E. James, "American Geography at Mid-Century," in James, *op. cit.,* p. 17.
[31] *Ibid.,* p. 18.
[32] *Ibid.,* p. 12.

they are employed to explain and describe spatial relationships, associations, and interactions.

Because geography draws so many concepts and methods of inquiry from other disciplines, it is a synthesizing discipline similar in many ways to history. A major difference is that geography organizes data in spatial dimensions or regions while history organizes data in time dimensions; together, they provide information for synthesis or integration of time and space relationships. No other discipline actively attempts to draw so much from both the natural sciences and the social sciences, which is undoubtedly one of the reasons why geography holds such an important place in the social studies curriculum.

Geography in the Social Studies

Educators today are concerning themselves with planning a social studies curriculum for kindergarten through grade twelve or kindergarten through college. Whatever is accomplished in the improvement of the social studies must be viewed in relation to all of the social sciences. Basic social science concepts introduced early are strengthened and deepened in a spiral manner as the student matures.

Phillip Bacon has raised the question as to what constitutes the proper role of geographers who wish to contribute to the development of geography as a subject for study in the schools, and he answers it, in part, by saying that geographers must learn to communicate with teachers and others who are engaged in making the curriculum.[33] Professional geographers must give to teachers the kinds of knowledge needed in developing curricula, which knowledge will reflect geography as an area of study in the ways geographers understand their discipline.

Geography teachers are going to have to think of geography teaching more broadly than they have in the past, for present-day geography teaching must place heavy emphasis upon *people* and their relationship to the environmental circumstances in which they find themselves. Teachers may possess much geographical information without having developed a geographical point of view and

[33] Phillip Bacon, "An Introduction to Geography in the Curriculum," in Hill, *op. cit.*, pp. 3–4.

without having gained that insight into human problems which comes from seeing differences in problems and in ways of coping with them in different localities and regions.

Geography has numerous contributions to make to the content and method of all education since it is a study of the interaction of physical, cultural, and biotic elements as well as the influence of man's environment upon his needs, interests, problems, and activities. There is a need for education in geographic thinking and for the geographic interpretation of today's problems. A program of geographic instruction should begin in the grades and continue into high school and on into college. If young people are to understand the world in which they live, the schools must help them to realize that the world has grown smaller, and that nations once far removed in space and time are now only hours away. Teachers must encourage their pupils to interpret geographically what they hear, read, and see if they are to develop an awareness of the dynamic geographic relationships of which they are a part.

James says it is time that the hard core of geography be returned to the social studies, that geography be taught as the analysis of the meaning of place and position on the earth, and of the significance of the areal association of phenomena.[34] This calls for knowledgeable understanding of word and map symbols, and for the problems related to showing the curved surface of the earth on a plane. It consists of an understanding of the geography of the contemporary world made meaningful by reference to historical processes which will create the future and out of which the present was created.

There is widespread disagreement as to whether more geography is taught better when included as a part of the earth science or behavioral science curriculum, or when presented as a separate subject. Whatever the decision, geography is and must always be a part of the social studies program. Perhaps there is good argument for teaching geography from these several approaches as students progress from grades K–12. While it is beyond the scope of this chapter to suggest how all of the nine concepts of geography mentioned earlier may be developed, an attempt will be made to

[34] James, *New Viewpoints, op. cit.,* p. 9.

show how some may be implemented at various levels in the curriculum.

The elementary and junior high school program

Examination of currently used textbooks indicates repeated emphasis on basic geographic concepts. For example, in one seventh-grade textbook the following are included: [35]

1. The world is made up of many different peoples living in many different kinds of places.
2. The natural environment in which people live helps to explain why they live and make a living in the ways they do.
3. The skills people develop, their education, their cultural and spiritual heritage, their stage of economic development, all help to explain why people live the way they do.
4. The varied ways of living in the world are not odd, but reasonable, when seen in terms of the environment in which people live and their education, skills, and heritage of ideas. Understanding *why* people live in the ways they do encourages an attitude of respect for and realistic understanding of other people.
5. Man lives in a changing world; people everywhere are changing their ways of living and will continue to change them.
6. All people everywhere are interdependent; they depend on people in their own community, in their own country, and in other countries.
7. Community living is a common experience all over the world. A study of the geography of real communities helps pupils recognize the importance of the individual person and his relation to the group.
8. The geography of any part of the world today is largely an outgrowth of its geography in earlier times. Historical geography helps pupils understand the world in which they live today.
9. Making a living is a major concern of all people. The study of geography helps develop an appreciation of the importance and dignity of different kinds of work.
10. Government is of critical importance in people's lives and helps to explain the ways men live and work and think.
11. People by working together can usually achieve more than when working alone. Cooperation leads to a better life for all.
12. Intelligent use of natural resources is of vital importance to people everywhere.

[35] Clarence W. Sorensen, *A World View* (Morristown, N.J.: Silver Burdett Co., 1964). Study of the fourth-grade text verifies the fact that such ideas are emphasized in the early years of school.

Concepts and generalizations such as those listed above may also be found in units of study. One very rewarding unit for seventh graders in the metropolitan Knoxville area was based on a study of the local community during which the pupils were asked to prepare questions and hypotheses related to the study of their home community.[36] Together with their teacher they listed questions or topics for study, suggested purposes of such a unit of work, and made decisions on the most significant topics to be studied. As the unit of work progressed, the pupils used a variety of content gleaned from books, magazines, newspapers, and resource persons who were invited to work in the classroom with the children in an attempt to recognize more accurately and to identify their particular roles in the community. Field trips were made to industries, to points of historic interest, and to governmental offices. With the development of the unit, the pupils recognized that they were gaining understandings related to concepts 2, 3, 5, 6, 8, 9, and 11 in the previous list. To further clarify each concept, the teacher had students gather visual materials, and arranged them in selected areas about the room, thus providing added opportunity for the students to engage in analytical and comparative studies.

In another unit entitled "Five Great Natural Resources and How Men Use Them," the same teacher and pupils developed an understanding of why people living in certain environments make their living as they do, and of the interdependence of men in all nations (concepts 2 and 6). They took a look at people who made their living directly from natural resources. People were studied at their work on all six inhabited continents including those who live in highly mechanized societies as well as those who follow ways of the past. Other concepts related to the study of hunters and trappers, fishermen, ranchers, herders, farmers, forestry and mineral workers were stressed. The students became aware of the changing world as they explored the activities of workers who seem bound to the past. Every effort was made to find how *change* is affecting these workers who depend *directly* on natural resources for their livelihood.

The concept that the geography of any part of the world today is largely an outgrowth of its geography in earlier times was developed

[36] Jane C. Humble, Knox County Schools, Knoxville, Tennessee, personal communication, 1964.

by the same teacher and group in a study of South America. Specific ideas stressed were:

1. To understand how people live and make a living in South America, the main features of the continent must be kept in mind: (a) high, cold Andes on the west; (b) vast Amazon lowland, hot, rainy, forested; (c) plains reaching southward, in places dry, in other places wet enough for grass and crops.
2. More than one half of workers are rural people who make a living directly from natural resources. South America produces raw materials and imports manufactured goods. (Here the class looked for the latest facts to discover *changes*.)
3. Most of the people and cities are near the edge of the continent. The countries turn their backs to each other and face toward the ocean. Films were used and pictures and articles on Brazilia were examined to show how man is attempting to open up the interior. The ensuing difficulties were discussed.
4. South America was first occupied by Indians, and later colonized by people from Spain and Portugal who brought with them ideas and ways of life of those countries.

The concept that government is of critical importance in people's lives and helps to explain the ways men live and work and think was developed by the same teacher and her students in a study of the Soviet Union. By the close of the school year the pupils had developed an appreciation of the earth as the habitat of man, and of the world as the home of many different peoples living in many different kinds of places.[37]

The senior high school program

While more emphasis has been placed on geography in the elementary and junior high schools there is an increasing need for more geography in the senior high school, many people feeling that at least one year of geography should be required of all secondary students. For many students high school is the end of formal education and these students therefore particularly need "functional and challenging opportunities to observe, analyze, interpret and synthesize various aspects of the geography of their own region and other regions of the world." [38]

[37] Jane C. Humble, personal communication, 1964.
[38] Mary Viola Phillips, "Suggested Sequences for Geographic Learning," in Hill, *op. cit.,* p. 44.

Several kinds of courses, depending on what has been taught before and the needs of children in a given school, have been recommended for grades ten, eleven, and twelve by a committee of the National Council for Geographic Education. At the tenth-grade level, three kinds of courses are generally taught: World Geography, World Patterns of Economic or Commercial Geography, and Economic Geography with emphasis on world distribution and exchange. At grade eleven, two different courses may well be considered: Geography of Latin America and Other Special Areas (depending on current world problems) and Geography of Local Areas within the framework of Historical Geography of the United States. At grade twelve, four courses are recommended: Geography of World Cultures, Geography of Selected Areas, World Political Geography, Geography of Current World Problems. Some persons would add as alternative courses in any one of the three grades, a course in Physical Geography or Earth Science (as either a one- or two-semester course) and one in Conservation or Resource Management.[39]

Each of the courses recommended by the committee has much to commend it, since each affords students the opportunity to think geographically in a variety of frames of reference, and to renew and utilize skills, techniques, attitudes, concepts, and generalizations learned in earlier years and to develop them to a higher degree.

James strongly recommends the use of culture areas as a frame of organization where geography is taught as a part of the social studies curriculum. He sees the culture area as an excellent opportunity for blending the study of geography and history and has identified seven culture areas for study: European, American, North African-Southwest Asian, Oriental, Soviet, African, and Pacific.[40] The American culture area has a rich heritage from the European, and because no major wars have been fought on its soil, it has had an unexcelled opportunity to explore new ideas and to move ahead in science and technology and in the fields of social and political relations. These ideas and inventions may not be applied per se to the

[39] *Ibid.*, pp. 44–50.
[40] See Preston E. James and Nelda Davis, *The Wide World: A Geography* (New York: Macmillan, 1959), for a characterization of these areas.

further development of other culture areas but they may be of value to them and in our understanding of them.

Skills and Techniques

Certain skills and techniques are essential to or very useful in both the learning and teaching of geography. Barton suggests that geographic instruction might be more effective if teachers were more certain of the meaning and use of such terms as "geography techniques," "geography abilities," and "geography skills." [41] Geographic techniques are the methods or procedures which enable one to use maps, atlases, and other tools and aids, and to think geographically. They often involve a sequence of activities. While it cannot be assumed that all children have equal ability to study geography and to learn to think geographically, it can be assumed that teachers may help design methods and procedures by which natural talents can be exploited with varying degrees of rapidity and efficiency. Geography skills include both a knowledge of and ability to carry out geographic activities. Many of these skills represent the development of facility in making, using, and interpreting the tools of geography. The innate ability of the child and the techniques used in the teaching process will determine how completely and rapidly he develops a new skill.

Many of the techniques pupils will use in learning geography are similar to those used in learning biological and physical sciences, or history and other social sciences. Teachers, however, tend to associate some of the tools of learning more closely with geography than with other subjects. Hence, the techniques of reading globes, maps, atlases, profiles, cross sections, and weather instruments are usually developed in the study of geography. While developing skill in using such tools, geography teachers will also use skills used by teachers in other disciplines, such as "observing, selecting, measuring, recording, sketching, organizing, analyzing, and interpreting." [42]

[41] Thomas Frank Barton, "Geography Skills and Techniques," in Hill, *op. cit.*, p. 52.
[42] *Ibid.*, p. 53.

Some Problems of Geographic Education

Since the map and globe are basic tools in geographic study, it is essential that the child learn to use them purposefully; this learning should start at an early age. Several excellent books have been written illustrating globe and map skills and concepts which should normally be developed as the child progresses through grades one to twelve.[43] The child must be oriented properly to such study and introduced only to those principles and facts which he can be expected to master at various stages. Maps and statistical techniques are often complex since they are based on a knowledge of arithmetic and geometric concepts not easily understood by some pupils. Studies in scale and ratio, in latitude and longitude, and in space and time concepts should be given specific attention. The teacher should probably see to it that a great deal more time is spent in the early years of school in introducing the child to geography. Since the map is a kind of picture on which certain kinds of data are shown, the child needs to learn to "read" maps of many types. Learning to make maps leads to learning to read maps.

Effective geography teaching presupposes considerable knowledge about the environment in all of its aspects in both large and small areas. The child must be taught what to look for in the landscape and how to interpret it. If he cannot go into the out-of-doors for field observations, he must be led consciously into ways of gathering necessary information about areas from photos, maps, graphs, articles, films, and books. The vocabulary of geography is large and often technical, and without direct experience with a wheat field, irrigation system, or a marble quarry, for example, the child may have difficulty in arriving at an understanding of related geographic concepts. Effective teaching has taken place when the child demonstrates the ability to synthesize and coordinate elements of

[43] Elaine Forsyth, *Map Reading,* Geographic Education Series (Bloomington, Ill.: McKnight and McKnight, 1944). Mamie L. Anderzhon, *Steps in Map Reading* (Chicago: Rand McNally, 1949). Parmer L. Ewing and Marion H. Seibel, *Fun with the Globe,* Sets I-II (Chicago: A. J. Nystrom, 1958). Ruby M. Harris, *The Rand McNally Handbook of Map and Globe Usage* (Chicago: Rand McNally, 1959).

the physical and cultural environment and to see the geographic relationships operating within and between them.

Whether geography is taught as a separate subject or as part of an integrated social studies program is the responsibility of curriculum planners. Instruction in geography should be part of the school curriculum, grades K–12, and on to the college and university for those who are zealous of understanding themselves and their country in relation to other peoples and nations around the world. The subject matter of geography is both rational and desirable, and its methods lead to results which are interesting and useful, e.g., training for better citizenship or preparation leading to a career in teaching and research, government service, resource management, or regional planning. In helping to bridge the gap between the physical and social sciences, geography makes a distinctive contribution to education.

SUGGESTED READINGS

THE STUDY OF GEOGRAPHY

Bowman, Isaiah, *Geography in Relation to the Social Studies* (New York: Scribner's, 1934). Identifies the several disciplines in the social studies field and emphasizes the need for geography in the curriculum.

Dickinson, R. E. and O. J. R. Howarth, *The Making of Geography* (Oxford: Oxford Univ. Press, 1933; University Microfilms Inc., Ann Arbor, Michigan). An excellent study tracing the development of geographic ideas from the earliest civilizations to the thirties of the present century.

James, Preston E., and Clarence F. Jones, eds., *American Geography: Inventory and Prospect* (Syracuse, N.Y.: Syracuse Univ. Press, 1954). Contributed to by many scholars and is the most comprehensive survey of American geography.

Hartshorne, Richard, *The Nature of Geography*, (Lancaster, Pa.: The Association of American Geographers, 1939; Edwards Brothers, Inc., reprinted with corrections, 1961). Excellent for its presentation of the development of geography, the relation of history and geography, and the nature of geography as a science.

———, *Perspective on the Nature of Geography* (Chicago: Rand McNally, 1959). A valuable, brief reassessment of the author's earlier work identifying the scope and methods of geographic study.

KOHN, CLYDE F., ed., *Geographic Approaches to Social Education,* Nineteenth Yearbook (Washington, D.C.: National Council for the Social Studies, 1948). A symposium on the goals, objectives, and tools of geography together with implications for the curriculum.

METHODS IN TEACHING GEOGRAPHY

ANDERZHON, MAMIE LOUISE, *Steps in Map Reading* (Chicago: Rand McNally, 1949). An excellent workbook for map-reading.

CASPER, BERNIECE M., "Scope and Sequence of Geographic Education in the Modern School Curriculum Grades Four Through Twelve," *Journal of Geography,* IX (February), 53–58, 1961. Good for any who are planning a curriculum.

EWING, PARMER L., AND MARION H. SEIBEL, *Fun with the Globe,* Sets I–II (Chicago: A. J. Nystrom, 1958). Useful for developing global concepts in grades 3–8.

GREENHOOD, DAVID, *Down to Earth: Mapping for Everybody* (New York: Holiday House, 1944). A good handbook for all who are interested in making or using maps.

HALVERSON, L. H., *Geography via Pictures* (Chicago: National Council for Geographic Education, 1960).

HARRIS, RUBY M., *The Rand McNally Handbook of Map and Globe Usage* (Chicago: Rand McNally, 1959). An excellent source of material on the kinds of maps and globes appropriate for use at the various grade levels, goals for learning with these tools, and suggests a variety of techniques and exercises for use in the classroom.

HILL, WILHELMINA, ed., *Curriculum Guide for Geographic Education,* Geographic Education Series (Normal, Ill.: National Council for Geographic Education, Illinois State Normal Univ., 1963). An excellent guide on the significance of geography in the curriculum and contains valuable material on major concepts, sequences for study, skills, and techniques and resources for geographic education.

JAMES, PRESTON E., ed., *New Viewpoints in Geography,* Twenty-ninth Yearbook (Washington, D.C.: National Council for the Social Studies, 1959). An interesting and timely symposium of points of view and ideas expressed by both research personnel and teachers of geography representing all levels of the curriculum.

Journal of Geography, published monthly from September through May by the National Council for Geographic Education (Chicago: A. J. Nystrom). The single best magazine for geography teachers. It carries both substantive and methodological articles of current interest.

MCKINNEY, W. R., *Geography via Use of the Globe* (Chicago: National Council for Geographic Education, 1963).

ODELL, CLARENCE B. AND DALE EDWARD CASE, eds., *Cartecraft Teach-*

ing Aids (Chicago: Denoyer-Geppert Company, 1960). Excellent both in the substantive and methodological fields.

PEATRIE, RODERICK, *The Teaching of Geography* (New York: Appleton-Century-Crofts, 1950). A valuable guide to some of the content to teach in geography and how to teach it.

PENNSYLVANIA DEPARTMENT OF PUBLIC INSTRUCTION, *Course of Study in Geography for Secondary Schools* (Harrisburg, Pa.: State Department of Public Instruction, 1951). Contains valuable materials for curriculum builders.

PHELPS, JEWELL, *Geography via Television* (Chicago: National Council for Geographic Education, 1959).

RICH, STEWART, AND L. YOUNG, *Geography via the Use of Slides, Film Strips, Motion Pictures and Opaque Projectors* (Chicago: National Council for Geographic Education, 1961).

THRALLS, ZOE, *The Teaching of Geography* (New York: Appleton-Century-Crofts, 1958). A well-organized, simple guide to instruction in geography.

UNESCO, *Some Suggestions On The Teaching of Geography* (Paris: UNESCO, 1949). An attempt to present geography as a means to securing better international understanding.

4   Political Science

Vernon R. Iredell
Department of Political Science
University of Tennessee

THE THIRD EDITION OF WEBSTER'S NEW INTERNATIONAL DICTION-
ary includes among its definitions of political science one which is
very different from any appearing previously. According to this
definition, political science is "a field of inquiry devoted to an analysis of power in society." [1] Though this idea is new to Webster's, it is
not new to American political scientists. The notion that they
should focus their attention on power began to appear in the 1920's
and slowly gained ground until by the end of World War II it was
generally accepted. It carried political scientists from the study of
governments into a consideration of how all organizations, from
General Motors to the local Baptist Church, "govern" themselves.
Not only did the new field of study stretch far beyond the traditional
boundaries of political science and invade other social sciences but
also many came to feel that it did not form a cohesive whole. For
these reasons and others, dissatisfaction with the new definition developed. Actually, the vanguard of political science was beginning

[1] By permission. From Webster's *Third New International Dictionary*.
Copyright 1961 by G. & C. Merriam Co., Publishers of the Merriam-Webster
Dictionaries.

to move away from it about the time Webster's third edition was being published. The remaining definitions of political science in this new edition tend to be either highly experimental or circular. Thus we will doubtless do best to retreat to the first definition given in the second edition. Political science is "that branch of the social sciences dealing with the organization and government of states." [2]

The Emergence of Political Science

The study of political science is extremely ancient. Two of the most celebrated products of classical Greek civilization, Plato's *Republic* and Aristotle's *Politics,* are primarily concerned with it. In American colleges and universities, political science was at first attached to other disciplines, particularly history. It began breaking away about the time of the Civil War but even as late as the turn of the century few independent departments of political science existed. Half a century later almost all of our colleges and universities were teaching political science courses and several hundred were offering political science majors. Seventy percent of the institutions offering such majors had independent departments of political science.

Simultaneously with the development of political science came the development of a body of professional political scientists. By 1906, they were numerous enough to establish their first major professional organization, the American Political Science Association. Of course, many college students who major in political science ultimately enter other fields, and a large portion of these choose law. Nonetheless, it has been estimated that by 1958 there were about 10,000 political scientists in the United States. Over 90 percent of them worked either for academic institutions or the government. They were about equally divided between these two types of employment. As a result of the heavy demand for political scientists in government, a substantially larger proportion are employed outside of academic institutions than is the case with any other group

[2] By permission. From Webster's *New International Dictionary, Second Edition.* Copyright 1959 by G. & C. Merriam Co., Publishers of the Merriam-Webster Dictionaries.

categorized as social scientists in this book, with the exception of psychologists.

Two Basic Approaches

Two alternative approaches have traditionally been used in classifying the subject matter with which political scientists deal. One centers around the idea of *functions* and the other around the idea of *levels*. The primary function of government is the regulation of interaction between individuals and groups. The possibility of breaking it down according to functions arises from the fact that in order for government to perform its primary function it must perform a number of secondary ones. For instance it must make laws and apply them. All governments must perform these same functions no matter what individuals or groups they are governing. The possibility of breaking political science down according to levels, on the other hand, arises from the fact that men live in a series of groups arranged like a set of concentric circles. Individuals group themselves into families, families into cities, cities into states, and so on. The whole field of political science can be covered by either of these two approaches. They are related to each other like the two sets of bars that make up a grid, one set running from top to bottom and the other from left to right, but both covering the same broad area.

International Relations

When one divides the subject matter of political science according to levels, he finds at the top a field for which there is no really adequate name. It is often called "international relations," but this name is a bit broad for it seems to cover both economic and political relations. Another name often used is "international politics." This can be used, in contrast to "international economics," to indicate that part of international relations with which political scientists should concern themselves. Yet it is often used instead as a name for a further subdivision within that part of international relations. When used in this way it is contrasted with international law and international organization. It refers to the less organized and formal aspects of the political dealings which nations have with one another. Domestically, the word "politics" is often used in a similar sense.

National Government

At the next level we find the study of national governments. Since we live in the United States we subdivide this field into American government and foreign or comparative government. Those who study the latter field are constantly confronted by two contrary temptations. One is the temptation to deal with each government investigated as a unique whole which is, in turn, part of a larger whole, the society within which it exists. Those who treat governments in this way try to explain how each government grows organically out of the society surrounding it and how its parts form a seamless whole. This approach renders true comparison difficult. The alternative is to begin with the assumption that there are several distinct political functions which must be performed for any society, as for instance, the legislative, executive, and judicial functions; and then to compare the way in which they are performed in various societies. In recent times the former approach has probably been dominant though the latter has received considerable impetus in the last few years from the behaviorists about whom more will be said later.

The most basic concept we customarily use in comparing governments was originated by Greek thinkers. It is the tripartite distinction between autocracy (rule by one man), oligarchy (rule by a few), and democracy (rule by the many). Most of the additional concepts used in comparative government have their origin in the attempt to explain the governments of Europe and North America. It is only in the last few years that political scientists have become vitally concerned with other parts of the world.

Present-day autocracies are of two fundamental types: old fashioned monarchies, which are fast dying out, and modern dictatorships. The word "dictatorship" goes back to a Latin word for rulers who were temporarily given absolute power during times of emergency. Modern dictatorships are a different sort of phenomenon. The majority of those which appeared before World War II are usually characterized as "dictatorships of the right." They appeared mainly in Western countries and their supporters frequently argued that weak pacifist democracy was ultimately undesirable and must be replaced. Since World War II many non-Western dictatorships have appeared in both the Communist and underdeveloped countries. Their supporters usually do not argue that democracy is ultimately bad, but rather that it is temporarily unworkable in the situation facing these countries. Democracy, at the other end of the spectrum, has also changed since classical times. It was the Greeks rather than the Romans who initiated democracy. Their democracy was direct, that is, the citizens gathered as a body to make basic decisions. Such democracy can be found today in a few New England town meetings but in the main our modern democracy is indirect, that is, the citizens as a whole elect representatives who make the basic decisions for them. There are several ways in which we can classify modern democracies. First of all, we can divide them into constitutional monarchies and republics. These can be equally democratic. The only difference is that in the first the monarch remains but in most modern constitutional monarchies, like Great Britain, he has been deprived of almost all his powers except those which are ceremonial in character. The word "republic" is used in several senses but when contrasted with constitutional monarchy it refers to a system, like ours, in which there are no vestiges of monarchy. Modern democracies can more significantly be divided into presidential democracies like ours and parliamentary or cabinet democracies like the British. In the former, the head of the executive branch of the government is chosen by the people as a whole; while in the latter, he is chosen by the legislature or at least in some manner which reflects its will, and he can be dismissed by it.

One of the most fundamental characteristics which has distinguished modern dictatorships from modern democracies is that the rulers in the former frequently exercise power in an arbitrary manner while the rulers in the latter usually exercise it in accordance with strict constitutional limitations. A constitution is a basic set of rules widely agreed upon in the community. Sometimes, as in the United States, it is written; and sometimes, as in Britain, it is not. A second fundamental difference between modern dictatorships and democracies is that the dictatorships tend to be totalitarian in character. In many, though not all, of the dictatorships, the government controls in minute detail the everyday lives of the citizens. The democratic governments of today tend to be nontotalitarian, though it is doubtless true that they exercise more control over the everyday lives of the citizens than democratic governments did in earlier times. Finally, the distinction between unitary and federal systems should be mentioned. Under both, the functions of government are divided between a central government and a number of regional governments. Under the unitary system, all power ultimately rests in the hands of the central government, which can do anything it wishes. Under the federal system, power is ultimately divided between the central government and the regional governments, each of which can perform only those functions constitutionally allocated to it. The claim is often made in the United States that a federal system is more democratic than a unitary one because it gives the people a greater chance to govern themselves. The argument sounds impressive when stated abstractly but when one looks at political realities it loses some of its force. It is hard to contend that in practice the American federal system is more democratic than, for instance, the British unitary one.

In what direction is the world moving? How are the various sorts of governmental systems doing in the struggle for survival? In the economically developed countries the picture is most encouraging. In recent times the number of such countries governed democratically has increased and their governments have become more democratic. Of the nineteen countries which Banks and Textor classify as "developed," all but three are usually considered to be democracies. Of these three, Czechoslovakia and East Germany would doubtless be democracies also were it not for Russian pressure. The one additional country they classify as "developed" is Russia itself.[3]

In the case of the underdeveloped countries, the picture is not so bright. Until the end of World War II most of them were ruled by colonial powers. Such rule was obviously not democratic. As they have achieved their independence a large majority of them, despite certain democratic pretenses, have established what are, in fact, non-

[3] Arthur S. Banks and Robert B. Textor, *A Cross Polity Survey* (Cambridge, Mass.: M.I.T. Press, 1963), p. 65 and paragraph 41.

democratic systems. What will happen to these systems when the crises of birth and the first stages of development have passed no one now knows. Finally, it must be added that today both democratic and autocratic governments control the everyday lives of their citizens more extensively than they used to and that they are now more centralized.

State and Local Government

Let us now step down to the next level. In some countries like the United States and Germany, this is an intermediate level. We call it "state" government while the Germans call it "land" government. In other countries like Britain there is no intermediate level; the next level below national government is local government, that is, the government of counties, municipalities, and a variety of special districts charged with looking after schools, utilities, and the like. In the United States, municipal government has been a particularly lively field in recent years. Ever since our nation was born, a constant trend toward urbanization has been apparent. In 1790, 5 percent of our population was urban, by 1900 the figure had risen to 40 percent, by 1960 to 70 percent. Not only have our citizens come increasingly to live in urban centers but they have also come increasingly, particularly in recent years, to live in a relatively small number of extremely large urban centers. Today, according to the 1960 census, almost two-thirds of them live in 212 gigantic metropolitan areas which cover only 7 percent of the nation's land area. These gigantic metropolitan areas and many smaller ones as well have been struggling with traffic congestion and slums at their cores, the flight of higher income groups to their suburbs, and numerous other problems.

Classification by Functions

Let us now turn to the classification of the same subject matter by functions. At the heart of this classification, political scientists have usually placed the field of law. Within that field one finds international law, the major part of which regulates relations between nation-states.[4] In addition there is municipal law which applies within nation-states. Municipal law can in turn be divided into public and private law. Public law regulates governments, while private law regulates lesser groups and individuals. Public law in turn can be divided, in countries having written constitutions, into constitutional law and administrative law.

Though no final agreement has been reached in defining the functions of government, the writings of Montesquieu, most notably the *Spirit of the Laws* published in 1748, and modern practice both give rise to the notion that government performs three major functions *with respect to law*. On the basis of this notion, formal government can be divided into a legislative process and branch which makes law, a judicial one which interprets it, and an executive one which enforces it. Many universities have courses in legislative institutions and processes and judicial institutions and processes. The field of administration deals mainly with executive institutions and processes. The principles with which these courses deal apply at all levels of government.

In addition to these formal institutions and processes, there exist informal ones. They lie at the borderline between the political and the nonpolitical and are usually not clearly provided for in constitutions. The institutions or groups involved are the public and lesser entities within it like parties and pressure groups. The processes involved are those by which these entities influence the course of governmental action. In the nineteenth and early twentieth centuries, political scientists devoted themselves almost exclusively to exploring the formal aspects of government. More recently, the most creative thinkers among them have concentrated their attention largely on the informal aspects.

Political Theory and Methodology

There are two remaining fields of importance within political science which were not shaped by either the logic of levels or functions. In

---

[4] In recent decades the internal subdivisions within international law have grown increasingly similar to those within municipal law.

a sense all of political science is descended from political philosophy but the fields of political theory and methodology bear a rather special and intimate relationship to it. If we are to understand how they arose we must dip briefly into the history of philosophy. Philosophers once studied all that is fundamental and important. In time, however, so much that falls within this category came to be known that no one could cover it all. Various parts of philosophy began to break away from the mother field and establish themselves as independent disciplines. Psychology was the last major field to do so. It is significant that the great American thinker William James (1842–1910) was equally well known as a philosopher and a psychologist. The splitting off of the various parts of philosophy led to a redefinition of its role. Some said that it should concern itself primarily with analyzing and transmitting to new generations the general theories it had once produced, that is, that it should become a branch of history. Others said that philosophy should take the territory that was left to it and continue its exploratory ventures there. This led to the blossoming of epistemology, that is, the study of what knowledge is and how it is gained.

Political philosophy is that branch of philosophy that traditionally dealt with politics and government. It underwent an evolution similar to that of philosophy in general. As the various branches of political philosophy, which we have been discussing, broke off, some political philosophers concentrated primarily on analyzing and transmitting to new generations the general theories about politics produced in the past. In present-day American universities, courses which take this approach are usually labeled "political theory" courses. Others sought to study what political knowledge is and how we gain it. Courses taking this approach are usually labeled "methodology" courses.

The great tradition of thought with which political theorists deal had many facets. In the main, however, it was an armchair search for the best possible sort of government. Though the common people must have speculated on this subject from time to time, their speculations had little effect on the course of human thought or action until recently. The history of political theory from the classical period until the nineteenth century was mainly the story of a succession of great minds. The nineteenth century brought substantial changes. The intellectual ferment of the first half of that century gave rise to the *"isms."* According to R. R. Palmer: [5]

So far as is known the word "liberalism" first appeared in the English language in 1819, "radicalism" in 1820, "socialism" in 1832, "conservatism" in 1835. The 1830's first saw "individualism," "constitutionalism," "humanitarianism," and "monarchism." "Nationalism" and "communism" date from the 1840's. Not until the 1850's did the English-speaking world use the word "capitalism" (French *capitalisme* is much older); and not until even later had it heard of "Marxism," though the doctrines of Marx grew out of and reflected the troubled times of the 1840's.

In the second half of the nineteenth century, these *"isms"* spread and their hold on people deepened. As a result they were transformed into "ideologies." An ideology is a body of concepts that tells a group how to conduct its life in whole or part. In recent times large groups of people have clung to ideologies as those of earlier times clung to religious creeds. Ideologies have in fact been called "secular religions."

Why did these ideologies appear? One reason was the fact that Western man began to realize in the nineteenth century that he was caught up in a rush of progress which could vastly alter the life not only of the elite but of the masses as well. Until this time the masses had always lived in poverty and misery and it had looked as if they always would. Not only were hopeful changes affecting the masses taking place, but the masses were increasingly in a position to gain some understanding of these changes and to play a role in directing them. The West was ceasing to be made up primarily of inert peasants. The Industrial Revolution, which got under way in the preceding century, was dumping ever increasing numbers of people into cities. It is in cities that new ideas have usually appeared and it is there that militant groups can most easily organize. The masses were beginning to be educated by the new mass education and informed and stimulated by the new mass press; the rise of modern democracy was beginning to give them a role in shaping their destinies. The problems of society were increasingly their problems, not somebody else's.

[5] R. R. Palmer, *A History of the Modern World* (New York: Alfred A. Knopf, 1951), p. 441.

Nationalism, Liberalism, Conservatism

Before proceeding further we should perhaps say a word about a few of the more important of these ideologies. The most powerful of all has doubtless been nationalism. Nationalism is the idea that one's ultimate loyalty should be to the nation (i.e., cultural group) and state (i.e., political unit) to which one belongs. It is one's duty to make these two into one and to help them achieve some high destiny. Today scattered signs appear that nationalism may eventually give way to internationalism. In the West nationalism is still dominant though internationalism is gaining ground, as indicated by the development of the European Economic Community. In the less developed parts of the world where nationalism is new, it is extremely strong and boisterous. Even here, however, larger loyalties are not entirely absent as the growth of the Pan-African dream indicates.

Among the most important of the remaining ideologies are liberalism and conservatism. Liberalism has meant many different things. It is descended from a Greek word meaning "free." Freedom and faith in progress have always been close to its core. In the nineteenth century the word was used to refer to those who sought freedom by limiting the power of government. At first they put their faith in checking the power of monarchs through the writing of constitutions. Their political outlook was closely related to an economic outlook which is usually called "capitalism" today. "Capitalism," used in this sense, refers to an economic system in which government interference is minimal. "Capitalism" is also called by many other names, one of which, significantly enough, is "economic liberalism." In time many people came to feel that they could prevent the government from interfering with the citizens' freedom not only by limiting its power but also by increasing the citizens' power to control it. Perhaps it would be more accurate to say that this feeling was really there from the first, but in the early days liberals did not want all of the people to have power over the government, only the enlightened few. As time passed the liberals worked simultaneously to spread enlightenment among the many and to give them increasing control. Also it gradually became obvious that government was not the only social institution which is capable of limiting freedom; economic oligarchies of the sort that developed in this country at the end of the nineteenth century can do so as well. It also became obvious that a person's freedom is increased not only by checking the power of social institutions but also by using social institutions to open up new possibilities for action. Thus people calling themselves "liberals" in a sense reversed their position as the years passed. Once the many had come to control government, they began advocating that its powers should be increased insofar as increasing them was necessary to regulate the power of the economic oligarchies and open up new possibilities for action. Today the word "liberal" is used frequently in Europe and at times in this country to refer to the nineteenth-century notion that the powers of government should be strictly limited, particularly in the economic field. In the United States, however, the word has been used mainly in recent years to refer to the notion that the powers of government should be expanded to regulate the economic oligarchies and open up new possibilities for action. "Liberalism" of this latter variety was clearly dominant during the period of the New Deal. As the post-World War II period unfolded and frustration built up in the international field, the liberal philosophy went into eclipse. The eclipse can perhaps best be dated from August 1948 when Whittaker Chambers testified against Alger Hiss before the House Un-American Activities Committee. There followed the radical rightism of McCarthy and the calmer conservatism of Eisenhower. "Liberalism" was widely blamed for the trying international situation. In the Kennedy-Johnson era, "liberalism" again became the official philosophy of the day. The unfinished business of the Roosevelt era was once more taken up, but there was a growing feeling among thoughtful liberals that much of that business was almost done, that liberalism would have to take a new tack in the not too distant future.

Today in the United States the word "liberal" is usually contrasted with the word "conservative." The conservative position has never been as fully worked out and analyzed as its opposite. Conservatism, as an ideology, is usually said to have its roots in the reflections of the English thinker and statesman Edmund Burke (1729–1797). He trusted sentiment more than the liberals of his day and reason less. The tendency to mistrust reason has become an important part of the conservative creed and doubtless helps explain the fact that it has received less intellectual attention than its opposite. At the heart of conservatism is the desire to keep what one has. Conservatives find plans for improvement less appealing than established traditions. Throughout most of history the few have experienced wealth and pleasant living while the many have known poverty and suffering. Since the birth of the possibility of progress in the West, only the few wealthy have had reason to be content with things as they are. The hope of the poor has been change. Thus conservatism has tended to be the philosophy of the few. It has been wary of complete democracy for only in a system which is less than democratic can a conservative elite maintain control and protect itself. It is interesting to speculate as to what will happen to the basic historical distinctions between liberalism and conservatism as the many come to be well off.

Just as the meaning of "liberalism" has shifted through the years, so has the meaning of "conservatism." In the period when modern conservatism was born, the landed aristocracy of Europe was the economic elite that dominated society. Conservatism was its philosophy. With the rise of modern trade and industry, dominance tended to pass into the hands of the business oligarchy. As we have indicated, the philosophy it espoused was new in the nineteenth century and was called "liberalism." In some places it is still called that as we have also indicated. In the United States, however, once "capitalism" became established we began calling it "conservative." This was, after all, a reasonable thing to do, for at its core conservatism is the philosophy that maintains established orders. The alteration of meaning was made easy in the United States by the fact that we never really had a landed aristocracy here with which to tie the notion of conservatism. We did perhaps have the beginnings of one in the ante-bellum South, but modern historians usually feel that these beginnings were less significant than our sentimental memories have often suggested.

Capitalism, Socialism, Communism

In addition to the ideologies already mentioned, we should say a word about capitalism, socialism, and communism. They are all essentially economic ideologies which have strong political implications. During the early modern period an economic theory known as mercantilism, which provided that governments should participate extensively in the economies of the states they rule, dominated the scene. Once modern commerce and industry became strong enough to stand by itself, however, mercantilism was replaced by capitalism, which became the official philosophy of the middle class. The great landmark in the rise of this latter theory was the publication of Adam Smith's *Wealth of Nations* in 1776. The core of capitalism is the idea that a government should interfere in the economy as little as possible. National economies, left alone, will to a large degree regulate themselves.

As industry continued to grow, a larger and larger laboring class developed. Socialism became the official philosophy of this class in Europe though in the United States it never gained wide popularity, perhaps in part because of our recent experience with individualistic frontier life. Socialists believe in extensive government control of the economy which extends as far as government ownership of the means of production and distribution. They also believe in a number of closely related ideas, including the re-emphasis of social values as opposed to individual values and cooperation as opposed to competition. Socialism represents an attempt not only to improve the means of production and distribution, but also an attempt to reintegrate the individual into society in such a way as to make his total life more meaningful. Elements which can, with considerable justice, be called "socialistic" are to be found in human society long before the rise of modern socialism. "Socialistic" elements appear in the life of certain primitive tribes and in the life of the early Christians. It is in the nineteenth century, however, that the first really serious attempts are made to establish socialism in the modern world. The early nineteenth-century socialists are usually called "Utopian Socialists." It was their objective to establish small communities where the good life, as they saw it, could be lived despite the general misery of surrounding society. The Frenchman Charles Fourier and the Englishman Robert Owens were probably the most famous of the Utopians. It should be noted, however, that it was in the United States rather than Europe that the greatest number of Utopian Socialist communities arose. The latter part of the nineteenth century and early part of the twentieth century saw the rise of vast interdependent societies, the consequent fall of the Utopian Socialist dream and the rise of state socialism. The unit which was to own the means of production and distribution was no longer to be a local community but a nation-state. Some state socialists have believed in democracy and others in autocracy.

Communism is, historically speaking, a variety of socialism. When the word first came into use in the 1840's, it seems to have implied a sort of socialism under which the community would distribute goods and services in accordance with the needs of its members. Later on the word was used as a name for the brand of socialism advocated by Karl Marx and the brand put into practice in the Soviet Union in 1917. Though both Marx and the Russian leaders taught that goods and services should ultimately be distributed in accordance with need, they taught many other things as well. Sometimes they agreed and sometimes they disagreed. On some points they were clear and consistent and on others they were not. Politically speaking, the chief difference between Marx and the Russians is probably the fact that Marx favored democratic rule followed by the eventual disappearance of government while the Russian Communists established a dictatorship. It is true that Marx talked about a brief transition stage in which a "dictatorship of the proletariat" would rule, but he meant by this a regime in which the vast majority (i.e., proletariat) would organize themselves internally in a largely democratic way and dictate to a tiny minority (i.e., the remnant of the bourgeoisie). The Russian dictatorship has become less oppressive since Stalin's death, but it remains a dictatorship and there is little prospect that it will become otherwise in the foreseeable future.

There are many other ideologies which we could mention. Those we have discussed, however, are probably the most significant at present. All of them are both economic and political in character though the relative importance of the two components varies. Human society is a cohesive whole which always defies those who try to break it down into basic elements. During the age of mercantilism it was extremely difficult to separate politics from economics. Later, under capitalism, when government gave up, to a considerable degree, its control over the economic realm, separation became easier. Now again with the rise of socialism it has become more difficult.

Ideology has never been as strong a force in the United States as in Europe. Our pragmatic spirit has promoted more interest in getting on with the everyday tasks of life than in dreaming of ideal societies. There is some evidence that even in Europe people are losing interest in ideologies. Some think that they are destined eventually to disappear. In the past, as we noted above, there have always been a few rich and many poor. The rich have been powerful and cultured and the poor, weak and primitive. Industrialism has been drastically changing this pattern. Present-day ideologies have resulted in large part from the process of change. They have been the means by which the groups involved have tried to guide the process so that it would benefit them. But the process may be reaching its end. Many feel that in the United States we already have the technological means of completely eliminating poverty though we seem unable as yet to organize society so as to make use of them. If poverty is eliminated then the present ideologies, born out of the struggle to eliminate it, will no doubt disappear. What will replace them? Other ideologies? Some say yes. Others, as we have already indicated, reply no. Ideologies are after all a relatively recent phenomenon. Perhaps they are a transitional form of thinking and feeling which is imperfect because it pretends to a sort of absolute validity which in actual fact it lacks. Either more truth must be found or pretense must be dropped.

Methods of Inquiry

If ideology fades from the scene what will replace it? We can best approach the problem of answering this question by recalling where we are and how we got here. We suggested earlier that the tradition of political philosophy gave rise to two contemporary fields, political theory and methodology. We have been tracing the history of the subject matter with which political theory deals and have discovered that the story culminated in the rise of popular ideologies the ultimate value of which most scholars have come to doubt. A few penetrating thinkers have been sprinkled among the popular ideologists of recent years, but the trend toward academic specialization has turned most first-rate minds away from the building of general theories of politics. The drive to pursue fundamental issues has instead been largely poured into the specialized field of methodology. In recent times a great number of methods of getting at political truth have been used by political scientists. Some have approached politics from a historical point of view and others from a legal point of view, to name but two. The most talked about approach in recent years, however, has been the scientific. A great many political scientists have been engaged in trying to build a science of political phenomena similar to sciences like physics and biology which deal with natural phenomena. It is to developing this approach that most methodologists have devoted their efforts. Many believe that it will replace the ideological one.

Those who have been trying to build a science of politics usually call themselves "behaviorists" or in some cases "behavioralists" in order to distinguish themselves from psychological behaviorists. Political behaviorists usually trace their lineage back to Arthur Bentley, whose once much neglected but now famous book *The Process of Government* appeared in 1908. It was not until the 1920's, however, that the movement really got under way. The following decade saw the rise of the "Chicago School." It was so called because its leaders, Charles Merriam, T. V. Smith, and Harold Lasswell, were professors at the University of Chicago. Though all of them helped strengthen the link between the study of politics and "science," the contribution of Lasswell to this undertaking was undoubtedly the most substantial. During the post-World War II period, behaviorism has become increasingly rigorous and increasingly dominant among those in the vanguard of American political science. Though many European students of politics have been influenced by science, rigorous behaviorism is overwhelmingly an American phenomenon.

Just what are the behaviorists trying to accomplish? This is a question which they do not answer with one voice, as they are themselves forever pointing out. If they can be said to have a common goal it would seem to be, as David Truman has put it, "the development of a science of the political process." [6] By "science" they usually mean a study which uses a method similar to that used by the natural sciences, though they are constantly troubled by the realization that any given subject matter can best be studied by a method that is to some degree uniquely tailored to fit it. In a recent article, David Easton, one of the most respected commentators on behaviorism, listed first among the assumptions underlying its method

[6] David B. Truman, "The Implications of Behavior Research," *Items*, Vol. 5, No. 4 (New York: Social Science Research Council, 1951), p. 38.

the belief that "There are discoverable uniformities in political behavior. These can be expressed in generalizations or theories with
explanatory and predictive value." [7]   What Easton seems to be saying
is that something comparable to the laws of physics can be found in
the political world.   It should be noted, however, that he intentionally avoids stating the assumption in this simple way.   Why?   Because the behaviorists doubt that they will find anything as simple
and absolute as a law of physics in the political world.   A bit later
on Easton lists "measurement and quantification" as important
characteristics of the method but again he qualifies the statement by
making it plain that these means are to be used "not for their own
sake, but only where possible, relevant, and meaningful in the light
of other objectives." [8]   Perhaps the essence of behaviorism can best
be summed up by saying that it is a search for political laws with the
aid of quantification.   It must speedily be added, however, that
this summary would be wholly unacceptable to many who consider
themselves behaviorists and would appear too stark to most of them.
Some of the needed qualification has been outlined earlier by quot-
ing from Easton.

Certain of the fields discussed in this book are almost always
categorized as social sciences while others are not.   Those almost
always so categorized are cultural anthropology, social psychology,
sociology, economics, and political science.   Of these five, political
science is the last to try to make itself into a "science" in the sense in
which we have been using the word.[9]   The fact that it has at last
set out to transform itself has greatly increased the unity of the social
sciences in recent years.   Their unity has been further increased by
the fact that political behaviorists have tended to borrow a great part

---

[7] David Easton, "Introduction: The Current Meaning of 'Behavioralism'
in Political Science," in James C. Charlesworth, ed., *The Limits of Behavioralism in Political Science* (Philadelphia: American Academy of Political
and Social Science, 1962), p. 7.

[8] *Ibid.*, pp. 7–8.

[9] Some claim that economics entered the race after political science or
even that it has not yet done so.   This claim rests on the fact that economics
has largely stood aloof while the other social sciences have increasingly drawn
together under the roof of sociology.   Yet economics began developing its
own "science" long ago and became adept at model building and the use of
exact measurement even before some of the other social sciences were born.
Present-day econometrics may not be "sociological" but it is certainly "scientific."

of their method not directly from the natural sciences but from the other social sciences, particularly sociology. It surprises many to learn that political science has set out to become "scientific" only recently. After all, it is the only social science which actually contains the word "science" in its name. This fact is due, however, not to any long-standing desire on the part of students of politics to be "scientific" in the modern sense, but rather to the fact that the word "science" once had a much broader meaning than it has today. It is in fact descended from the Latin word "*scientia*" which meant pretty much what "knowledge" means at present. The word "science" became connected to politics and government while it still had this broader meaning. Thus Washington and Jefferson both refer to the "science of government" in their writings; and in the ninth of the Federalist Papers, Alexander Hamilton uses the phrase "science of politics."

The one area in which the behaviorists have unquestionably made substantial contributions is voting behavior. Unfortunately, voting is a procedure which does not appear in all political systems, only in democracies. Furthermore, the generalizations which have been arrived at are not very broadly applicable. The impressive thing has not been the discovery of general principles, but the use of sophisticated techniques of measurement to produce accurate and detailed pictures of particular elections and voting trends.

What, specifically, have the students of voting behavior discovered? Their most extensive studies have dealt with this country so we shall confine our remarks to findings concerning it. First of all, they have investigated who votes and who does not. They have found that since 1916 there has never been an American presidential election in which more than two-thirds of those eligible voted. A higher percentage of rich people vote than poor ones, a higher percentage of well-educated people vote than poorly educated ones, a higher percentage of Jews and Catholics vote than Protestants, a higher percentage of city people vote than country people, and a higher percentage of men vote than women. People between 35 and 55 are more likely to vote than either younger or older people. A higher percentage of westerners vote than people from any other region and a lower percentage of southerners. Finally, it should be added that this pattern is not a fixed one. For instance, ever since women gained the right to vote by the adoption of the Nineteenth

Amendment in 1920, the percentage of women voting has been constantly increasing. Why? Perhaps because old traditions and habits change slowly.

Studies have also been made of who people vote for. It has been discovered that family tradition has a great influence here. Three out of four young people voting for the first time select candidates of the same party their parents support. Of course, many children do break with family tradition. At times such breaks result from marriage. Wives tend to vote with their husbands. At times they result from a change in the overall political situation. Young people seem to be highly sensitive to tides of political persuasion which are rising during the period when they first become conscious of political problems. They tend often to associate themselves with these tides and maintain the association even in later years when the tides have changed. Thus the Great Depression seems to have made permanent Democrats of many people who first became conscious of political problems during the 1930's. During the 1950's a great number of young people became Republicans. What party one favors also depends to a large degree on the social groupings to which one belongs. Table A sums up in detail the findings of one research center concerning this matter. It not only indicates certain long-run relationships but also various temporary shifts. It covers, of course, only selected aspects of the overall picture. Furthermore, the way in which it presents these aspects tends, at places, to be misleading. This is almost always so of summary statements. One interesting example comes in the correlation between education and voting. The table seems to indicate that the more formal education one has, the more likely one is to vote Republican. Actually this is so only up to a point. The people in the society with the most formal education of all, the intellectuals, usually vote Democratic. This is particularly so of political scientists and other social scientists.

Although the behavioral approach has been most successful when used in dealing with voting, it has also been used in the study of judicial and administrative decision-making and in the study of numerous other matters as well. The greatest deficiency of the scientific or behavioral approach to politics is that it provides no way of answering ethical questions, that is, no way of deciding what citizens and politicians should and should not do. Fundamentally

TABLE A

Voting Trends Among Numerous Social Categories Since 1948
(Presidential Vote, 1948–1960)

| | Percent Democratic of Two-Party Vote for President | | | |
	1948	1952	1956	1960
A. Sex				
Female	53	41	38	47
B. Race				
Negro	68[a]	80[a]	64[a]	70
C. Age				
Under 24	70[a]	43[a]	45[a]	43[a]
23–34	61[a]	46	41	53
35–44	61	46	42	51
45–54	47[a]	42	39	55
55–64	43[a]	35	33	44
65 or over	50[a]	37	44	39
D. Type of place of residence				
Urban metropolis	[c]	49	53	64
Suburban metropolis	[c]	34	37	52
Cities over 50,000	[c]	52	34	51
Towns, 2,500–50,000	[c]	37	37	42
Rural	[c]	40	42	47
E. Religion				
Protestant	47	36	36	36
Catholic	67	52	46	83
Jewish	[b]	72[a]	77[a]	89[a]
F. Occupation of head of household				
Business and professional	20[a]	31	32	50
Clerical	50[a]	35	45	49
Blue-collar	76	55	40	57
Farm operator	65[a]	37	43	32
G. Union membership				
Union member	82[a]	61	57	65
H. Education				
Grade school	68	48	41	55
High school	54	43	44	53
College	24[a]	27	31	36

[a] Means fewer than 100 cases: sampling error may be sizable.
[b] Too few cases to compute a stable proportion.
[c] Data not available.

this is so because a science, as we use the word today, is a quest for laws. Actually this is overstating the objective somewhat. As we have already seen, most political behaviorists suspect that they cannot find "laws" as rigorous as those of physics. What they are looking for is somewhat less rigorous "uniformities." Yet the more these "uniformities" resemble "laws," the more able the behaviorists will be to create a rigorous science and hence the happier they will be. Now ethical rules only have significance where absolute laws do not govern behavior. If people are ultimately like stones and their behavior is completely determined by laws like that of gravitation, then ethics is not worth worrying about. Why tell a stone what it should and should not do when it cannot help doing what it does? The method of science is best suited for dealing with areas of reality where ethics is irrelevant. The more important ethical questions are in an area, the less adequate is the method of science for dealing with it.

Traditional Approaches

If one is not satisfied with any of the modern ideologies or with science, where can he turn? One possible direction is back toward the past. Those who look for answers there are usually called "traditionalists." This term covers a multitude of approaches including various sorts of eclecticism. It does not refer to a turning back to any particular political forms or customs, however, as much as to a return to older ways of studying and viewing government. Perhaps the two most consistent approaches which go under the name "traditionalism," are the "approach of practical politics" and the "approach of natural law." The "approach of practical politics" grows, in the main, out of an appreciation for great statesmen rather than great thinkers. Those who adopt it feel that both the believers in ideology and the believers in science are caught up in deceptive and

---

Table A is based on a table appearing in Robert K. Carr, Marver H. Bernstein, and Walter F. Murphy, *American Democracy in Theory and Practice,* 4th ed. (New York: Holt, Rinehart and Winston, 1963), p. 264. Their source is a press release of the University of Michigan Survey Research Center. Several minor changes have been made in the table on the basis of an unpublished recomputation of the figures by Mr. Richard T. Lane of the Survey Research Center.

impractical abstraction. They say that the most significant political problems are the day-to-day problems which face citizens and statesmen. They advocate the use of "common sense" in determining both the means to be used and the ends to be sought. They feel that ends should be practical and specific not ideal and general. For instance, they would rather see people concern themselves with preventing the spread of Communism to Brazil than with the elimination of Communism from the world.

The "approach of natural law" arises from the study of the great political philosophers of the past. Those who have turned to them in recent years have been particularly interested in finding in their works an answer to the great problem left unanswered by science, that is, the problem of ethics. The answer they have found is natural law. It is for this reason that I have characterized their approach as the "approach of natural law." The concept of natural law is usually said to have been developed by the Stoics, a school of philosophers which was born in ancient Greece after Greek civilization had begun its decline. The concept was taken over by Roman thinkers and then by Catholic thinkers, thus entering the modern West. It has been reshaped so many times through the centuries that defining it in a brief and accurate way has become difficult. In general, however, it can be said that natural law is thought by its advocates to be a perfect kind of law inherent in the universe which man can discover. The laws which men make and courts apply should be made in accordance with this higher law. The doctrine of natural law underlies the famous passage in our Declaration of Independence which says, "We hold these truths to be self-evident, that all men are created equal, that they are endowed by their Creator with certain unalienable Rights, that among these are Life, Liberty and the pursuit of Happiness." In recent times the idea of natural law has lost ground in the West. In Catholic circles, however, it remains strong and furthermore it has experienced a revival in non-Catholic circles in the last few years. In academic political science the revival has been led by Leo Strauss. It has come to the attention of the general public mainly through a book by Walter Lippmann entitled *The Public Philosophy*.

One major difficulty seems to have hampered this revival of natural law. How can one determine what the law tells him to do and not to do? During the Middle Ages most ordinary citizens learned the injunctions of the law from the Church. For them the immediate source was authority. Those intent on reviving natural law have also tended, in practice, to rely on authority. In their case, however, it has been the authority of the great political philosophers of the past. According to tradition, however, the ultimate means of discovering the law is not authority but "right reason." Today this phrase seems somehow to have lost its meaning. The hidden assumptions on which the method rested seem to have eroded away. In fact the whole idea of an external moral law has become for many an alien concept. The voice in the burning bush is now explained as psychological projection. It seems somehow to belong to an age of monarchy rather than an age of democracy. Perhaps a new law can be found within. This approach to the problem does not necessarily mean the end of social order. If looking within meant that each individual would find a unique law, it would indeed spell chaos, but those who have looked inward most intently in recent years, like Freud and Jung, have found in the depths general principles belonging to all humanity more often than they have found individual whims.

Political Science in the Curriculum

Finally, we must turn from our consideration of political science itself to a consideration of its place in the curricula of our schools. It is vital that political science and the other social sciences be given increasing attention. Our knowledge of nature and our ability to use it to produce plenty or destruction has greatly outdistanced our knowledge of society and our ability to organize it so as to ensure plenty rather than destruction. This is one of the most significant and widely acknowledged insights of our age. It is also one of the most badly neglected, a fact which was long ago clear in our colleges and is becoming increasingly so in our high schools. Why? Certainly in part because our society cannot operate without training many people extensively in technology and the natural sciences. Often there is not much time left over for other sorts of training. Yet as the grave necessity for a more adequate comprehension of society becomes obvious, this excuse loses force. Our inability to face all of the complex challenges of the modern world simultaneously, together with habit, has caused us, at times, to attempt to solve social problems by unsuitable technological means. For instance, we have tried to pretend to ourselves for some years that an ever greater use of our knowledge of technology in the military field will bring us peace and freedom. It is becoming increasing clear that it will not. In our struggle with Russia we have come upon exasperating difficulties which increased military power can do little to eliminate. Still we hesitate to turn to the social sciences because they have not produced much of a solid sort as compared with the natural sciences, partly, no doubt, because they have been neglected but also for other reasons. Those who desire to apply the scientific method to the study of man and society usually suggest that the shortcomings of the social sciences arise from the fact that the significant variables they must deal with are very numerous and experimentation is difficult. Others feel that the shortcomings arise from the presence of free will and the problem of values. Whatever the cause, our knowledge of society is less impressive than our knowledge of nature and in addition it is more difficult to apply. The application of knowledge about things changes our way of life only indirectly while the application of knowledge about people changes it directly. Even though such change has become necessary our resistance to it remains great.

What should our schools teach about man and society? First, they should be honest and acquaint students with the depths of our ignorance, with the desperate need for further knowledge. They must help students take a more creative and even experimental attitude toward human problems. Second, the schools must help students see that the world of man and society is an interrelated whole. As we have already suggested the subject matter of the various social sciences overlaps greatly. But in the colleges and universities, until very recently, they were becoming increasingly compartmentalized. This made useful application of their insights difficult. Analysis may thrive amid compartmentalization but wise action can only be taken by those who see the whole picture. Now the behaviorists have happily taken up the job of unification. The new unity they have been creating has, it is true, some defects. It is based on premises that allow one to say a lot about what is but very little about what should be. Furthermore, it has been created largely by considering sociology to be the heart of the social sciences and there are grave questions as to whether sociology really is the heart and as to whether, as presently constituted, it possesses the clarity and depth necessary to the fulfillment of its new role. These are serious problems but they cannot be solved by turning back toward compartmentalization.

What aspects of government should courses dealing with man and society contain? First, they should present the most significant facts. Just what these are is, of course, open to debate. Certainly basic information concerning our institutional arrangements and how they differ from those of others should be included. Second, students should be introduced to significant ideas in the realm of values. They should be taught to deal not simply with what is but also with what should be. Here even greater problems arise for there is much less agreement about the latter subject than the former. Some people believe that schools should "sell" a certain set of values while others believe that they should prepare students to engage in free inquiry.

Most schools in the Western world were once operated by the Church. They propagated its doctrines and did so in its language, Latin. As nation-states came to dominate the scene they changed the institutional structure of education. A majority of schools came to be state-operated. They began to inculcate loyalty to the state and the traditions and practices of its citizens. Instruction increasingly took place in the various national languages. The idea that the main job of the schools was to produce good Christians gave way before the idea that it was to produce good citizens. Jean Jacques Rousseau (1712–1778) is usually said to have been the most significant proponent of this modern view. The notion that schools should train people for citizenship has its virtues, as we shall suggest in a moment. All too often, however, the enterprise degenerated into a disgusting attempt to persuade children that their nation was the only real value in the world and that it was always right. In 1948 and 1949 an extensive opinion-sampling study was conducted in nine countries under the auspices of UNESCO. It is perhaps indicative of the state of the world's education, among other things, that "all the groups studied were in agreement on one point: their own nation was the most peace-loving of all." [10] Teaching which

[10] Otto Klineberg, *The Human Dimension in International Relations* (New York: Holt, Rinehart and Winston, 1964), p. 36. His source: W. Buchanan and H. Cantril, *How Nations See Each Other* (Urbana: Univ. of Illinois Press, 1953).

twists or disregards facts and does not prepare children to think critically about their country's policies does not do the children or the country any ultimate good. In January of 1964, events in Panama clearly demonstrated that the person who waves the flag in the wrong place at the wrong time is no real patriot. In a world where nations were less intimately and constantly in contact with one another and where friction between them could not produce atomic war, excessive nationalism was costly but the price could be paid. Today the price is far too high.

Not only has the blind inculcation of nationalism become clearly undesirable but so has the blind inculcation of tradition. We live in a rapidly changing world. Once desirable traditions are forever becoming out of date and furthermore some of our traditions probably never were desirable. It is clear, from any objective reading of history, that "Jim Crow" has been an American tradition. A majority now clearly hopes that it is ceasing to be one. Perhaps Andrew Carnegie went too far when he spoke of "an ignorant past whose chief province is to teach us not what to adopt, but what to avoid . . ." Perhaps Henry Ford did too when he insisted in an interview that "history is more or less bunk." [11] It would seem likely, however, that it is not going too far to assert that an uncritical clinging to tradition is no wiser in the social realm than in the technological.

Not only must the advocacy of strident nationalism and the blind acceptance of tradition be avoided but slanted propagandizing for any position as well. Deep and lasting conviction does not result from the unreasoned presentation of one-sided accounts. There is always the danger that someday those who have been indoctrinated will catch a glimpse of the other side. Propaganda is a powerful tool but it is becoming clear that it was for a time overrated. Fact all too often catches up with fantasy and when it does, fantasy is apt to be the loser. A teacher dealing with political values is probably best advised to present all major positions in as clear and objective a manner as possible. The strongest points of each should be developed as convincingly as they themselves permit. The weakest points should be thoroughly explored even when doing so is painful. Internal contradictions should be analyzed and an attempt

11 Richard Hofstadter, *Anti-Intellectualism in American Life* (New York: Alfred A. Knopf, 1963), p. 241.

should be made to see how assumptions concerning fact correspond with reality. Finally, the teacher should move on with the students to try to choose from among traditional positions or to create a new one. It should not be a matter of dictating what the students are to select, it should rather be a matter of helping them to make a thoughtful choice. General consensus should be sought but not imposed. Pressure arising from the lack of time or the hostility of uninformed citizens may make the adoption of this approach difficult. The wise teacher does not undertake the impossible. The good teacher, however, does all that can be done to advance true understanding and that is often far more than timid souls believe is possible. The approach outlined here not only leads to strong and reasonable conviction but it also familiarizes students with the very essence of democratic living. Only insofar as we help students to work out value problems in this way do we prepare them to maintain and improve democracy. Whether this goal is a worthy one had best be left for the reader to decide.

SUGGESTED READINGS

Most of the books listed below contain good bibliographies which will help the student locate further material on each field covered.

THE STATE OF THE DISCIPLINE

Easton, David, *The Political System: An Inquiry into the State of Political Science* (New York: Alfred A. Knopf, Inc., 1953). A distinguished analysis which is too complex for most general readers.

Hyneman, Charles S., *The Study of Politics: The Present State of American Political Science* (Urbana, Ill.: Univ. of Illinois Press, 1959). A general survey.

Van Dyke, Vernon, *Political Science: A Philosophical Analysis* (Stanford, Calif.: Stanford Univ. Press, 1960). A thoughtful critical analysis.

THE FINDINGS OF THE DISCIPLINE

Political science as a whole

Dahl, Robert A., *Modern Political Analysis* (Englewood Cliffs, N.J.: Prentice-Hall, 1963). A brief and easily understood volume in which the author works out a largely behavioral method for analyzing government and politics. He does so by building a model on the basis of which one can identify the differences and similarities between various sorts of governments. Thus the book is a valuable introduction to the content as well as the method of political science.

LIPSET, SEYMOUR MARTIN, *Political Man: The Social Bases of Politics* (Garden City, N.Y.: Doubleday, 1960). A brilliant series of essays by one author on the sociological foundation of politics.

LIPSON, LESLIE, *The Great Issues of Politics,* 2d ed. (Englewood Cliffs, N.J.: Prentice-Hall, 1960). A basic text which surveys the fundamental issues which must be settled in the quest for good government.

MACIVER, ROBERT M., *The Web of Government* (New York: Macmillan, 1947). An easy to read but classic analysis of government from a sociological point of view.

RODEE, C., T. J. ANDERSON, AND C. Q. CHRISTOL, *Introduction to Political Science* (New York: McGraw-Hill, 1957). A basic text which surveys the various fields which make up political science.

International relations—general

MORGENTHAU, HANS J., *Politics Among Nations: The Struggle for Power and Peace,* 3d ed. (New York: Alfred A. Knopf, 1960). A basic text which presents a comprehensive theory based on the concept of power.

PADELFORD, NORMAN J., AND GEORGE A. LINCOLN, *The Dynamics of International Politics* (New York: Macmillan, 1962). A basic text which is eclectic and factual.

International relations—theory

HOFFMANN, STANLEY H., *Contemporary Theory in International Relations* (Englewood Cliffs, N.J.: Prentice-Hall, 1960). A collection of readings accompanied by a thoughtful commentary.

International relations—international law

BRIERLY, J. L., *The Law of Nations: An Introduction to the International Law of Peace,* 6th ed. Humphrey Waldock, ed. (New York: Oxford Univ. Press, 1963). Unquestionably the best brief account of international law in the English language. It contains no bibliography but bibliographic material on international law can be found in the works by Morgenthau and Padelford mentioned above.

International relations—international organization

CLAUDE, INIS L., JR., *Swords into Plowshares: The Problems and Progress of International Organization,* 3d ed. (New York: Random House, 1964). A thoughtful and well-written account of international organization which focuses mainly on the United Nations.

GOODRICH, LELAND M., *The United Nations* (New York: Thomas Y. Crowell, 1959). A solid factual account.

Comparative government—general

BANKS, ARTHUR S. AND ROBERT B. TEXTOR, *A Cross Polity Survey* (Cambridge, Mass.: M.I.T. Press, 1963). A comprehensive attempt to arrive at basic generalizations concerning governments by statistical methods. The book consists of an explanation of the methods used followed by a great number of factual statements printed just as they came from a computer. It is not a book to sit down and read from cover to cover but it is a valuable source of information and an interesting example of the application of the "scientific" approach to politics.

Comparative government—Europe

BEER, SAMUEL H. AND ADAM B. ULAM, eds., *Patterns of Government: The Major Political Systems of Europe*, rev. ed. (New York: Random House, 1962). A basic text dealing with Britain, France, Germany, and Russia which adopts the behavioral approach.

CARTER, GWENDOLEN M., AND JOHN H. HERZ, *Major Foreign Powers: The Governments of Great Britain, France, Germany, and the Soviet Union*, 4th ed. (New York: Harcourt, Brace & World, 1962). A basic text which adopts the traditional approach.

Comparative government—the underdeveloped countries as a whole

ALMOND, GABRIEL A. AND JAMES S. COLEMAN, eds., *The Politics of the Developing Areas* (Princeton, N.J.: Princeton Univ. Press, 1960). A classic behavioral study of the governments of Africa, Asia, Latin America, and the Middle East.

Comparative government—Africa

CARTER, GWENDOLEN M., ed., *African One-Party States* (Ithaca, N.Y.: Cornell Univ. Press, 1962). A collection of essays by various authors covering Tunisia, Senegal, Guinea, The Ivory Coast, Liberia, and Tanganyika.

———, *Five African States: Responses to Diversity* (Ithaca, N.Y.: Cornell Univ. Press, 1963). A collection of essays by various authors covering the Cameroun Federal Republic, the Congo, Dahomey, the Rhodesias and Nyasaland, and South Africa.

SPIRO, HERBERT J., *Politics in Africa: Prospects South of the Sahara* (Englewood Cliffs, N.J.: Prentice-Hall, 1962). A brief, up-to-date survey.

Comparative government—Asia and the Middle East

KAHIN, GEORGE McT., ed., *Major Governments of Asia*, 2d ed. (Ithaca, N.Y.: Cornell Univ. Press, 1963). A collection of essays by various authors covering China, Japan, India, Pakistan, and Indonesia.

SHARABI, H. B., *Governments and Politics of the Middle East in the Twentieth Century* (Princeton, N.J.: D. Van Nostrand, 1962). Basic generalizations followed by a country-by-country account.

WARD, ROBERT E., AND ROY C. MACRIDIS, eds., *Modern Political Systems: Asia* (Englewood Cliffs, N.J.: Prentice-Hall, 1963). A collection of essays which cover Japan, China, and India in detail and survey the rest of Asia and the Middle East as well.

Comparative government—Latin America

DAVIS, HAROLD E., ed., *Government and Politics in Latin America* (New York: Ronald Press, 1958). A collection of essays which take the subject-by-subject rather than country-by-country approach.

NEEDLER, MARTIN, *Latin American Politics in Perspective* (Princeton, N.J.: D. Van Nostrand, 1963). A brief, up-to-date survey.

American government—general

BURNS, JAMES M., *The Deadlock of Democracy* (Englewood Cliffs, N.J.: Prentice-Hall, 1963). An analysis of the major weaknesses in the American system of government.

BURNS, JAMES M., AND JACK W. PELTASON, *Government by the People*, 5th ed. (Englewood Cliffs, N.J.: Prentice-Hall, 1963). A basic text.

CARR, ROBERT K., MARVER H. BERNSTEIN, AND WALTER F. MURPHY, *American Democracy in Theory and Practice*, 4th ed. (New York: Holt, Rinehart and Winston, 1963). A basic text.

FERGUSON, JOHN H., AND DEAN E. McHENRY, *The American System of Government*, 7th ed. (New York: McGraw-Hill, 1963). A basic text.

American government—the Constitution and the courts

CORWIN, EDWARD S., AND JACK W. PELTASON, *Understanding the Constitution*, 3d ed. (New York: Holt, Rinehart and Winston, 1964). A very brief, easy-to-follow, article-by-article analysis of the American Constitution.

MASON, ALPHEUS T., *The Supreme Court from Taft to Warren* (Baton Rouge, La.: Louisiana State Univ. Press, 1958). The best history of the court in the recent period.

PRITCHETT, C. HERMAN, *The American Constitution* (New York: McGraw-Hill, 1959). An excellent extended analysis of the American Constitution.

WARREN, CHARLES, *The Supreme Court in United States History*, rev. ed. (Boston: Little, Brown, 1928). The standard history. It does not cover the recent period.

American government—the executive and administration

CORWIN, EDWARD S., *The President: Office and Powers,* 4th ed. (New York: New York Univ. Press, 1957). The presidency treated from a legal point of view.

NEUSTADT, RICHARD E., *Presidential Power: The Politics of Leadership* (New York: John Wiley and Sons, 1960). The presidency treated from a political point of view.

PFIFFNER, JOHN M. AND ROBERT V. PRESTHUS, *Public Administration,* 4th ed. (New York: Ronald Press, 1960). A basic text which synthesizes the behavioral and traditional approaches to administration.

SIMON, HERBERT A., *Administrative Behavior,* 2d ed. (New York: Macmillan, 1957). A pioneer work which takes the behavioral approach to administration.

WOLL, PETER, *American Bureaucracy* (New York: W. W. Norton, 1963). A good treatment which is current and brief.

American government—the legislature

GALLOWAY, GEORGE B., *The Legislative Process in Congress* (New York: Thomas Y. Crowell, 1953). A balanced traditional political and legal discussion of the organization and functioning of Congress.

American government—politics

BINKLEY, W. E., *American Political Parties: Their Natural History,* 3d ed. (New York: Alfred A. Knopf, 1958). The standard history of American parties.

KEY, V. O., JR., *Politics, Parties and Pressure Groups,* 5th ed. (New York: Thomas Y. Crowell, 1964). The standard textbook treatment of the entire field of politics.

TRUMAN, DAVID, *The Governmental Process* (New York: Alfred A. Knopf, 1951). The classic behavioral study of interest groups.

American government—state and local

ADRIAN, CHARLES, *State and Local Government: A Study in the Political Process* (New York: McGraw-Hill, 1960). A behavioral text.

DAHL, ROBERT A., *Who Governs?* (New Haven, Conn.: Yale Univ. Press, 1961). A pioneer behavioral investigation of the power structure of a local community.

EDITORS OF FORTUNE, *The Exploding Metropolis* (New York: Doubleday, 1958). An excellent journalistic account of the major problems now facing American cities and means for dealing with them.

Traditional political theory—general

SABINE, GEORGE H., *A History of Political Theory,* 3d ed. (New York: Holt, Rinehart and Winston, 1961). The standard American text.

Traditional political theory—American

GRIMES, ALAN PENDLETON, *American Political Thought*, rev. ed. (New York: Holt, Rinehart and Winston, 1960). A broad historical survey of the most important intellectual movements related to politics written by a political scientist.

HOFSTADTER, RICHARD, *The American Political Tradition* (New York: Alfred A. Knopf, 1948). A very readable account concerning key thinkers and trends written by a historian.

Ideologies

EBENSTEIN, WILLIAM, *Today's Isms,* 4th ed. (Englewood Cliffs, N.J.: Prentice-Hall, 1964). A brief account which is comprehensive and up-to-date.

HUNT, R. N. CAREW, *The Theory and Practice of Communism,* 5th ed. (Baltimore: Penguin Books Ltd., 1963). An excellent brief account of Communism.

LANE, ROBERT E., *Political Ideology: Why the American Common Man Believes What He Does* (New York: Free Press of Glencoe, 1962). An attempt through depth interviewing to get at what a small sample of Americans actually believe about politics.

MAYO, H. B., *An Introduction to Democratic Theory* (New York: Oxford Univ. Press, 1960). A defense of democracy rooted in the outlook of traditional English philosophy.

THORSON, THOMAS LANDON, *The Logic of Democracy* (New York: Holt, Rinehart and Winston, 1962). A defense of democracy rooted in the outlook of contemporary logical positivism.

Methodology

DAHL, R. A., "The Behavioral Approach," *American Political Science Review,* Vol. 55, pp. 763–772. A very brief explanation of the behavioral approach to politics.

EULOW, HEINZ, *The Behavioral Persuasion in Politics* (New York: Random House, 1963). A brief defense of an extreme behavioral position.

STORING, HERBERT J., ed., *Essays on the Scientific Study of Politics* (New York: Holt, Rinehart and Winston, 1962). A series of articles attacking the behavioral position by various traditionalist scholars.

THE CURRICULUM AND THE DISCIPLINE

AMERICAN POLITICAL SCIENCE ASSOCIATION, *Goals for Political Science* (New York: William Sloane Associates, 1951). A discussion of the teaching of political science in colleges and universities. Chapter VIII is devoted to "Better Teamwork Between High Schools and Colleges."

5   Economics

Ronald H. Wolf
Department of Economics
University of Tennessee

ALTHOUGH SOME INDIVIDUALS HAVE "TIME ON THEIR HANDS," MANY of us find the days too short and life too brief to enable us to do all the things we would like to do. The typical teacher, having completed the evening meal, may find numerous activities to which she could devote her time: grading a set of examination papers, answering letters, calling on a sick friend, preparing tomorrow's lessons, watching television. With the evening not long enough to accommodate all of these activities, the teacher must use some method of choosing which of these alternatives she will pursue.

Any one who has faced the problem of allocating, budgeting, or distributing his time among various alternatives has a point of contact in his experience with that social science which we call economics or, less frequently, political economy. In seeking to build upon this point of contact, the author will discuss the nature of economics, set forth its recent important findings, disclose the methods of inquiry and the essence of understanding needed about the unique organization of knowledge in the subject, point out the basic methods in establishing economic truth, indicate the major theories used to explain events, to bridge gaps in knowledge, and to predict the future, and, finally, to hint at the role of economics in the social studies.

137

What Is Economics?

Although in some quarters the search for essences and rigorous definition has been discarded in favor of a certain calculated vagueness and flexibility of definition to fit the problems at hand, the author assumes that understanding and communication will be enhanced if there is some general agreement as to what is included and not included in a particular social science. A student of economics ought to have some guidelines which will help him select, out of the great mass of data, that which is economic. Otherwise, we shall be in danger of losing the benefits of division of labor in the social sciences.

Economics defined

In one of the first treatises devoted specifically to economics, Adam Smith writing in 1776 defined political economy as "an inquiry into the nature and causes of the wealth of nations." Wealth, according to Smith, is "the annual produce of the land and labour of the society." [1]

Between 1880 and 1920, a British economist, Alfred Marshall, influenced greatly the study of economics. His textbook, *Principles of Economics,* was widely used, going into numerous editions. According to Marshall: [2]

> Political economy or economics is a study of mankind in the ordinary business of life; it examines that part of individual and social action which is most closely connected with the attainment and with the use of the material requisites of wellbeing. Thus it is on the one side a study of wealth; and on the other, and more important side, a part of the study of man.

During much of the Marshallian period, Frank A. Fetter was a brilliant contributor to economic understanding in the United States. In his textbook Fetter defined economics "briefly, as the study of men earning a living; or, more fully, as the study of the material world and of the activities and mutual relations of men so far as all

[1] Adam Smith, *The Wealth of Nations,* Modern Library Edition (New York: Random House, 1937), p. 652.
[2] Alfred Marshall, *Principles of Economics,* 9th ed. (New York: Macmillan, 1961), Vol. I, p. 1.

these are the objective conditions to the gratification and to the welfare of men." [3]

Among contemporary textbooks, the most widely used is Paul A. Samuelson's *Economics: An Introductory Analysis.* After stating that "economists today generally agree on a definition like the following one," Samuelson goes on to define economics as "the study of how men and society *choose,* with or without the use of money, to employ *scarce* productive resources to produce various commodities over time and distribute them for consumption, now and in the future, among various people and groups in society." [4]   Campbell R. McConnell, in another popular text, defines economics as "the study of man's behavior in producing, exchanging, and consuming the material goods and services he wants." [5]   In his lectures to students in introductory economics, the writer has often employed this definition: economics is the study of how societies allocate their scarce resources to produce goods and services and how they distribute the goods and services to meet human needs and wants.

Comparing earlier definitions of economics with those more recent, one notices a good deal of similarity, yet there is one striking change.   In some of the more contemporary definitions, goods and services have replaced wealth.   Adam Smith broadened the term "wealth," the material means of satisfying human desires which have value in exchange, to cover not only the products of the farm, forest, mine, and sea, but also the manufactured products of the factory. It remained for later economists to broaden economics to include the services which can be performed to meet human needs and wants. In fact today the value of services in our total production is greater than the value of goods.

Subdivisions of economics

The breadth and complexity of economics has led to the creation of subdivisions in the study of economics.   It is common today to

[3] Frank A. Fetter, *Economic Principles* (New York: The Century Co., 1925), p. 3.

[4] Paul A. Samuelson, *Economics: An Introductory Analysis,* 6th ed. (New York: McGraw-Hill, 1964), p. 5.   Italics in the original.

[5] Campbell R. McConnell, *Economics: Principles, Problems, and Policies,* 2d ed. (New York: McGraw-Hill, 1963), p. 3.

speak of microeconomics and macroeconomics, both of which may be national economics or international economics.

Microeconomics focuses on the parts whereas macroeconomics deals with the whole or aggregates. Microeconomics is concerned with individual industries and specific product prices. Macroeconomics is concerned with total output and the total price level.

Microeconomics is itself broken down into a number of specialized areas including antitrust policy, consumer economics, labor economics, managerial economics, and price determination. Macroeconomics in turn includes such areas as economic fluctuations, output and employment analysis, price level determination, and stabilization and growth policies. International economics includes such subdivisions as development, finance, and trade.

Questions to which economics seeks answers

Economizing, or the practice of economics, is necessary because the means wherewith a society can meet its needs and wants are scarce relative to the alternative uses in which they might be employed in meeting those needs and wants. Thus economics involves a choice among alternatives, a method of establishing priorities when a society would like to have or do more than its resources permit. There are certain basic economic questions which every economic system, whether capitalist or socialist or mixed, answers in one way or another. These questions are: What to produce? How to organize production? How to produce? For whom to produce? When to produce?

What to produce? Since the resources are not great enough to do everything that a society might like to do, an economic system must provide a mechanism for making the selection. The decision can be the authoritative one of a dictator, a group of "wise men," a group of "good men," or some other recognized authority. In capitalistic democratic economies, the bulk of these decisions are made by private business firms or voluntary associations according to signals furnished by the household sector in buying goods and services. A smaller share of the output results from the decisions of governmental authorities who make choices as the elected representatives of the people. Thus in a democratic market economy the households ultimately determine the bill of goods of that society by the way they vote their dollars and ballots.

How to organize production?   Every society must decide what are to be the respective roles of private enterprise and government enterprise in the production of goods and services.   In the United States about 80½ cents of each dollar of household income go to pay the prices charged by private enterprise for goods and services, about 1½ cents go in gifts to voluntary associations (mainly religious) to maintain their services, approximately 12 cents go in taxes to finance the general activities of government, and approximately 6 cents are saved.   In socialist economies a much larger share of the goods and services, perhaps practically all, will be produced by government enterprise.

How to produce?   In answering the question, How to produce?, the economic injunction is: Be efficient!   Since we must economize, we attempt to get the most for the least, the greatest output for the least input.   The engineer can furnish perhaps several recipes on how to build a bridge.   The home economist can tell us several ways to bake a cake.   The economist reminds both to choose the recipe that is economical, the formula that gives the greatest value for the least cost.   And cost ultimately is opportunity cost, that which we have to give up in order to obtain that which we have selected.

For whom to produce?   The output of goods and services which is available for consumption may be looked upon as a large pie.   How are the pieces to be cut?   Should everyone receive an equal piece?   Should the pie be cut on the basis of individual need, a larger piece to the person who "needs" more?   Should the pie be cut on the basis of the "contribution" made in producing the pie, the productivity principle?   In the United States we mainly rely on the latter in distributing the output of finished goods and services.   Those who have furnished their resources to the productive sector have had them evaluated by the market and received for them a money income which constitutes a means of claim on the available supply of goods and services.

In our economy we do recognize that there is an element of truth in the principle of equality and in the needs principle.   To

141

reduce extreme inequality in income and claims to product, we employ progressive income taxes and inheritance taxes. In recognition that some minimum provision must be made for those who cannot make a contribution to production, we transfer income to them in the form of grants or pensions thus allowing them to claim a portion of the pie.

When to produce? Every economic system answers the question, What provision shall be made for the future? Shall we "eat, drink, and be merry today for tomorrow we die"? Or shall we assume that we shall live tomorrow and have needs and wants then that we shall want to satisfy? A society that consumes all of its wheat this year will have no wheat to plant for next year's crop. A society that employs all of its resources to produce consumer goods may well produce at a lower level tomorrow than it would if it tightened its belt today, devoted some of its resources to the production of capital goods now which could subsequently be used to enlarge in the future the output of consumer goods and services.

Goals of economics

Most economists accept as the main goal of economics the establishment of an economic order which maximizes satisfaction of human needs and wants consistent with the desire for leisure. Earlier economists thought that satisfaction might be measured and interpersonal comparisons made. They attempted to evaluate the effect of income distribution on the maximization of satisfaction. However, satisfaction has not proved to be measurable. Contemporary economists in capitalistic economies assume that if all the resources voluntarily forthcoming in an economy are utilized, then that economy is doing all that it wants to do in the way of satisfying human needs and wants. It is maximizing. An economy organized along authoritarian lines would presumably be maximizing if all the resources it could command were utilized. An economy can measure its progress over time by computing and comparing from year to year its output of goods and services on a per capita basis.

The subjective nature of satisfaction and its lack of measurability have led some economists, especially those who wished to make economics more scientific, to espouse an alternative goal. Professor

C. E. Ayres, one of the best known of these "institutional economists," has urged practitioners to abandon "maximizing satisfaction" as the goal of economic order and to substitute for it the establishment of an economic order which maximizes acceleration of the technological process. He argues that such a goal offers greater promise of objectivity because the results of different technologies and changing technologies and the effects of various policies on the technological process can more easily be measured scientifically.[6] The main regiment of economists, however, continues to march under the old banner.

Data with which economics deals

Economics deals with that aspect of human behavior which has to do with individual and group activity related to the production, exchange, and consumption of goods and services, i.e., making a living. It relates man to the material world and thus touches the natural sciences. It relates man to other men and thus is a social science. Human decisions and human actions provide the facts which economic science seeks to gather, sort, relate, and understand. In fact "every hour in the streets and stores one may witness thousands of acts, such as bargains, labor, and payments, that are the data of economic science."[7]

A good deal of economic data can be quantified since they consist of transactions which take place using a common unit of account, money. Included in the data available to economists are the record of the inputs and outputs of the productive sector, the income of and its disposal by the household sector, and statistics regarding the accumulated wealth, number of households and consumers, enterprises, and producers.

Government agencies and trade associations assemble a vast amount of facts and figures which provide the raw material that economists seek to comprehend in advancing their understanding of how an economic system works. The greater availability of data has made it easier for the economist to formulate and test his hypotheses, theories, and laws regarding the working of an economic system.

[6] A recent statement of Professor Ayres' position will be found in his book *Toward a Reasonable Society* (Austin: Univ. of Texas Press, 1961).

[7] Fetter, *op. cit.*, p. 4.

Finally, the data with which economics deals include the economic historian's record of the economic experiments and experiences of history. This record may serve to illuminate contemporary observation, add to the total of economic knowledge, and make clearer what policies to pursue in the attainment of economic goals.

What economics is not

Economics does not concern itself with either the ultimate meaning of human existence or with the nature and destiny of man. Nor does it deal with final values. Economists may suggest economic goals that a society may pursue and indicate the ways and means whereby these goals may be attained. They may indicate the economic costs of pursuing various policies whether economic or noneconomic. Economics does not answer the question as to why goals should be pursued.

Economics does not concern itself with the technical aspects of making things. For knowledge of bridge building the student should consult engineering. For knowledge of how to make cookies the student should refer to home economics. A knowledge of economics, however, will illuminate the practice of engineering and home economics by calling attention to the economic implications of alternative technical recipes.

Economics does not concern itself with the how of managing a business firm or a government agency; nor does it concern itself with the keeping of accounts. For answers in these areas the student should consult experts in business administration, public administration, and accounting. A knowledge of economics will help managers and accountants understand the relationship between their special areas of knowledge and economics, and make clear to them the economic implications of their behavior.

Important Findings in Economics Today

One names the important findings in economics today with some trepidation, knowing that the word "important" signifies that a value judgment is being made. When an economist makes such a selection he makes it from the standpoint of his own knowledge of economics, which in any case will be incomplete. Thus the items presented here are not to be thought of as exhaustive by any means and yet it is believed that there is widespread agreement among economists as to the importance of these findings.

Harmony of interests in the market economy

As an alternative to the economic systems of restraint and preference of his day, Adam Smith presented his "obvious and simple system of natural liberty." Relying primarily on private enterprise and the price system, he showed how in a market economy self-interest could be utilized to promote the public interest. Competition among buyers of goods and services that were in great demand would result in price increases and higher profits. Since the principal way to secure an income in a market economy is to provide either a labor service or the use of one's property in production, the higher prices and profits would attract resources into the production of those goods and services that were in great demand. Thus in a market economy society gets the goods and services it wants by relying on the self-interest of the producers who stand to gain more if they provide what buyers want. In such an economy there is an element of paradox. A person sets out to serve himself but in the end he benefits society, which was no part of his intention.

Unfortunately this profound but limited truth which relates self-interest to the public interest has at times been interpreted to mean that any self-interested pursuit of gain is in the public interest, that in economic activity people may be left to their own devices. But such a conclusion by no means follows. Modern awareness of economic behavior indicates that the conflict between the economic interests of the individual and the economic interests of others is partially harmonized in the market economy. There remain substantial areas of economic activity where interests are not harmonized. Reference will be made to two of these areas.

A large part of economic activity takes the form of exchange transactions in which the interest of the buyer is opposed to that of the seller. The buyer ordinarily wants low rather than high prices, good rather than poor quality, ample rather than niggardly service. The seller wants high prices rather than low, less quality rather than more, a minimum of service rather than a maximum. Thus in the area of buying and selling there is no automatic harmonization of interests. There is rather a conflict of interests which gives rise to possible exploitation and thus the need to establish institutional arrangements which provide for "just" or "reasonable" prices, quality, and service. Presumably, justice requires something in between the extreme desires of the conflicting parties.

Moreover, individual decisions to spend or to save may be in harmony with the interests of others but are not necessarily so. In a period of unemployment, decisions to spend may create the demand for goods and services that stimulates production and puts men back to work. In such a situation, decisions to save, although beneficial to the saver, may depress the demand for goods and services, discourage production, and limit the job opportunities of the unemployed. When resources are fully utilized and inflation threatens, decisions to save may mitigate price increases and thus protect the welfare of those who are without income or who are on a fixed income. In such a situation, decisions to spend now before prices rise, or rise higher, while beneficial to buyers, contribute to an upward pressure on prices to the detriment of those without or on fixed income. Harmonization of interests in a market economy, modern economics finds, is a limited truth. A good deal of modern economics must of necessity devote its attention to the achievement of justice in the resolution of these conflicting interests where there is no automatic harmonization of interests.

Competition: fragile and enduring

According to Adam Smith, free enterprise or free competition was the remedy for exploitation and inefficiency. If legally free to compete in any market where prices and profits indicated an opportunity, business concerns would enter and soon put an end to any exploitation. Moreover, since competition serves to embarrass and endanger the inefficient, it spurs enterprise to be as efficient as, or more efficient than, its rivals. Apparently Smith thought that competitive impulses sprang eternal in human behavior if only government did not restrain them. He admitted that rivals tended to conspire to eliminate competition among themselves but relied upon the potential competition that would enter should they succeed in doing so. To Smith competition must have been more or less automatic and spontaneous because he advocated repeal of the antitrust laws of his day—the laws against engrossing, forestalling, and regrating.

Smith's laissez-faire approach to competition, his belief in its automatic, spontaneous, and enduring nature, appears overly optimistic in the light of contemporary economic understanding. In an economy where technology may necessitate a substantial investment in plant and equipment, entry though legally free may in fact not be easy or feasible, with the result that existing firms do not feel compelled to buy and sell under competitive pressures.[8] One of the insights of modern economics is that competition to be effective must be present in the market, not just potential, at least where entry is difficult.

Moreover, government must take positive steps to maintain, promote, and restore competition.[9] Left to their own devices, individuals and firms may compete but logic, experience, and observation unite in indicating that they are even more likely to eliminate the competition that incessantly restrains and prods. Left to themselves, competitors may merge their firms into one, agree to fix prices, eliminate rivals by exclusive marketing practices, and control the prices of others by discriminatory tactics. The antitrust laws of the United States and of other countries are evidences of affirmative action by government to strike down anticompetitive arrangements and behavior to make competition an effective controlling and prodding device.

Achievement of full employment

Starting with the assumption of man's unlimited needs and wants and the limited nature of the resources available to meet these needs and wants, the early economists logically concluded that resources should tend to be fully used. When experience indicated that this was not always the case, economists readily admitted that individual goods and services might be in excess supply at going prices but

[8] A recent analysis of this problem will be found in J. S. Bain, *Barriers to New Competition* (Cambridge, Mass.: Harvard Univ. Press, 1956).

[9] For a carefully reasoned statement of the modern view, see Vernon A. Mund, *Government and Business,* 3d ed. (New York: Harper & Row, 1960), Chapters 3 and 4.

argued that the excess supply would drive prices down, demand would be greater at the lower prices, and the goods would sell. If the price dropped below the cost of production of some of the firms, the latter would have to shift out of the market and into the production of other goods where price-cost relationships indicated a more favorable return. Thus, assuming free enterprise and complete price flexibility, economists taught that a market economy tended automatically to move toward equilibrium at full employment.

Modern economists no longer expect to achieve full employment in a market economy through adjustments in demand and supply via flexible prices. The development of economic knowledge in the past thirty years reveals that the earlier explanation confused static and dynamic analysis, i.e., what may be true at any one moment of time compared to what happens over time. Although there is substantial evidence in logic, experience, and observation to support "the law of demand" that at any one moment of time more goods would be taken at lower prices than at higher prices, there is no reason to believe that declines in price over time necessarily increase sales. When prices are falling, buyers may in fact buy less than they had been buying at higher prices because they postpone purchases anticipating even greater declines in the future. Furthermore, when prices are rising, buyers may in fact buy more at the higher prices than they bought earlier at lower prices because they expect that prices may rise even higher in the future.

It is one of the findings of modern economics that society must take positive steps to assure full employment.[10] The problem is one of securing an aggregate demand for goods and services commensurate with the ability of the economy to produce at the full employment level. Two principal devices are available to bring about the desired equality: monetary policy and fiscal policy. In using monetary policy, the monetary authority attempts to induce or discourage spending by controlling the supply of credit available for borrowers. Resulting changes in the rate of interest serve either to increase or reduce the desirability of spending on credit. In using fiscal policy,

[10] The reader will find the new approach set forth in the book of the British economist John Maynard Keynes, *The General Theory of Employment, Interest and Money* (New York: Harcourt, Brace & World, 1936). The work is heavy going for the nonprofessional economist. A clear, concise treatment of the subject will be found in Howard S. Dye, John R. Moore, and J. Fred Holly, *Economics: Principles, Problems, and Perspectives* (Boston: Allyn and Bacon, 1962), Chapter 7.

governments determine the level of their spending and the sources of their revenue purposely to raise or lower total spending, increasing expenditures or reducing taxes to raise the level of aggregate demand, lowering expenditures or increasing taxes to decrease the level of total demand.

Conditioners of economic development

As specialists, economists like to emphasize the economic conditioners of economic activity. In the past a good deal of effort has been directed toward the study of the economic factors that contribute to economic progress. Economists have paid attention to the quantity and quality of the resources that are available for production—the labor supply with its skills and technical know-how and the material resources both natural and artificial, natural resources being inclusive of such factors as land, forests, metals, minerals, and water and artificial resources being inclusive of such items as plant, equipment, machines, and tools. They have long emphasized that an increase in the quantity and quality of resources is prerequisite to economic development.

It is one of the findings of modern economics that more than economic resources are necessary to have economic growth. A nation's educational institutions may be preparing its members to play roles in the economy which will accelerate economic progress. Illiteracy, on the other hand, can be a powerful deterrent to growth and a lack of knowledge and wisdom can leave abundant resources unutilized. A society's political system may either be conducive to development or inhibit it. Economies with resources have, nevertheless, languished in economic progress because of governmental instability. A society's ethical, moral, and religious values spur economic growth or they hinder it. Asceticism, dishonesty, and lethargy can offset the advantages of abundant economic resources. A society's sociological characteristics, including its class structure, cultural patterns, family traditions, and interpersonal relationships, may have either a positive or negative impact on the economic development of that society. Thus today's economists have become increasingly aware that noneconomic factors which are within the borders of other disciplines must, nevertheless, be taken into consideration by the economist because they break out of the confines of their own specialized fields of knowledge and have an economic impact.

Government intervention in international trade

Impressed by the increase in productivity when a nation resorts to division of labor and specialization, Adam Smith and his followers extended the analysis to the international economy. It is only reasonable, economists argued, that nations specialize in the production of those goods and services in which they have a comparative advantage and then exchange their specialties for those of others. In this way the world's resources would be used efficiently; output and satisfaction would be maximized. Economists accepted the principle of laissez-faire in international trade long after they had abandoned it in domestic trade, although they occasionally made concessions for government intervention on behalf of national defense and infant industries.

It now appears that a laissez-faire policy of government "hands off" is no more desirable in international trade than it is in domestic trade. The lack of uniformity around the world in the establishment of standards of fair competition and employee welfare, in the achievement of full employment, and in the elimination of exploitation, discrimination, and disorder distorts the performance of the market mechanism in international exchange, as it does when those elements are present in the domestic economy. Modern economics is finding that positive steps must be taken to establish "rules of the game" in international trade just as they have been found necessary in domestic trade. Moreover, there is an awareness in modern economics that something is lost in an economy when division of labor and specialization are carried to extremes and a broad, balanced range of output sacrificed. When such rules are established and such an awareness is taken into account, then international trade and international competition can be powerful factors in promoting the efficient use of resources and in raising the level of living around the globe.

Predictions of the future of capitalism and socialism

According to the Marxist interpretation of the development of capitalist economies, the latter are eventually doomed to pass away and be replaced by socialist economies. This outcome is certain, the socialist argument runs, because the capitalist system carries within it its own seeds of destruction. Usually it is asserted that the capitalist system of private property in the material means of production leads to injustice in that workers do not obtain all of the value of that which they produce. Out of this injustice, say the critics, flow ever-recurring capitalist crises involving increasing concentration of economic power, intensification of competition, falling profits, and larger armies of unemployed. Capitalism stresses efficiency and freedom at the expense of security and order, it is said.

On the other hand, spokesmen for capitalism have asserted that socialist economies are pragmatically impossible because they are inconsistent with the realities of the world in which they must operate. The principal charge against socialism is that it assumes a doctrine of the nature of man which is out of contact with reality. The offer of security, it is asserted, ultimately will lead to less security because incentives to produce goods and services will be less. Security and order are purchased, the argument runs, at the expense of efficiency and freedom. Proponents of the capitalistic market economy assert that the lure of profit and the hope of gain, the fear of loss and the embarrassment of want are powerful incentives to keep men on the job so that the world's work gets done.

Modern economics finds that both of these predictions need re-examination in the light of changing situations. The capitalistic system has proved to be much more flexible than its earlier critics thought. Government intervention has served to change economic institutions to check, offset, rechannel, or reverse certain economic trends thought by the critics to be inevitable. Antitrust legislation and government control have served to mitigate or offset the concentration of economic power. Institutionalizing collective bargaining; minimum wage, maximum hour, and health and safety legislation; and countercyclical policy designed to maintain full employment have served to enhance and make more secure the position of labor. Governments in advanced capitalist countries now assure their residents a minimum level of security through unemployment insurance, old-age pensions, workmen's disability compensation, and welfare payments. To rise above the minimum level of living provided still requires personal effort, inheritance, or luck. Thus incentive remains.

On the other hand, a socialist economy has now operated for

over forty years and there appears today no sign of imminent collapse. Its growth in production of goods and services has been more rapid than one might have expected, bearing in mind the inefficiencies and compulsions of such a system. It is possible that socialist economies, too, are undergoing or will undergo modifications in their economic institutions so as to enhance their workability. Furthermore, it is possible that technology has so advanced that a nation's production machinery can endure an element of inefficiency and yet turn out a level of output of goods and services that will tolerably satisfy a society. In conclusion, one may say that modern economics is finding both economic systems less vulnerable to their internal contradictions and errors than earlier critics had supposed.

Methods of Inquiry and the Organization of Knowledge

Economics as a social science is a body of knowledge about human beings in their economic relations with each other and with the material world. Since human behavior provides the raw material out of which economists erect the body of economic knowledge, the beginning of understanding lies in a doctrine of the nature of man. Moreover, economics shares with other social sciences the problems involved in the application of the scientific method to the study of human behavior. Economics is further complicated by the fact that it deals with both the measurable and the immeasurable. Finally, it is necessary to understand how economists organize their knowledge and use words in talking about it.

The nature of man revealed in economics

The mainstream of economic thinking west of the Iron Curtain, at least since the days of Adam Smith, has revealed a rather ambivalent attitude toward the nature of man. On the one hand, there has been an emphasis upon man's rational nature, his reasoning ability, his rational economic behavior. On the other hand, there has been a preference for a market economy rather than one that is centrally planned, because of the belief that no one person or one group has sufficient mental capacity to maximize economic order and justice amid all the complexities and conflicts in economic behavior. This ambivalence appears in Adam Smith, where a good deal of confidence is placed in rational behavior and yet there is a lack of confidence in the ability of one person to know another person and to make his decisions for him. Thus, in the end, Smith falls back on an individualism which makes each person the best judge of his abilities, interests, and satisfactions.

Not only is man finite in the thinking of most economists but he also exhibits a universal and persistent tendency to self-centeredness. Observation has led economists to conclude that human beings are more interested in the welfare of themselves and their immediate families than they are in broader and more remote interests. Economists as early as Smith believed that the output of goods and services for the satisfaction of society's needs and wants will be greater if primary reliance is placed upon this tendency toward self-interest rather than the possibility of benevolence. It was Smith's observation that society will get more bread if it makes it worth the baker's while than if it appeals to his sympathy for hungry humanity. Thus, most economists have assumed that self-interest is universal and lasting, and that economic wisdom requires that economic systems take this into account if they are to achieve their objectives. Economic policy attempts to channel, regulate, or control self-interest where its expression is not consistent with the public welfare. Economists do not deny that human beings are capable of benevolent, charitable, heroic, and self-giving acts. They simply assert that a workable economic system must take into account the behavior of most of the people most of the time.

Perhaps the principal dissenter from the doctrine of man assumed by most economists was Karl Marx. Although agreeing with the orthodox economists in regard to human behavior in a capitalistic economy, Marx believed that the root of human selfishness lay in the institution of private property. Once property was socialized, he reasoned, men would have no cause for self-centeredness and could be educated to unselfishness. Marx's hypothesis is now undergoing testing in the Soviet Union. The persistence of antisocial behavior in that country leaves his hypothesis unverified at present.

Use of the scientific method in the study of economic behavior

Economists use the scientific method in advancing their knowledge of economic behavior. They gather the facts and figures which they

153

judge to be economic in nature or relevant to the economic, often relying on the assistance of the accountant, historian, and statistician. They group those facts and figures which appear to be of the same kind or to belong together, thus bringing some order to the raw data and reducing the number of individual items that must be studied. Economists study the groups of facts and figures to see if they can detect any relationship between them. Upon noting a possible relationship, they form a tentative hypothesis or explanation which they then proceed to verify or test by applying the hypothesis to additional facts of the same kind which had suggested the hypothesis. If testing indicates the correctness of the hypothesis, economists believe that an addition has been made to the stock of reliable economic knowledge.

In all of this search for economic knowledge, the scientific ideal is that truth is pre-eminent, every other consideration must be subjected to it. The scientist must be objective. The scientist is supposedly so dedicated to the pursuit of truth that his personal comforts, interests, and preferences are submerged. In the natural sciences such a submersion is not easy but it is easier than it is in the social sciences because the object of study belongs in another world from that of the subject. However, in the social sciences the subject is himself a part of the process, the object which he is studying. Thus, his economic interests are present when he engages in the study of economic behavior and they may distort his objectivity.

A second consideration must be understood in regard to the application of the scientific method to the study of economic data. It is sometimes said that facts do not speak for themselves, or if they do, they are not speaking very loudly. This may be true especially if the facts collected, whether of choice or necessity, are limited in number. In such a situation the economist in a hurry or the one without a sensitive ear, may attempt to speak for them, stating the hypothesis first and then searching for facts and figures which support the preconception. Facts and figures that do not fit the hypothesis are either ignored or distorted, the progress of economic knowledge is delayed, not advanced, and the task has to be done again. The facts may not be speaking but to avoid this misuse of the scientific method the economist must be sure they are not speaking before he speaks for them.

In the third place, he who uses economic knowledge must be

aware of the difficulties of predicting economic behavior. In the natural sciences, explanation and prediction go hand in hand. This is possible for two reasons. The range of freedom in the behavior of natural phenomena is usually narrower than is the range of human behavior. Thus, the explanation of human behavior may be much more complex and the assignment of the degree of importance to be accorded to the various factors exceedingly difficult. Thus, prediction becomes extremely hazardous. Moreover, insofar as we know, natural objects about which predictions are made are not conscious of such predictions. Thus, the mere fact of prediction does not influence behavior. However, in economics, as perhaps also in the other social sciences, explanations of past human behavior may be well established, but forecasts of similar behavior in the future may fail because those about whom the predictions are made, with knowledge of those predictions, may consciously change their behavior to will a different result.

The measurable and the immeasurable in economics

Economics, perhaps more than some of the social sciences, deals with data that lend themselves to quantification. Practically from the beginning of the organized discipline, mathematically-minded economists have introduced mathematics into the study of economics. Even before that there was political arithmetic. Moreover, those associated with the development of the science of statistics early saw a place for their tools in the study of economics. Today, econometrics, which combines the use of statistical data in the mathematical formulations of economics, a task made easier by the technological development of data processing and computing machines, attracts wide interest in the profession. Inputs, outputs, exchange ratios, consumption, and inventory stocks of goods can all be quantified in real and monetary terms.

Nevertheless, there are large areas of economic behavior where quantification is difficult or impossible. Utility and disutility, satisfaction and sacrifice are not measurable in any objective manner. It is often difficult if not impossible to measure the exact contribution of relevant factors to the total result, for example, the factors that contribute to economic growth. It may be said that their presence will help and their absence will hinder but it is difficult to say how much. Moreover, in achieving economic justice through economic policy, judgments must be made which require a weighing of conflicting interests and goals and of advantage against disadvantage, all of which are immeasurable.

Organization and communication of knowledge

The data which economists have at their disposal are commonly classified into aggregate and sectoral, real and monetary. In communicating economic understanding, economists use a specialized vocabulary which is sometimes confusing to the nonprofessional because the words are either unfamiliar or they are familiar but they are being used in a sense different from their ordinary, nontechnical meaning.

For a picture of the total economy, economists study aggregates. They utilize data which give totals over a period of time: the output of goods and services, the purchases of goods and services, changes in inventories. They also group data to obtain totals at any one moment of time: the wealth of the economy, the supply of money, bank deposits, employment and unemployment, the price level, number of enterprises, number of households, the population. Aggregate economic data are important in the study of the problems of economic growth and stability.

For some purposes, sectoral data are needed. The problem of the concentration of economic power is related to specific product markets. The economist wants information on the structure, behavior, and performance of particular industries and product markets. He wants to know how prices are determined in individual markets, and the price, cost, and profit relations in them. According to the economist's criteria of judgment, some markets may be performing badly. The coal industry may be sick, the economy may have a farm problem; in such cases the economist finds it useful to have his knowledge organized on a sectoral basis so he can deal with the problem at hand. Rather than looking at employment in the aggregate, the economist may wish to study the change in employment in various industries or in various grades of jobs over a period of time. For these reasons, economists have found it useful to classify their knowledge according to its macro (aggregate) or micro (sectoral) character.

It is the real goods and services themselves which actually satisfy human needs and wants. It is the real resources, whether human or material, which are the vital ingredients of production. Thus the economist is interested in real data. However, few economic transactions are barter transactions today. Most of them involve the use of money or its substitute, credit. Money serves as a unit of account, a medium of exchange, a standard of deferred payment, and at times a store of value. It is a common denominator which facilitates measurement and comparison. Moreover, its introduction into the economy introduces an element which complicates the achievement of general equilibrium at full employment. As a result of these considerations economists find it helpful to organize their data both in real terms and in monetary terms.

Finally, it is important for the nonprofessional who comes in contact with economics and economists to understand how the discipline uses words. Economics has many terms which are not used except in a technical sense: marginal revenue, marginal cost, marginal firm, marginal productivity, oligopoly, product differentiation, elasticity, factors of production, propensity to consume, just to mention a few. In such cases there is no ambiguity, it is simply a matter of learning the meaning of the terms. However, economists sometimes use ordinary words but give them a specialized, technical meaning. For example, the stranger to economics may, upon hearing the word "investment," think of the stocks and bonds which he owns. In economics the word investment is used to refer to business spending for plant and equipment, and government and foreign spending for all goods and services. The purchase of stocks and bonds is not considered investment. Or, take another example. The word "rent" is commonly used in business to refer to the price paid for the use of someone's durable property or the income received from allowing someone else to use one's property. Many economists restrict the use of the word "rent" to the price paid for the use of land or the income received from allowing the use of one's land. Similarly, the word "capital" in its root meaning has reference to a fund of money or one's wealth stated as a financial sum, but many economists use it to refer to the plant and equipment which have been acquired through the expenditure of money. Without a grasp of the meaning of the economist's technical words or the technical meaning he sometimes gives to ordinary words, the stranger to economics will find a good deal of the discipline baffling and ambiguous.

Basic Methods of Establishing Truth in Economics

Truth is a rather elusive thing to define or describe. On an elementary level it is defined as fact, fidelity, and veracity; it is agreement with reality. There may be higher levels of truth in philosophy and theology where, it is said, truth may involve that which is "more true than fact." However, economists concern themselves with the lower levels of truth, with factual truth, reliable information, sound knowledge.

Impressionistic, intuitive truth

In the absence of scientific methods in the search for truth, mankind has often had to resort to impressionistic, intuitive truth. Undoubtedly, those with able, inquisitive, and keen minds have discovered truth out of experience and observation. Their insights have stood the test of time. The great difficulty, however, with knowledge so gathered is the risk that it will prove to be fragmentary, incomplete, and unreliable. Impressions and insights may be gathered from too few observations, too little experience. Our senses may delude us. Unique experiences may be blown up into universal generalizations. If the data are not present to permit the use of surer methods to truth, impressionistic, intuitive truth may have to be relied upon. When it is, it should be held tentatively and tested at the first opportunity.

Inductive, deductive, scientific truth

Modern economists prefer to use the scientific method as a surer way of getting at the truth in economics. The scientific method as applied in the natural sciences involves the controlled experiment. However, in economics, as in the other social sciences, this method of the laboratory cannot be used because individuals cannot be isolated in order to observe their economic behavior or if they could be, their behavior would be different than it would be in the real-world situation and thus not comparable.

"Deprived of the possibility of actual experiments," writes Professor Lloyd G. Reynolds, "the economist resorts to *intellectual experiments*. The process of intellectual experiment begins with *observations of behavior*." [11]   To observe, the economist needs to know what has gone on and what is going on, he needs a record of the events, a statement of the facts and figures.   In observing the data, he may detect certain regularities.   When he finds *x*, he finds *y*.   He then sets up the regularity as a hypothesis: if *x*, then *y*.   His next step is to test or verify the hypothesis by applying it to new data to see if, in fact, it has general application.   Using statistical tools, the economist attempts to find out with what degree of assurance he can say that when he finds *x*, he also finds *y*.   Where prolonged testing reveals that the evidence is overwhelming in support of the truth of the hypothesis, it becomes a law.

If *x* and *y* are always associated, the economist will then ask why.   Is there a causal relationship between the two?   If so, in what direction?   Is there a third factor affecting both?   In going behind the facts, the figures, and the observed relationships, the economist is seeking "a general explanation that accounts for or combines a number of laws, just as Newton's theory of gravitation 'explained' Kepler's laws." [12]   In such a case the economist is theorizing and his explanation is a theory.   It is said that "a theory in this . . . sense cannot be as well established as the laws on which it rests, since it is further removed from the facts." [13]   Professor Rendigs Fels says that "economic theory is largely deductive. . . .   The analyst tries to specify all the conditions under which *b* logically and inevitably follows *a*." [14] These conditions are the theorist's assumptions.

Testing economic truth

At the present time, there is a methodological controversy engaging the attention of economists.   It concerns the testing of the validity of

[11] *Economics: A General Introduction* (Homewood, Ill.: Richard D. Irwin, 1963), p. 8.   Italics in the original.

[12] Rendigs Fels, *Challenge to the American Economy: An Introduction to Economics* (Boston: Allyn and Bacon, 1961), pp. 488–489.

[13] *Ibid.*, p. 489.

[14] *Ibid.*

a theory. In the past, economists have argued that the assumptions must be realistic, that is, that the facts must be in the assumptions. Then one could safely proceed by logical reasoning and reach sound conclusions. Theories whose assumptions were not in accord with the facts were deemed to be poor, unreliable theories.

Professor Milton Friedman has urged that theories be tested not by the realism of their assumptions but by their validity in prediction.[15] For example, the law of identity has been a part of economic knowledge for a long time. It states that in a competitive market, cost, including a normal profit, and price will tend to be equal in the long run. The economist's theory of perfect competition explains why the law is true; but the realism of the assumptions of the theory have often been challenged. However, since Friedman finds a good deal of evidence that the law of identity is true in the real world and since the theory of perfect competition explains why the law is true, he believes that the theory is valid because it predicts the result which we actually observe in the real world. The issue is still unresolved. Friedman has some supporters; [16] others remain uneasy.[17]

Although some economists have been satisfied if economic laws and theories have met any one of three tests: sound logic, historical experience, or empirical observation, economics is on surer ground when it submits its hypotheses to all three tests. Moreover, economics is true to the spirit of science when it remains open to, and welcomes, all methods and paths that lead to truth.

Major Theories for Explanation and Prediction

Theory may be an explanation of what is taking place. It may also be an explanation of what would take place under different condi-

[15] "The Methodology of Positive Economics," in *Essays in Positive Economics* (Chicago: Univ. of Chicago Press, 1953).

[16] For example, Fels, *op. cit.*, p. 494.

[17] For a discussion of Friedman's position see Eugene Rotwein, "On 'The Methodology of Positive Economics,'" *Quarterly Journal of Economics*, 73:554–575 (November), 1959; Ernest Nagel, "Assumptions in Economic Theory," *American Economic Review*, 53:211–219 (May), 1963; Paul A. Samuelson, Discussion, *Ibid.*, pp. 231–236.

tions. Thus, theory is relevant to the question, What does society want to have take place? Theory is also closely related to policy, for policy is the creation of the conditions which theory indicates are necessary if certain results are to follow

Theory is useful, too, in bridging gaps in knowledge and in fore-casting the future. The economist who uses theory does not have to study every similar situation afresh in detail. If he can study some of the like situations and then abstract the unifying significant factors in them, he can formulate his theory and apply it to similar but un-known situations with confidence that the same results are taking place. In this case, theory is bridging a gap in knowledge. So, too, the economist expects that like situations will yield the same results in the future that they are yielding in the present and have yielded in the past. He uses theory to forecast future behavior.

Economics has two major areas of theory: price theory and employment theory. The first attempts to explain how prices are determined, the second, how the level of employment is deter-mined.

Price theory

In explaining price determination in a market economy in the short run, whether for factor services or products, economists have been in general agreement that price is a function of demand and scarcity (supply). The early economists, however, wanted to go behind the theory of demand and supply to see if there was a more fundamental explanation of price. In studying those products which were pro-duced and thus had a cost of production the early economists noticed that in the short run there was no predictable relationship between the cost of producing the item and the price at which it was sold when production and sale were carried on under conditions of competition. Under conditions of competition in the long run, how-ever, the economists observed that there was a tendency for price and cost to come into an equality. To this observed tendency, economists gave the name "law of identity" or "empirical law of cost."

Since the cost of producing a product and its selling price tend to be equal in the long run under conditions of competition, economists sought an explanation for this identity. Is there a causal relationship? Early economists developed the cost-of-production theory of value which explained the identity by saying that cost of production determines price, that the price of a product depends upon the expenses incurred in its production. Starting with the factor markets where demand and supply determine price, economists followed production through various stages which added value (cost) until finally the product was finished and ready for the consumer's use.

At first glance, the cost theory of price seems plausible enough. Businessmen certainly hope that the price of the product will cover its cost and leave something over. They may try to set prices which cover cost and sometimes succeed. However, as a general explanation of how prices are determined the theory proved to be inadequate. The mere fact that cost had been incurred in the product's production did not assure that the product would sell in the market at a price which would cover that cost.

As a substitute for the cost-of-production theory of price other economists developed the imputation theory of value.[18] According to this theory, the flow of value begins with the determination of prices in the finished goods markets under the theory of demand and scarcity. Value then flows back through the various stages of production until the factor service markets are reached. Thus intermediate goods and the factor services have a value which is derived from their use in finished products. Costs, in the imputation theory, broadly viewed are more likely to be reflections of price than determinants of it. However, the imputation theorist declines to assert that the price of any particular product determines its cost because intermediate goods and factor services reflect a value which alternative uses bestow upon them.

The identity of price and cost in a competitive market is no longer explained in terms of causation. It is explained by the physical adjustments which are made in supply and the financial adjustments that are made in cost when price and cost are not equal.[19]

[18] The reader desiring to pursue this topic in detail should consult Frank A. Fetter, "Cost-Prices, Product-Prices, and Profits" in *Economic Principles and Problems*, Walter E. Spahr, ed., 3d ed. (New York: Farrar & Rinehart, 1937), I, pp. 503–520.

[19] The modern view is carefully developed by Vernon A. Mund, "The Financial Adjustment in the Empirical Law of Cost," *American Economic Review*, 26:74–80 (March), 1936.

Moreover, the financial adjustments that are made in cost both illuminate and illustrate the imputation theory of value.

Employment theory

Although the total demand for goods and services and the total output of goods and services may not be equal in the short run, economists have noticed that in the long run the two tend to be equal. To explain this identity, J. B. Say, a French economist, theorized that "supply creates its own demand." Thus, there ought never to be any general overproduction in the long run because what was produced could and would be demanded. No supply of labor would go unwanted. Competition and flexible prices would assure full utilization of an economy's resources. Say's proposition received such widespread approval that it was acclaimed an economic law, "the law of markets."

The period of prolonged depression and stagnation which began in 1929 cast doubt on Say's theory of employment. A new theory was needed that would better explain the employment situation in the real world. J. M. Keynes and others have developed a modern employment theory which stresses the importance of aggregate demand in creating employment opportunities. Instead of "supply creating its own demand," modern theory affirms that "demand creates supply," up to the level of full employment. By emphasizing the necessity of effective demand if output is to be encouraged, modern employment theory makes clear why mankind's vast needs and wants can exist along with a high level of unemployment.[20]

Economics in the Social Studies

Economists do not know everything that they would like to know about the workings of an economy, but they know a good deal and are learning more. In fact, they already know a good deal more than the people of the United States have been willing to accept and use in economic policy. In my opinion, this hesitation stems in

[20] For an excellent literary presentation of both the old and the new theories of employment, see Dye, Moore, and Holly, *op. cit.*, Chapter 7.

part from a lack of economic understanding on the part of a large segment of the population. To the extent that teachers of elementary and secondary social studies can incorporate economic knowledge into their work and push back the wall of economic illiteracy, so much the easier will come public acceptance of economic policy designed to create the conditions necessary to ensure the desired economic results.

The writer has attempted to make clear what economics is all about, to disclose recent developments in economic knowledge, to set forth what one needs to know about the peculiarities of economics and the distinctive organization of economic knowledge, to indicate the principal methods of establishing truth in economics, and to present the two major areas of economic theory. Which of these elements of economics can be used in the classroom, in the final analysis, will have to be determined by educators since they are the ones best able to determine the mental capacity of children and youth. The writer will indicate, however, some factors that economists would like to see emphasized in the classroom, if possible.

Appreciation of the specialized nature of economic knowledge

The student should be made to realize that economics is a complex subject to which experts are giving their full attention. Its complexity requires a spirit of humility on the part of both those who know nothing of the subject and those who devote their lives to its comprehension. It is appropriate that the uninformed do not pose as experts; it is also appropriate that the experts do not pose as the unhesitant possessors of the truth. One of the problems in economic education is that so many people believe that they already know the truth in economics without formal study or without continuing study.

In writing for college students about to begin the study of economics, Professor Reynolds [21] makes this helpful suggestion:

> Forget what you think you know about economic issues, because much of what you "know" is wrong. The greatest difficulty in discussing economics is that people already know the answers. They see no need for examining evidence or for careful reasoning, and commit the

[21] Reynolds, *op. cit.*, p. 13.

simplest logical errors with unashamed cheerfulness. The purpose of this course is mainly to unteach you what passes for "commonsense economics" among the general public. Any positive knowledge you may acquire beyond this is a sheer bonus.

Recognizing economics as a social study

A major criticism made by a committee of economists who examined and appraised the economic content of selected textbooks used in high school economics, social problems, and United States history courses was that too much emphasis was placed on describing how economic activity affects the individual as a consumer and a worker and too little emphasis was devoted to analyzing how an economic system works, the role of allocation machinery including the price system, and the aggregate problems of economic growth and stability.[22] Perhaps a good deal of the emphasis on the individual and his problems reflects the pedagogical interest in stimulating learning by relating the student to the subject in a "life-situation approach."

Economists would like to see economics taught as a *social* science. According to Professor Fetter: [23]

In the main, economics must be understood as a social study for social ends, not a selfish study for individual advantage. The individual interest must be recognized, but treated as within, and subordinate to, the larger social interests.

The solution may lie in relating the life-situation approach to the broader aspects of economics as a social science.

Straight thinking on economic subjects

Two elementary errors in sound reasoning are frequently found by economists when they appraise economic comprehension. One is the commission of the logical error of the fallacy of composition, and the second is the commission of the analytical error of failing to take into account the two-sided nature of economic activity.

In the first place, individuals frequently reason that what is true

[22] Special Textbook Study Committee of the Committee on Economic Education of the American Economic Association, Report, "Economics in the Schools," *American Economic Review,* 53:ix–xi (March), 1963, Pt. 2, Supplement.

[23] Fetter, *Economic Principles,* p. 9.

of a part is also true of the whole, what is true for themselves must be true for the economy as a whole. For example, an individual can easily learn either from logic, experience, or observation that a person can spend himself into bankruptcy. From the standpoint of society as a whole, however, a higher level of spending may be the essential prerequisite to rapid economic growth and full employment. A society can spend itself into prosperity, and it can attempt to save too much.

In the second place, much of economic activity is recorded as transactions between two parties. People frequently look at such transactions from the standpoint of how it affects them without taking into consideration the economic implications of the other side of the transaction. Much confusion in economic thinking follows from this failure to consider both sides of the coin. A business firm can easily see how a reduction in wages would mean lower costs and higher profits. However, wages which are a cost of production from the viewpoint of the business firm are a form of income to the person receiving them. One side of the coin is cost, the other side is income. The very cut in wages that seems so desirable from the standpoint of costs and profits also means a loss in income and, as a result, less ability to purchase the goods and services the very same firms are producing.

In summary, it may be said that economics is a complex, difficult subject. The role that economists would like economics to play in social studies may be beyond the realm of the possible. From the standpoint of the public welfare, however, it is desirable that economic education be as widespread as possible. To whatever extent it can be included, economists will feel a deep sense of gratitude to educators. And economists hope that whatever of economics is introduced into the classroom will meet the standards of truth established in the discipline.

SUGGESTED READINGS

INTRODUCTORY ECONOMICS

Dye, Howard S., John R. Moore, and J. Fred Holly, *Economics: Principles, Problems, and Perspectives* (Boston: Allyn and Bacon,

1962). According to a reviewer, "To a greater extent than perhaps any other recent introductory textbook, it presents clearly and forcefully the basic tools necessary to 'think, talk, and write about economic topics' in a competent manner." The book includes a strong historical emphasis which provides perspective to understand the contemporary economy.

FELS, RENDIGS, *Challenge to the American Economy: An Introduction to Economics* (Boston: Allyn and Bacon, 1961). In the first two parts of the book the author uses policy problems to teach the fundamental concepts of economics. In the third part he uses the puzzle kind of problem to teach deductive theory and reasoning. The book has been acclaimed as "a superior elementary economics text."

HEILBRONER, ROBERT L., *The Making of Economic Society* (Englewood Cliffs, N.J.: Prentice-Hall, 1962). The author skillfully combines economic history and economic theory to present the basic elements of economics in prose without recourse to mathematical equations or geometrical drawings. An excellent book for the layman.

REYNOLDS, LLOYD G., *Economics: A General Introduction* (Homewood, Ill.: Richard D. Irwin, 1963). Written by a man with many years spent in studying and teaching economics, the book contains a wealth of economic knowledge. It has an unusually large amount of information on the Soviet economy and stresses economic growth.

SAMUELSON, PAUL A., *Economics: An Introductory Analysis,* 6th ed. (New York: McGraw-Hill, 1964). Reportedly the most widely-used textbook in economics, Professor Samuelson's book modernizes Marshall by incorporating into the main body of economic knowledge the developments in analysis of the past thirty years. The author gives special emphasis to the Keynesian approach to aggregate monetary economics. Much use is made of geometrical drawings in the presentation of economic ideas.

SOULE, GEORGE, *Economics: Measurement, Theories, Case Studies* (New York: Holt, Rinehart and Winston, 1961). An excellent book for the student who wants to get acquainted with economics largely through prose and yet who wants an introduction to the geometric models used in economics. An interesting feature of the book is the case studies which provide practice in using economic tools of analysis.

READINGS IN ECONOMICS

MARK, SHELLEY M. AND DANIEL M. SLATE, eds., *Economics in Action: Readings in Current Economic Issues,* 2d ed. (Belmont, Calif.: Wadsworth, 1962). A well-balanced collection of readings drawn from a wide range of sources and stressing divergent points of view, the book includes among its authors such prominent economists as Milton Friedman, John Kenneth Galbraith, Clark Kerr, and Walt Rostow, and such public figures as the late President John F. Kennedy, William McChesney Martin, Walter Reuther, and Nelson Rockefeller.

McCONNELL, CAMPBELL R. AND ROBERT C. BINGHAM, eds., *Economic Issues: Readings and Cases* (New York: McGraw-Hill, 1963). The editors have gathered an assortment of readings that cover the macro, micro, and international areas of economics including such less frequently treated topics as the problem of creeping inflation, growth problems and costs, structure and performance of markets, the social balance question, and tax reform. The book contains an unusually large number of readings not hitherto used in books of this sort.

HISTORY OF ECONOMICS AND ITS METHODOLOGY

OSER, JACOB, *The Evolution of Economic Thought* (New York: Harcourt, Brace & World, 1963). This new, concise treatment of the history of economic thought will give the reader an appreciation of various individuals who contributed to economics as a discipline and also a grasp of the various schools of economic doctrine that flourished from time to time. The excerpts from the original sources seem especially well-chosen and should whet the reader's appetite for further reading in them.

RUGGLES, RICHARD, "Methodological Developments" in Bernard F. Haley, ed., *A Survey of Contemporary Economics,* Vol. II (Homewood, Ill.: Richard D. Irwin, 1952). The author includes in his survey of methodology the process of economic research, methodological approaches, recent developments in specialized techniques for economic research, and methodology in current economic research. The reader should also read the Comments which follow Professor Ruggles' presentation.

MACROECONOMIC POLICY

GALBRAITH, JOHN KENNETH, *The Affluent Society* (Boston: Houghton Mifflin, 1958). Professor Galbraith's economic history and economic analysis are not always of the highest order but his writing is always powerful and provocative and bristles with hypotheses for his colleagues to test. Here he presents his case for greater emphasis on the public sector, feeling that the United States is now, broadly speaking, affluent in the production of private goods and services.

MYRDAL, GUNNAR, *Challenge to Affluence* (New York: Pantheon Books, 1963). This book raises questions about Professor Galbraith's position, critically examines current economic policy designed to promote stability and growth, and suggests new paths that policy should take.

MICROECONOMIC POLICY

MUND, VERNON A., *Government and Business,* 3d ed. (New York: Harper & Row, 1960). Hailed by Professor Henry W. Spiegel as "the outstanding text on *Government and Business,*" the book is the fruit of the scholarship of an economist who has devoted over thirty years to the study of the problem of economic power and the alternative policies which societies use in dealing with it. The author carefully integrates economics and law in his analysis.

STOCKING, GEORGE W. AND MYRON W. WATKINS, *Monopoly and Free Enterprise* (New York: The Twentieth Century Fund, 1951). Called by Professor Marshall E. Dimock "the most complete study of this subject ever undertaken," this book contains a comprehensive picture of the concentration of economic power in the United States, an incisive analysis of the economic implications of such concentration, and an exhaustive review of our public policy designed to promote competition and a free society. The book also contains numerous suggestions for implementing public policy to make it more effective.

ECONOMIC EDUCATION

AMERICAN ECONOMIC ASSOCIATION, "Economics in the Schools: A Report by a Special Textbook Study Committee of the Committee on Economic Education," *American Economic Review,* 53: Pt. 2, Supplement (March), 1963. A penetrating examination and appraisal of the economic content of selected textbooks used in high school economics, social problems, and United States history courses. The report should be required reading for all who are concerned with economic education.

COMMITTEE FOR ECONOMIC DEVELOPMENT, *Economic Education in the Schools: A Report of the National Task Force on Economic Education* (New York: Joint Council on Economic Education, 1961). A comprehensive report which shows the need for economic education and the need for a rational approach to economic problems, presents in summary fashion the nature and scope of economics, and makes recommendations to implement economic education in the schools.

————, *Study Materials for Economic Education in the Schools: Report of the Materials Evaluation Committee* (New York: Joint Council on Economic Education, 1961; rev. 1963). This report contains a bibliography of carefully screened economic materials which are designed to be understood by students at the high school level.

6   Anthropology

Alfred K. Guthe
Department of Anthropology
University of Tennessee

Asked to define his field, an anthropologist is generally quick to respond that it is the study of mankind. If this response prompts further questions, the answer becomes more involved. Biologists and doctors of medicine study man. Psychologists and sociologists study man. Historians study man. Economists study man. Thus, man is the subject of many studies by many different disciplines. Each of these studies has a defined approach or goal toward which research is oriented, thus limiting research to certain areas of human behavior or the human organism. The goal of anthropology is broader, more general, than any of these. Yet, it too limits the character of anthropological research.

What Is Anthropology?

The goal of anthropological research is an understanding of the relationship between man as a biological entity and his adaptations to his environment. These adaptations constitute culture. The means by which food is obtained, prepared, and eaten are part of culture. The manner in which man views his environment is a part of culture. This environment may be viewed as friendly or hostile.

It may harbor supernatural powers which must be pleaded with or cajoled into performing acts favorable to man's continued life. It may consist of matter which is to be converted into various forms deemed useful or meaningful by men. Culture also includes those ideas shared by groups of men and the languages by means of which these ideas are communicated. It includes the patterns of behavior developed to relieve those anxieties and those areas of potential social conflicts which may exist because of the biological nature of man.

Yet anthropologists have found it difficult to agree on one definition of culture. A recent study [1] listed 164 concepts and definitions of culture. Some of these stressed one characteristic of culture; some stressed others. Still, most anthropologists would agree that culture is unique to man, that it is learned not inherited, that it is a more or less integrated system of behavior and products of this behavior. One definition which is frequently encountered in anthropological texts was published in 1871. E. B. Tylor wrote, "Culture or Civilization, taken in its wide ethnographic sense, is that complex whole which includes knowledge, belief, art, morals, law, custom, and any other capabilities and habits acquired by man as a member of society." [2]

Let us return to the goal of understanding the relationship between man and culture. There can be no doubt that man's physical characteristics affect his culture. Man has an upright posture. This frees his forelimbs from the function of locomotion and enables him to manipulate tools. It also influences the design of clothes, if he wears them. They are supported at the waist or on the shoulders. Furniture and houses are designed to accommodate the physical form and the biological needs of man.

In order to study this relationship between man and culture, it is necessary to collect and record data pertaining to both. To achieve a comprehensive understanding, this study must be made of all mankind. The world is the laboratory of anthropologists. Human beings must be studied in their natural habitat. But this

[1] A. L. Kroeber, and C. Kluckhohn, *Culture* (Papers of the Peabody Museum of American Archaeology and Ethnology, Harvard University), Vol. 47, No. 1, 1952.

[2] Edward B. Tylor, *Primitive Culture* (New York: Henry Holt & Co., 1874), Vol. I, p. 1. Originally published in London, 1871.

study must also extend back in time to include former cultures and forms of mankind no longer living. Thus the study must encompass a time span of several thousand years. The scope of this study and the increasing body of pertinent knowledge has required specialization within the field. It has become practical for anthropologists to concentrate on either the physical characteristics or the cultural achievements of man. In fact, the need for specialization has resulted in the definition of areas of study within each of these. Their nature will be discussed in the next section of this chapter.

The range of diversity with which an anthropologist must deal is great. This diversity exists in both the physical and cultural subdivisions. But since many other fields of research consider various aspects of man, one is able to draw pertinent concepts and techniques of analysis from them. The frame of reference within which they are used may be different from those of the field within which they were developed. Their application is no less sound, for man remains the common denominator. A more accurate definition of anthropology is that it is a generalizing science in which data are organized and analyzed to provide a greater understanding of the relation between man and culture.

Major Branches

Understanding this definition enables one to grasp the unity underlying the varied and somewhat diverse areas of anthropological interest. The lack of cohesion between the studies called anthropological is more apparent than real. Thus, while one report may deal with blood group antigens [3] and another with residence and marriage concepts,[4] the conclusions provide further information bearing on the nature of man as a biological organism or a producer and user of culture. Possession of similar percentages of blood groups does suggest possible genetic relationships between people with dif-

[3] M. Layrisse, Z. Layrisse, and J. Wilbert, "The Blood Group Antigens in Goajiro Indians," *American Journal of Physical Anthropology,* 19:255–262 (September), 1961.

[4] Peter Kloos, "Matrilocal Residence and Local Endogamy: Environmental Knowledge or Leadership," *American Anthropologist,* 65:854–862 (August), 1963.

ferent or similar cultures. The possibility of a historic relationship should be checked. Residence patterns, which are related to land tenure and use, are in turn related to methods required to provide sufficient food (a biological need) for a people.

Physical anthropology

Those studies concerned chiefly with the biological attributes of man are classified as physical anthropology. Not only blood groups, but other genetically derived attributes such as eye color, skin color, stature, and the distribution of body hair are of interest to those attempting to define the physical characteristics of man and the explanations for their diversity. Another area of interest in this subfield is the recapitulation of human evolution. During the past 100 years, evidence gathered indicates that our present species (*Homo sapiens*) existed over 30,000 years ago. This evidence consists of skeletal remains found situated in deposits of known geological age or in association with cultural remains for which radiocarbon dates have been obtained. Many of these skeletal remains are of a fragmentary nature yet their structural and morphological details indicate a close similarity to modern man. There are skeletal remains of still other forms which closely resemble our species. Yet the resemblance lacks the closeness required for classification into our species. Many of these remains are in even older geological deposits. The evidence thus indicates that our present species has descended from earlier forms. The changes occurring during this descent can be described. In some cases where the association with cultural remains is clear, the relationship between the two can be studied.

The value of this kind of data lies in the definition of human characteristics and the structural changes that have taken place through thousands of years. The degree to which these changes have affected cultural development appears relatively small. If one were to list the additions to our culture during the last 100 years, this list would greatly exceed one containing the changes which have taken place in the biological structure of man. It is clearly evident that although the capacity to produce and perpetuate culture is inherent in the human organism, factors other than changes in the physical characteristics of man are largely responsible for culture change and cultural diversity.

This is not intended to imply that the nature of culture is more complex than the nature of the human organism and its development. The two variables with which anthropologists deal are of a different order. One is organic, the other is more than organic. The latter is culture which, while dependent upon the organism for its perpetuation, does not conform to organic principles in its development and content. Culture, it has been said, is man's way of adapting to his environment. But men at different times, in different places experience different natural environments. They even react differently to the same natural environment. Thus, something more is involved than a simple adaptation of the human organism to his natural environment.[5] This extra something is culture, that is, the ideas, knowledge, belief, and systems of behavior which man has learned as a member of society. These have developed through social interaction and because of their effectiveness in dealing with the natural environment.

Cultural anthropology

Up to this point we have discussed man as a biological entity. We must now acknowledge that the generic term "man" includes numbers of individuals—men, women and children. These individuals have for thousands of years lived in social groups. Some have lived, or live, in Australia. Others live, or lived, in Africa, Europe, Asia, Oceania, and the Americas. Their ways of life are, and have been, different. Members of each social group, or society, learned how to survive, to live together, to view their environment and communicate their thoughts in rather different ways. Each of these ways of life is referred to as a culture. The diversity in these cultures is obvious. Many have been recorded; many have not. The point is that the term "culture" is used when referring to the adaptations of all of mankind, or to just some adaptations which are followed by a particular society at one point in time.

The study of culture and the various cultures comprising that

---

[5] Alfred L. Kroeber, "The Superorganic," *American Anthropologist*, 19:41–54, 1917; and Leslie A. White, *The Science of Culture, a Study of Man and Civilization* (New York: Farrar, Straus, 1949).

totality developed by man through the years is the subject of cultural anthropology. Such a study can be undertaken in several ways. The orientation may be of a historical character; or it may involve an analysis of many cultures to determine their structural and general characteristics. Many cultural anthropologists use both approaches. The collection of original data is involved in the historical approach, as it is in scientific approaches. The interpretation of data normally draws upon the results of analyses or syntheses of many cultures.

Among those studies of culture generally considered historical in orientation are those in archaeology and ethnography. In each of these, original data are sought in the field. The focus is upon specific cultures and their content. The archaeologist recovers evidence pertaining to the culture of former societies. He is the excavator who seeks the record of a culture in the soil. The ethnographer obtains data through observing a living society. He records human behavior which he witnesses and the explanations for this from the participants. Since each of these activities results in records of cultures at a particular point in time, they may be said to be historical in orientation.

The interpretation of these original data generally involves comparisons of the data with those obtained by others. The result is the presentation of generalizations. These pertain to a broader view of the archaeology in a particular geographic area, or present the original data in a more general cultural perspective.

Some cultural anthropologists attempt generalizations based upon analyses of data pertaining to certain kinds of cultural phenomena. The following discussion of selected practices pertaining to the selection of marriage partners is illustrative. The comparison of data collected from several cultures on this subject permits generalization regarding attitudes associated with marriage. For example, child betrothal is a practice among the Kalinga, a tribe in the Philippines. This is arranged between the fathers of the pair. If agreement is reached, the fathers exchange gifts of meat. As long as the engagement lasts, gifts of meat and other foods are sent by each household involved to the other. The engagement will be broken if the girl's father refuses to accept a gift of meat from the boy's father. The ceremony of marriage is accompanied by two feasts. One is given by the girl's family, the other by the boy's family. The Kalinga regard the sharing of meat as a powerful institution unifying the group.[6]

Among the Mixe Indians, who live in the State of Oaxaca, Mexico, a betrothed boy will go to the girl's house each day and work for her parents. This follows the request and the presentation of gifts by the boy's father to the father of the girl. The boy will work for his prospective father-in-law for six months to two years.[7]

Another practice involves the marriage of the widowed to members of the affinal (in-law) group. The Comanches, who once occupied parts of Kansas and Colorado, consider it obligatory for a man to marry the widow of his deceased brother. It is also customary for a man to marry his deceased wife's sister.[8] This is a greatly abbreviated example of the procedure followed in seeking generalizations regarding cultural phenomena. But it suggests that the selection of a partner in marriage is viewed by some societies as a contract between families. Doesn't the same attitude prevail in our culture?

Such analyses are oriented toward particular problems. These may pertain to certain categories of cultural phenomena, or they may relate to certain characteristics of culture. The above example considers one of many institutions within the category of social organization. Selection of marriage partners is one of those institutions which determine the position of men and women in a society. Other analyses pertaining to social organization include the nature of the family, kinship systems and the status system. The categories of culture relate to language, subsistence, world views, social organization, and aesthetics.

Characteristics of culture which have been of considerable interest to anthropologists are those of integration and dynamics. In defining culture, it was stated that it is a system of learned behavior. This simply means that an individual must learn what behavior is

[6] R. F. L. Barton, *The Kalingas* (Chicago: Univ. of Chicago Press, 1949), pp. 38–46.

[7] Ralph L. Beals, "Ethnology of Western Mixe," *University of California Publications in American Archaeology and Ethnology*, 42:45–46, 1945.

[8] Ernest Wallace and E. Adamson Hoebel, *The Comanches* (Norman: Univ. of Oklahoma Press, 1952), pp. 135, 228–229.

expected of him as a member of his society. When he is confronted with a situation, how is he expected to react? Such knowledge is acquired through observation, instruction, and experience. Yet even a casual observer of a culture, even his own culture, notes that the concepts of accepted behavior change through time. However, the changes witnessed during a lifetime are not usually of a magnitude to alter the system completely. Yet because change does occur over a period of time, culture can be studied as a dynamic continuum. There is, then, a relationship between the integration of a culture and the changes taking place within it. However, one may study the integration of a culture during a given period of time and virtually disregard the dynamic character of the culture.

A study of a culture by an ethnographer is followed by a description of that culture. In order to determine the content of a culture, it is necessary to observe individuals and their behavior. After recording his observations, the ethnographer attempts to determine that behavior which most individuals exhibit under similar or identical stimuli. He seeks to determine that behavior which is characteristic of the members of the society. This is an abstraction from the behavior of several individuals. The description of the culture is a description of a system of behavior to which the members of that particular society conform to a marked degree. It can be said to be a pattern of behavior characteristic of that society. The recognition of this pattern is made possible by the relatedness of the behavior. This relatedness is referred to as the culture's integration, or the manner in which the several elements in the culture form a complete way of life.

Another approach to an understanding of a cultural system is to describe the relation of one trait to another and yet another. It is based upon the assumption that each trait in a culture must be functioning in relation to other traits in the culture for the system to exist. An explanation of a trait, therefore, must include its relation to other traits. For example, the description of a house must also state who lives in the house, what is kept within it and how the occupants are related, cooperate, and organize this group. The family structure is seen as a unit within a larger social group. This may serve to illustrate how a description of one unit of a culture includes a consideration of another. Such a description is analogous to a multigeared machine.   Such an approach to describing a culture is called the functionalist approach.

Anthropologists concerned with the changing character of culture find that studies of a culture's integration are incomplete.   If there is a system which integrates a culture, how does it accommodate or tolerate the changes which can be seen to take place when it is viewed over a period of time?   The concern is not so much an attempt to define culture in another manner as one to study it as a dynamic yet unified entity.   It is clear that cultures change.   Yet they still exhibit enough uniformity to permit the conclusion that they both change and persist.   It appears that the change is relative to the persisting quality of a culture.   Factors contributing to the persistence of a culture include tradition, habit adjustment, and the natural environment.   Factors contributing to change include the introduction of new ideas through invention and discovery or from other cultures through social contacts.   It has been shown that awareness of new ideas does not inevitably lead to their adoption by a society.   Some selective process is involved.   Apparently the new idea must be to some degree compatible with the already existing concepts and values before it will be adopted.   Furthermore, once adopted it may be utilized in a manner different from that employed by the donor society.

Recognition that a selective process is involved has led anthropologists to study situations where two cultures are in contact. Colonial and economic exploitation situations permit such studies today.   These studies are referred to as studies of acculturation when they involve the continuous contact of two cultures.

Those students concerned with the individual members of a society and the part they play in such culture-contact situations draw upon the field of psychology for pertinent concepts and techniques of analysis.   Information on the personality of these individuals and their awareness of their culture is sought or obtained.   For example, attention is given to such questions as, Are the well-adjusted members of a society more likely to accept new ideas than the less well-adjusted?

The organization of knowledge in the field of anthropology is oriented toward problems.   The nature of the problem may deal with the biological characteristics of man, culture per se, or the individual and culture.   But they all have a common goal of seeking information pertaining to the relationship between man as a biological organism and culture.

Key Concepts and Ideas

Following this exposition of several approaches used by anthropologists, it may be well to summarize some of the basic concepts or key ideas underlying them. In keeping with the goal of anthropology, these must relate to the biological characteristics of man and the manner in which this biological entity lives. They must establish what man is and how he lives.

There can be no doubt that man is an organism dependent upon water, food, and air for continued life. He also possesses a bony skeleton with its vertebral column and four appendages. So do other vertebrate forms. He is the product of a bisexual relationship. Thus he has a genetic structure, part of which is obtained from one parent, part from another. He must, therefore, differ to some degree from his parents and they in turn differ from their parents. At birth, man is in an immature state. Usually he is nursed at his mother's breast for a period of time. Mammals generally nurse their young. In these and other characteristics, the human organism develops in accordance with natural laws which apply to other forms of organic life. Therefore, the principles of organic evolution apply to the physical development of man.

As a member of the animal kingdom, man is classified in the same manner as other members of this kingdom. Taxonomists find that the human population of the world today shares such a number of similarities that men must be classified as members of one species, *Homo sapiens.* This is one species of the genus *Homo,* which is one of the genera within the *Hominidae* family of the *Primate* order. This order is one of several within the class *Mammalia.*

The physical characteristics of man, including an upright posture and a complex brain capable of using symbols, are a unique combination. Only man possesses this combination. Standing upright, he can use his forelimbs to grasp objects and to manipulate tools. His forelimbs are not required for locomotion. Through the use of symbols it is possible to communicate abstract ideas. Knowledge can be transmitted without recourse to demonstration. An individual can learn from another's experience. A language is based upon symbols. The written word, even the spoken word, is a symbol. It has a meaning upon which members of a society have agreed. Thus the ability to use symbols lies at the base of culture.

By transmitting his knowledge to others man can convey techniques employed in obtaining food, producing tools, and providing shelter. He can agree upon methods of organizing his society. Ideas pertaining to the universe can be exchanged and a system of beliefs agreed upon. Therefore, culture may be viewed as man's way of adapting to his social and natural environment. Yet one may easily note that different human societies exist and that many of these have different ways of thinking and living. It is evident, therefore, that a perfect adaptation of the human organism to his environment does not exist.

The totality of culture which has been developed by mankind through thousands of years consists of many different adaptations by many different societies. The ways of life followed by the Eskimo, the Polynesian, and the Neanderthal man are all part of the totality called *culture*. Yet each of these ways of life can be studied as a unit, described as a unit, and compared with other units. Each of these units is, or was, an integrated system of knowledge, beliefs, and customs which were learned by those who practiced them. The society following one system need not be aware of other systems. The Eskimo need not know of Polynesian culture or Navaho culture in order to survive or to experience a life which he considers full.

Each of these several ways of life is then an integrated system. The units comprising this system can be discerned and described. And each must be explained in terms of the system of which it is a part. The context within which a belief, custom, or food habit exists must be considered in order to understand it. Those who have learned how to hunt their food will not understand the process of plant cultivation. One who traces his descent through his mother's lineage may find the practice of tracing it through the father's lineage without purpose. It isn't likely to be consistent with other practices and concepts of his culture.

The idea that an understanding of another society's culture can be achieved only in terms of that system stems from the recognition that a culture is learned. As a member of society, one learns the ways of living which are shared by the group. In order to share these ways, there is agreement that certain events will evoke a known range of responses. These responses must be predictable to a large degree. Otherwise there would be chaos. Thus, each culture provides each society with guides to accepted behavior. Failure to comply with the meaning of the symbol "stop" in our culture could lead to the loss of life when approaching a thoroughfare. Our economic system would be considerably altered if we could not assume that a sum of money would be transferred from one account to another upon written order. In sharing a culture, one learns to conform with the patterns of that culture in order to continue to participate as a member of society.

Still it has been said that a culture is never a perfect adaptation to the environment. It can be argued, and justly, that a particular custom, practice, or belief is poorly adapted in its cultural matrix. But an ethnographic description of a culture is based upon observations made during a limited period of time. This does not permit a study of the changes taking place within it. Yet since change is inevitable, we know that some cultural elements are old, others are new. The old has not been discarded yet and the new is not well integrated within the system. Some imbalance in the system of the culture is to be expected. It is unlikely that changes will occur simultaneously in all areas of a culture. So change takes place, but a continuity also exists in a culture.

In electing to study all of man's ways of life, the cultural anthropologist becomes concerned not only with *how* man has adapted to his social and natural environment, but also with *why* he does *what* he does. So far we have considered how man lives. It has been noted that a number of ways have been developed to meet the requirements of life for the human organism. Some of these ways are more diversified than others. Can these diverse ways be classified or organized into categories? Do the cultures of all societies exhibit any regularities which permit the definition of a universal system developed by mankind?

It appears there are such regularities. The tables of contents for most introductory texts indicate this. The presentation of data describing how people do things follows a general order. This order has resulted from the comparison of cultures. Such comparisons are called cross-cultural because they examine certain elements, or clusters of elements, as they are manifested in several cultures. Several attempts have been made to define these categories of culture which are contained within all cultures.[9]   One which seems most useful has been presented by Herskovits.[10]   He defines five major groups of cultural phenomena: *material, social, intellectual, aesthetic,* and *linguistic.*   Those phenomena concerned principally with self-preservation constitute the material group.   The techniques employed in the subsistence quest, the shelters, clothing, and technology would be grouped under this heading.   The social group includes the systems by which the society is organized.   It would include the family and kinship system, system of government, clubs, associations, and concepts of property and commerce.

The intellectual group includes those ideas which explain the universe and the rationale giving meaning to life as well as the methods regulating individual conduct.   The concepts of religion and science are grouped herein.   The aesthetic group embodies those cultural phenomena which provide creative outlets.   Music, dance, poetry, fiction, sculpture, painting, and ornamentation constitute the content of this group.   The systems by which verbal communication is conducted constitute the linguistic group.

No culture is known which is devoid of elements pertaining to any one of these.   Yet some cultures will contain a greater number of elements assignable to one of these groups than another culture. This may reflect a differing emphasis upon one group of traits.   Our culture appears to emphasize the technological area.   Others may place greater emphasis on the social or intellectual area.

In establishing these five major groupings of culture, the classifier considered the principal purpose, or function, of the cultural trait or complex.   Since all cultures are integrated systems, the content of one group is not necessarily excluded from another.   Certainly there is a relationship between the family system and the food economy.   The techniques and practices associated with food cultivation usually include concepts pertaining to the intellectual group as well. There are prayers offered to seek help in a bountiful harvest.   There

[9] Clark Wissler, *Man and Culture* (New York: Thomas Y. Crowell, 1923), pp. 73–98; George P. Murdock, "The Common Denominator of Cultures," in Ralph Linton, *The Science of Man in the World Crisis* (New York: Columbia Univ. Press, 1945), pp. 123–142.

[10] Melville J. Herskovits, *Cultural Anthropology* (New York: Alfred A. Knopf, 1955), pp. 116–118.

are also dances (part of the aesthetic group) to promote rain. And, of course, the several ideas regarding how these acts are to be performed must be communicated by a system of language.

Since all cultures exhibit phenomena which can be classified within each of these groups, it suggests that mankind shares certain needs of a physical and mental nature. Each culture provides a system by means of which a society adapts to its total environment.

The key ideas of anthropology pertain to both human physical characteristics and the ways developed by this biological organism to promote survival and perpetuation.

Methods of Inquiry

Because all of mankind and culture is the subject of anthropological research, Shakespeare's comment that "all the world's a stage, and all the men and women merely players" might well be adopted as a slogan. No matter where man lives, or lived, he and his culture are of interest. When the vastness of the area, the millions of people who occupy it, and the variety of cultures once extant are contemplated, it is consoling to note that anthropology is a generalizing science.

Anthropology is also an empirical science. Concern with customary behavior by normal physical specimens in their natural setting leads anthropologists to go to the location where the data can be obtained. All original data are collected in the field. It is impossible to simulate these conditions in a laboratory. In the case of an ethnographer, this requires him to join the people whose culture he wishes to study. While with them he abstains from intentionally disrupting their routine. His role may be that of a participant-observer. However, when he returns to his own society he must translate the culture he studied into terms and concepts which will provide a clear understanding of this different way of life.

The anthropologist usually defines a research problem before entering the field. He then employs the most satisfactory methods of observing and recording data that are available. Technical devices such as recorders and cameras may be used. Technicians and specialists may be asked to accompany him into the field. While collecting data, preliminary attempts to classify them may be made. Hypotheses may even be formulated and additional data sought. Upon returning to the home office or laboratory, the procedure of analysis, classification, and formulation of hypotheses is completed. The criticism of colleagues is sought and the hypotheses reformulated, if necessary. It is clear that the scientific method is employed.

One of the principal anthropological contributions has been to expand the horizons of knowledge pertaining to man and culture. It has been demonstrated that human beings are capable of developing many forms of culture, and the cross-cultural approach has provided a new perspective. In summarizing anthropological achievements during the period between 1900 and 1950, Kroeber [11] wrote:

What the past half century has accomplished above all for anthropology is to transform a loose collocation of separate physical, social, cultural and linguistic interests, ancient and modern, primitive and civilized, into an integrated attack on the biological, the socio-cultural and linguistic phenomena presented by man—an attack held together by a common attitude. This attitude is expressed by the principle of the relativistic approach. It might equally be called the naturalistic approach. It insists on treating the customs and histories, the ideals and values, the societies and languages of man as being phenomena of nature to exactly the same degree as the biology of men, or for that matter of animals and men.

Cross-cultural studies have also demonstrated that certain cultural complexes tend to be associated. For example, a society obtaining food by hunting and gathering tends to be a small mobile one which moves about within a large geographic area. Their shelters are transportable or can be quickly constructed from available raw materials. Such groups tend to establish a spiritual relationship with nature, especially those parts of their natural environment upon which they depend for survival. Rites believed to encourage an abundance of edible animals are practiced.

An archaeologist readily uses such ethnographic information in interpreting the way of life indicated by the scraps of a culture which he has recovered and the evidence he has observed. Interpretation by analogy is a well-accepted practice. In the same way, an ethnog-

[11] A. L. Kroeber, "Anthropology," *Scientific American*, 183:94 (September), 1950.

rapher or cultural theorist can reasonably predict the general character of a culture by noting some of the basic attitudes of a group.

Principles for Judging the Significance of Data

The context within which the significance of data is judged will vary with individuals. An anthropologist's selection of what is significant and what is not will reflect his experience and training. Some might select other principles or theories as more significant than those which follow.

One of the most significant is that human behavior is learned as a member of a society. Today, the physical differences between human groups are far less than the similarities. Although different stocks of mankind are recognized, they are all classified as members of one species. In accordance with this theory, it follows that physical differences are to be viewed as physical differences only. They are *not* to be confused with sociocultural differences.

If we apply this principle to the racial integration problem in the United States, it appears that this distinction is not usually accepted. Euro-Americans do not discriminate against all dark-skinned people. Thus it is not simply a physical difference to which they react. Other factors influence these reactions. These factors include differences in behavior, beliefs, and attitudes. These are a part of culture which is learned. They reflect educational, environmental, and historical experiences. An approach to solving this problem must be sought in terms of culture. It would seem to depend upon education of the total society in the United States.

If culture is the major influence on human behavior, it is one's culture which influences an act of refusal, of acceptance, or thoughts, speech, belief system and concepts of morality and etiquette. As a system, a culture has a history. It has been found to provide satisfactory solutions to the problems of an individual, of a group, in the past. One begins to learn this system in infancy. As maturity is approached, more is learned of the accepted solutions to the problems encountered in one's society.

Yet with the variety of systems now recorded, it is clear that more than one set of solutions has been developed by humans. A culture is an integrated system. The nature of this integration may not be rational to an observer operating in terms of another culture's system. In order to understand a part of another culture, therefore, one must consider the total cultural context within which this part functions. One's avoidance of his mother-in-law may be a prescribed practice in the society. The use of a particular design may be connected with a spiritual belief and, therefore, must be used only as a symbol, not simply a decorative motif. Neither of these can be understood or adequately explained out of context.

Another basic principle is that the content of culture which one learns existed before one is born. It indicates that one learns the culture of the adult members of his society. The culture has a history; it changes through time. Our history books record these changes, so do the data of the archaeologist. On the other hand, a study of several cultures and the changes in their total content can be made. But the level of analysis will be different in that it will go beyond a single culture to include cross-cultural comparisons.

A view of culture in its totality covers a span of several thousands of years. Such a view provides information regarding the general trend of culture. It also provides insights into the general character of cultural change. This permits a view of culture as a phenomenon of mankind.

The consideration of changes within a particular culture provides information of a different level of significance. The mechanism producing changes within a specific culture can be ascertained. The appearance of new traits can be explained. They may have developed within that culture or they may have been borrowed from other cultures. The factors contributing to the acceptance of a new trait can be studied in relation to the factors resisting the acceptance of it.

This involves another principle which relates to patterning in culture. Since a culture is an integrated system, the introduction of new traits will produce a change in this system. If accepted, the new trait will lead to some modification in the related traits already in the culture. Recognition of the character of culture permits the development of techniques designed to bring about a desired change within a particular culture. Thus colonial endeavors and cold war procedures may become more effective. As a significant theory of anthropology, this combines those ideas gained by studying cultural change and the theory that a culture trait can be satisfactorily explained only when viewed within its cultural context.

Role of Anthropology in the Social Studies

Anthropological concepts provide a perspective for teachers of social studies. This perspective can be utilized in assessing the teachers' role in society, and in approaching their subject areas and the data within them. The nature of this perspective has been expressed in the following manner:

> This one remaining species of the genus *Homo* has far surpassed all competition in ability to reason. In the fields of discovery and invention his phenomenal achievements are incomprehensible to most of his kind. But, with his strange and conflicting notions about life and ways of life, his wisdom is sometimes open to question. Besides the adversity inherent in nature's apparent attitude to all of life, man has concocted more grief for himself than even the dinosaurs had to contend with. However, he is beginning to show some signs of a realistic interest in this aspect of his performance—and he is not yet a subject of paleontology.[12]

The role of education in our society is the same as that in other societies even though the nature of the educational process may differ. Although education in other societies may not involve a formalized structure to be followed five days a week for a specified period of time, it will always serve to inculcate the values, traditions, and background of a culture necessary for the continuation of that culture. In our society at least three groups of adults share this responsibility. One is the parental group, another the school teachers. A third group are those associations, or clubs, of adults with which the youth come into contact (YMCA, YWCA, Scouts, churches, hobby clubs, etc.). The function of these is to guide the child in learning the values, attitudes, goals, and systems of behavior accepted by his society.

Perhaps more than knowledge of our culture is now required in training our youth to cope with the world today. Familiarity with some of the diversity in culture can lead to a greater objectivity and

[12] Harvey C. Markman, *Fossil Mammals* (Museum Pictorial No. 4) (Denver, Colo.: Denver Museum of National History, 1952), p. 62.

187

depth in the interpretation of facts. It is clear that many methods have been devised to cope with the natural and social environment within which man finds himself. A recognition that these methods are as satisfactory for those who follow them as ours are for us can provide stimulating discussions. They may even assist in grasping the motivation of the behavior of children and youth. Due to the increasing mobility of the American family, a classroom may contain children with different social, intellectual, and geographic backgrounds. The character of classroom instruction must recognize this. The adult of tomorrow must be able to interpret events and actions in terms of their context. The goal of education may be one of objective understanding, not prejudice.

The objective viewpoint can also be of service when trying to judge the particular role of the school in a community. The methods developed by anthropologists in collecting data will be of use in determining how a community regards the school and its curriculum. Once this is achieved, a method for changing them can be developed, if necessary.

SUGGESTED READINGS

GENERAL

GOLDSCHMIDT, WALTER, *Exploring the Ways of Mankind* (New York: Holt, Rinehart and Winston, 1960). Applies the anthropological approach to human and cultural behavior in terms of 13 separate topics. An introduction to each topic is followed by readings to illustrate it. These pertain to exotic and modern American or western cultures.

HOEBEL, E. ADAMSON, *Man in the Primitive World,* 2d ed. (New York: McGraw-Hill, 1958). A useful introductory text. It includes the biological and cultural developments of man as well as the general categories of culture. Examples are taken from several cultures.

KLUCKHOHN, CLYDE, *Mirror for Man* (New York: Whittlesey House, 1949). A discussion of the techniques and concepts utilized by anthropologists in seeking to understand the relation between the varieties of the human organism, the environment and cultural achievements.

LINTON, RALPH, *The Tree of Culture* (New York: Alfred A. Knopf, 1955). The general development of culture is discussed, especially the growth of civilizations in southwest Asia, China, Africa, and India.

PHYSICAL ANTHROPOLOGY

ASHLEY MONTAGU, M. F. *Man: His First Million Years* (New York: American Library of World Literature, 1958). A summary of the physical and cultural developments of man. Today's ethnic groups and the general categories of culture are considered.

HOWELLS, WILLIAM, *Mankind in the Making* (Garden City, N.Y.: Doubleday, 1959). The evolution of man and a discussion of the races of man is preceded by a review of the evolutionary process and evidence pertinent to the emergence of man.

LASKER, GABRIEL W., *The Evolution of Man* (New York: Holt, Rinehart and Winston, 1961). A concise, objective discussion of human evolution. Significant discoveries, genetic principles, and the difficulties of interpretation are presented.

ARCHAEOLOGY

CHILDE, V. GORDON, *What Happened in History* (New York: Mentor Books, New American Library, 1951). The stages of cultural development in the Near East and Europe. Archaeological discoveries and inferences are combined with history.

COON, CARLETON S., *The Story of Man* (New York: Alfred A. Knopf, 1954). The history of culture, the interrelated factors of human evolution, races and environment are considered with a world-wide perspective. Covering some 650,000 years of human achievements in the first few chapters, the major portion of this volume reviews the growth of culture since 6000 B.C.

MARRIOTT, ALICE, *The First Comers* (New York: Longmans, Green, 1960). Describes archaeology as a means of learning the ways people lived in the past. A discussion of American archaeologists, the information they have obtained, and their techniques of investigation provides a stimulating account of American archaeology.

OTHER

BROWN, INA CORRINNE, *Understanding Other Cultures* (Englewood Cliffs, N.J.: Prentice-Hall, 1963). An introduction to cultural anthropology. The major categories of culture are discussed with data from several cultures to indicate the varied approaches to common human problems.

DAVIS, ALLISON, *Social Class Influences on Learning* (Cambridge, Mass.: Harvard Univ. Press, 1952). Studies of social class influences on learning.

MURDOCK, GEORGE P., *Our Primitive Contemporaries* (New York: Macmillan, 1936). Ethnographic descriptions of 18 discrete cultures in scattered parts of the world. These illustrate the range of subsistence patterns, social organization and religious concepts.

SPINDLER, GEORGE D., ed., *Education and Culture* (New York: Holt, Rinehart and Winston, 1963). A collection of 25 papers by educators and anthropologists discussing the application of anthropology to education. American and other educational systems are viewed as means of transmitting culture.

WARNER, W. LLOYD, *American Life: Dream and Reality* (Chicago: Univ. of Chicago Press, 1953). American values relative to those of other peoples.

7 Sociology

William E. Cole
Department of Sociology
University of Tennessee

Introduction

SOCIOLOGY IN AMERICA HAD ITS BEGINNINGS AS A SERIOUS COLLEGE
discipline during the first decade of the twentieth century. As a
separate high school subject, sociology has grown most since 1930.
Perhaps the Depression of the 1930's, with its resultant array of
social problems, gave some impetus to both college sociology and to
the study of sociology and social problems in secondary schools.
Considerable controversy continues to exist as to whether or not
high school sociology should be taught as a separate subject or
whether sociological materials should be an integral part of fused
social science offerings.

Contributions of sociology

The significance of any subject is highly variable, depending on how
it is learned, what features of it are internalized, and how much of
it is applied. Therefore, one can only comment on the usefulness
of sociology in a generalized fashion. Even so, some statement on the
importance of sociology is needed.

1. A knowledge of sociology should help a person understand his place in society, and his own roles, motivations, and responses.
2. Sociological knowledge, like psychological knowledge, helps one to understand the behavior of others.
3. Sociological knowledge should lead to an understanding of the social systems into which people are born and in which they live.
4. While sociology is first of all a normative social science, concerned with nondeviant conditions and behaviors, individual and group deviation is a fact; and sociology does aid in the understanding of deviation.
5. To many people working at professional and lower levels in sociology and in related fields, sociology serves a useful vocational purpose.

To the teacher and administrator, some knowledge of sociology is of almost inestimable value. The content of the learning process is the culture, whether this involves informal socialization—which is the learning of the content, roles, values, and norms of a culture—or the highly formalized content of formal education. The content of learning in early childhood socialization comes largely from the primary family, the peer group, the social class, and the community and its institutions. In the context of these systems, one matures. Many cultures are drawn upon in education and in adult socialization. The teacher, therefore, has in sociological knowledge a tremendous resource for understanding the social systems that socialize and educate. Sociology sheds light upon human motivation; behavior; value systems, as related to striving for goals; and individual and group deviation and disorganization.

Early roots of sociology

Sociology as a systematic field of study is largely the product of the latter half of the nineteenth century and the first half of the twentieth century. There is, however, a fair element of internationalism and time continuity in knowledge; and sociology is not the product of any one people or any one era. An important part of sociology is social theory. In back of social theory there is the unorganized and unsystematic social thought of many ancient peoples, civilizations, and cultures. These roots extend from preliterate cultures; through the Babylonian, Assyrian, Egyptian, Grecian, and Roman empires; and through the Oriental civilizations with their sacred vedas, Hindu epics, and philosophical religions of the period around 5000 B.C.

Professor Sorokin of Harvard cites more than a thousand men whose writings have influenced the development of today's sociology.[1] In Europe the roots of sociology go back to the ancient civilizations which we have mentioned. While knowledge here had continuity, it received little nourishment in the intellectual bleakness of the Middle Ages; however, the Renaissance and the Reformation gave knowledge and new growth as well as a new humanitarian interest.

To mention names of persons whose contributions were significant in the development of sociology is to be highly selective, perhaps overlooking persons whose contributions were as significant as those whose names are mentioned. The philosopher John Locke (1632–1704), with his emphasis upon scientific methods of acquiring knowledge, has at times been called the father of British empiricism.[2] About the same time, in Italy, Giambattista Vico (1668–1744) was attempting to systematize social thought; to explain human nature; and how man, through experience and reason, attains reliable knowledge and a system of values.[3] In the humanities and social sciences there is a fair degree of unity. For instance, there is a mutual interest between philosophy and social values. Both have a mutual interest in scientific method and value systems. Man is social by nature, said Vico, not because he possesses any "herd" instinct, but because of social conditioning. Vico's writings on culture unity were not unlike those of Max Weber and his linking of Protestantism with the development of capitalism.[4] Inkeles indicates that everyone agrees that four men were central figures in the development of sociology. These are Auguste Comte, Herbert Spencer, Emile Durkheim, and Max Weber.[5] Comte (1798–1857)

---

[1] Pitrim A. Sorokin, *Contemporary Sociological Theories* (New York: Harper & Row, 1928).

[2] Rollin Chambliss, *Social Thought* (New York: Dryden Press, 1954), p. 347.

[3] *Ibid.*, p. 374.

[4] Max Weber, *The Protestant Ethic and the Spirit of Capitalism,* trans. Talcott Parsons (London: George Allen and Unwin, Ltd., 1930).

[5] Alex Inkeles, *What Is Sociology? An Introduction to the Discipline and the Profession* (Englewood Cliffs, N.J.: Prentice-Hall, © 1964), p. 3.

gave sociology its name and most sociologists refer to him as the father of sociology. Comte's major works consisted of six volumes called *Positive Philosophy* and four volumes on *Positive Polity*.

In addition to naming the new social science, Comte made other important contributions to sociology. Sociology came into existence when the spirit and methods of inquiry, which had been so rewarding in investigations in the natural sciences, were being sought by those seeking knowledge of social phenomena. Comte sought to discover and describe laws of human nature as well as laws of human behavior. He felt that if laws could be established, then sociology might become a predictive science; and in this Comte was interested. Comte's concept of "social statics" is not greatly unlike that of social structure, and his concept of "social dynamics" is not greatly different from that of social function and behavior. To put the matter another way, social statics referred to the way the subsystems of a society were related, especially the institutions, and social dynamics referred to the way in which subsystems in whole societies functioned and changed. Comte wrote extensively on social change and social progress. He gave attention to both man's past and his future. He viewed culture as cumulative and social progress as continuing, even though generations come and go and nations rise and fall. He felt that modern man has no biological advantages over his barbarian ancestors when he comes into the world. On the other hand, man's potential for growth and for using and developing a culture shapes the kind of society and kind of world in which man lives. If society does not actually determine man's personal development, then it greatly conditions and modifies this development. Comte placed high value upon the comparative studies of societies just as do today's sociologists and cultural anthropologists.

Most sociologists agree that Herbert Spencer (1820–1903) produced the first detailed sociological analysis of society. This was his three-volume *Principles of Sociology,* published in 1877. Spencer's works were eagerly received in both Europe and America and did much to establish sociology as a field of study and research in both places.[6]

[6] See Herbert Spencer, *Principles of Sociology,* 3d ed. (New York: D. Appleton and Company, 1910).

Development of sociology in America

As we have said, sociology in America had its beginnings largely in the last quarter of the nineteenth century and the first quarter of the twentieth.

As is true today, early American sociology was strongly webbed with the influence of European scholars. For instance, probably the world's first journal in sociology was *The Sociologist,* which was published privately in Knoxville, Tennessee, by Albert Chavannes (1836–1903), who had immigrated from Switzerland with his family when he was twelve years of age. *The Sociologist* was published from 1883 to 1885. There is evidence that Chavannes read widely European works on sociology, including those of Spencer. Selections from Spencer's writings were published in *The Sociologist* from time to time.[7] Probably the works of Spencer, Durkheim, Comte, Pareto, and Weber have had the most influence upon American sociology. It is, of course, true that American culture was originally an extension of European culture for the most part.

A forerunner of the development of British sociology was the British social science movement which resulted in the founding of the British Social Science Association in 1857. It became the prototype of the American Social Science Association organized in 1865. While both of these associations were strongly problem-oriented, each served as a forum for fielding theoretical and methodological problems. More important was the fact that many of the early American social scientists were members of the Association.

As interest in the different social science disciplines grew, and as knowledge in each field increased, one by one the special interest groups began to pull away from the parent association. In 1874 the National Conference of Charities and Correction, now the National Conference of Social Work, was established. The American Historical Society was founded in 1884 and the American Economics Association in 1885. The political scientists established their own organization in 1904, and the American Sociological

[7] For more on Chavannes and *The Sociologist* see John B. Knox, "The Concept of Exchange in Sociological Theory: 1884 and 1961," *Social Forces,* 41:341–346 (May), 1963.

Society, now the American Sociological Association, was founded in 1906. The American Social Science Association disbanded in 1909. Since 1930 a number of regional sociological associations have been formed. In 1937, the Rural Sociological Society was founded; as was the American Catholic Sociological Society in 1938.

Many early American sociologists studied in European universities. William G. Sumner of Yale studied in Germany. He was also a strong apostle of Herbert Spencer and his theory of laissez-faire. Albion W. Small, who established the first department of sociology at the University of Chicago, studied the writings of Spencer and was a student of the German sociologist Ratzenhofer. Small studied in Germany. Franklin Giddings of Columbia was an avid reader of the works of Darwin, Tarde, Adam Smith, and Spencer. Thus it is that the roots of early American sociology were tied closely to those of European sociology. American sociology became more a specialized college subject. European sociology was less specialized. For example, a professor in a British university may teach a course in "Colonial Affairs" which requires a knowledge of all of the social sciences.

While the American Sociological Society was not established until 1906, earlier texts and books in sociology had helped to delineate the field and establish it as a college subject. One of the greats among early American sociologists was Lester F. Ward (1841–1913). While in government service, and before he went to Brown University to teach sociology in 1906, Ward wrote *Dynamic Sociology*, published in 1883. Interestingly enough, this book was condemned by the Czar of Russia in 1891. The Russian translation and its plates were burned in that year in the Public Square at St. Petersburg. Ward's *Dynamic Sociology* was extensively studied in America, as were his *Outlines of Sociology* (1897), *Pure Sociology* (1903), and *Applied Sociology* (1906). Ward was the first president of the American Sociological Society and the first American to be elected president of the Institut de Sociologie, an international professional organization of sociologists.

It is difficult to say when the first full-time teaching position in sociology was established in an American college or university. At least one university had a chair of sociology and economics as early as 1885. One of the earliest departments to gain both a national and an international reputation was that of the University of

Chicago. This department was established in 1893 under the chairmanship of Albion W. Small. The University of Chicago is usually given credit for having the first full-fledged sociology department in the world with an independent status. Franklin Giddings went from Bryn Mawr to Columbia as professor of sociology in 1894. Columbia established an outstanding department.

Mention should be made of at least three other early American sociologists who had a strong influence upon sociology. These were associated with college departments that became strong in their influence. William I. Thomas joined Small at Chicago and was a prolific scholar, as was Edward Alsworth Ross at the University of Wisconsin and Charles Horton Cooley of the University of Michigan. Cooley became famous for his work on social organization and especially for his theory of primary groups.[8]

The growth of sociology in colleges at the turn of the century is best indicated by the fact that in 1894 some 29 American colleges were offering at least one course in sociology. By 1902 the number had increased to 166.

The Field of Sociology

Definitions of sociology

Most sociologists today identify the field of sociology through the use of one of three statements. First, one might say that sociology has to do with human interaction. Interaction is the mutual influence of actors in social situations. Second, one might state that sociology is a study of plural behavior and behavior in plurality patterns. Two or more persons in interaction constitute a plurality pattern. Structurally, a dyad group of two persons is the simplest plurality pattern. A triad of three persons is much more complex in both structure and behavior. A third concept is that sociology is the

[8] For more on the development of American sociology and the nature of its early inception, see Floyd House, *Development of Sociology* (New York: McGraw-Hill, 1936). For a shorter and later treatise, see Roscoe C. Hinkle, Jr., and Gisela J. Hinkle, *The Development of Modern Sociology* (New York: Random House, 1954). See also, Harry Elmer Barnes and Howard Becker, *Social Thought From Lore to Science*, revised ed. (Washington, D.C.: Harren Press, 1952); and Harry Elmer Barnes, ed., *An Introduction to the History of Sociology* (Chicago: Univ. of Chicago Press, 1948).

systematic study of social systems. A social system is an operational social unit that is structured to serve a purpose. It consists of two or more persons of different status, with different roles, playing a part in an interaction pattern which is sustained by a physical and cultural base.

Max Weber characterized sociology as "a science which attempts the interpretive understanding of social action in order thereby to arrive at a causal explanation of its cause and effects." [9] If Inkeles' interpretation of Weber is correct, Weber regarded the social act or social relationship as the particular subject matter of sociology and interested himself mainly with the analysis of concrete institutions, such as religion.[10]

Emile Durkheim, like Herbert Spencer, considered societies as the proper units for sociological study. To Durkheim, sociology was "the science of societies." [11] He placed much value upon their comparative study.

Returning to contemporary sociologists, many sociologists do not define sociology as much as they characterize it. Johnson says that "sociology is the science that deals with social groups: their internal forms or modes of organization, the processes that tend to maintain or change these forms of organization, and the relations between groups." [12] Later we shall indicate some of the scientific characteristics of the social sciences as Johnson conceives of them.

Social systems

As was indicated previously, the writer prefers to define sociology as the study of social systems. All social systems are significant and meaningful to people who comprise their membership. To the teacher, the primary groups—those first in influence in the lives of individuals—are significant. For instance, the family and play groups, the clique, the gang, and courtship groups do much to shape

[9] Max Weber, *Theory of Social and Economic Organization,* trans. A. Henderson and Talcott Parsons (New York: Oxford Univ. Press, 1947), p. 88.

[10] Inkeles, *op. cit.,* p. 7.

[11] See Kurt H. Wolff, ed., *Emile Durkheim, 1858–1917: A Collection of Essays With Translations and a Bibliography* (Columbus: Ohio State Univ. Press, 1960).

[12] Harry M. Johnson, *Sociology: A Systematic Introduction* (New York: Harcourt, Brace & World, 1960), p. 2.

the behavior and the value systems of the young. All institutions—the family, school, church, government, and institutions of science and economic and political institutions—constitute the solid structure of any society. The nation-state is an all-encompassing social system containing many other social systems, perhaps the key ones being institutions.

When one analyzes social systems, one finds that they are made up of the following elements:

1. People or actors.
2. Acts or behavior.
3. Ends or objectives appropriate to the system or sought by persons in the system.
4. Norms, rules, or regulations controlling conduct or behavior in the system, particularly the means by which ends or objectives are sought and achieved.
5. Beliefs held by the people as actors in the system.
6. Status and status relationships of the actors in the system.
7. Role expectations, role performances, and role relationships of the actors in the system.
8. Authority or power of some individuals to influence the behavior of others.
9. Nonsymbolic facilities, such as buildings, laboratories, libraries, machinery, calculators, and other cultural items such as books, laboratory equipment, and communication facilities, all of which help the system to achieve its ends.
10. Instruments or other cultural items which are symbolic of the system, such as the cross, the rosary, the altar, the sacrament, the school crest, school songs and ceremonies.
11. Habitat or territory, where the system "lives," is located, or where one would go to find it.[13]

The school as a social system

The school is a social system made up of a variety of persons with different roles, statuses, and degrees of authority. The school seeks to achieve certain generalized objectives and often some very specific ones. In achieving these ends, it makes use of many cultural items,

[13] Adapted from William E. Cole, *Introductory Sociology* (New York: David McKay Co., 1962), Chap. 1, "Sociology as a Field of Study." See also Talcott Parsons, *The Social System* (New York: Free Press of Glencoe, 1951); Robert K. Merton, *Social Theory and Social Structure*, rev. ed. (New York: Free Press of Glencoe, 1957); and Harry C. Bredemeier and Richard M. Stephenson, *The Analysis of Social Systems* (New York: Holt, Rinehart and Winston, 1962).

some of which are symbolic, like the development of school loyalty through song, symbol, ceremony, and perhaps competition in sports. Language, gestures, signs, and symbols are used in the communication process as are the printed word and mass media such as radio, slides, screen, and television. Approved norms, such as honesty, and orderly steps and procedures for progression from one level to another are developed and are generally followed as the goals of the educational process are sought. Finally, the school has its own habitat, a building or buildings and perhaps a campus.

Within a school there are many social subsystems represented, such as social classes and families. The school has a variety of organizations, play groups, cliques, and other plurality patterns. Some of these are structured for purposes of instruction, discipline, extraclass activity, and guidance; and others simply develop informally from pupil-to-pupil relations.

Subdivisions of sociology

While the concept of sociology as a study of social systems is useful, more needs to be said about the content and subdivisions of the discipline. Inkeles [14] has developed a good analysis of the subject matter of sociology in the following outline:

A GENERAL OUTLINE OF THE SUBJECT MATTER OF SOCIOLOGY

I. Sociological Analysis
    Human Culture and Society
    Sociological Perspective
    Scientific Method in Social Science
II. Primary Units of Social Life
    Social Acts and Social Relationships
    The Individual Personality
    Groups (including Ethnic and Class)
    Communities: Urban and Rural
    Associations and Organizations
    Populations
    Society
III. Basic Social Institutions
    The Family and Kinship
    Economic
    Political and Legal

[14] Inkeles, *op. cit.*, p. 12.

Religious
Educational and Scientific
Recreational and Welfare
Aesthetic and Expressive
IV. Fundamental Social Processes
Differentiation and Stratification
Cooperation, Accommodation, Assimilation
Social Conflict (including Revolution and War)
Communication (including Opinion Formation, Expression, and Change)
Socialization and Indoctrination
Social Evaluation (the Study of Values)
Social Control
Social Deviance (Crime, Suicide, etc.)
Social Integration
Social Change

It is apparent from Inkeles' outline that the term "social systems" would constitute most of the units he refers to as "Primary Units of Social Life" and "Basic Social Institutions." Many aspects of social systems, both structural and functional, may be studied through sociological analysis. Inkeles' outline contains such items as might be covered in a basic introductory course in sociology, but it does reveal the content of the field and the nature of the subject matter, particularly those phases of the subject which are of value to teachers.

Within the discipline of sociology may be found a large number of specializations which, for convenience, may be grouped into the following branches:

General theory and *methodology,* having to do with the construction of both general theory and specific theories applying to one or more aspects of social structure or behavior, and problems of methodology including the improvement of methods of inquiry.

The sociology of institutions, such as art, the community, economics, education, the family, law, medicine and public health, politics, religion, and science.

The study of the group and the person, which deals with such specializations as culture and personality, personality and social structure, consensus and dissonance, small group dynamics and intergroup relations, including role and status relationships in groups.

Demography and social structure, which includes demographic composition, trends and behavior, rural and urban sociology, race and ethnic relations, occupational sociology, and social stratification.

Application of sociology to such areas as mental illness, social disorganization, crime and delinquency, mass communication, and teaching.[15]   In an attempt to inventory the current status of sociology, Merton and others, in the preparation of a book on the current status of sociology, *Sociology Today,* dealt with some thirty specialties.[16]

Even though the specializations indicated previously and also others are to be found in sociology, there are certain concepts, principles, and methods of inquiry that tend to unify the field.   We turn now to selected concepts and ideas that are of significance in planning social studies programs.   Let us say more about the concept of social systems, previously referred to, which is central to a widely held current view of sociology.

Concepts and Generalizations

The school as a social institution

As a social system the school is perhaps best described as a social institution.   This is true in terms of both the school and its function. Social institutions are social systems—clusters of people, behaviors, statuses, roles, and culture traits—which have slowly developed over long periods of time to serve the major elemental needs of people. Institutions change but one of their characteristics is continuity.   A generation is born, and another dies, but the institution as a social system goes on.

The major institutional complexes are: marriage and the family, government, education, recreation, religion, and science.   The economic institutions are: management, production, commerce, finance, and labor.

Each institution serves a constellation of needs, and institutions may overlap and somewhat duplicate each other in function.   For example, the school is primarily concerned with learning but the family is also involved closely with both the processes and products

---

[15] This breakdown of categories of sociology follows substantially that used by Robert K. Merton, Leonard Broom, and Leonard S. Cottrell, Jr., eds., in *Sociology Today* (New York: Basic Books, 1960).

[16] *Ibid.*

of learning. Fundamentally, then, education as an institutionalized social system was developed by society and, in instances, by the church, to make specific contributions to the socialization of the learner and to transmit selected aspects of the cultural heritage from one generation to another. While all levels of schooling are concerned with the transmission of knowledge and the development of approved behavior in its learners, only the higher levels of schooling —the universities and colleges—are greatly concerned with the development and extension of knowledge through research.

Although the nation-state functions as an institution, there is a close correlation between it and other institutions, especially those that are public. The nation-state, for example the United States, places a strong emphasis upon equality, freedom, and opportunity in its founding documents. These are reflected in the educational process in the freedom of the classroom and the attempt to make an elementary and, to a lesser degree, a secondary education available to all people. In the content of education, common subject matter materials and a common language are taught, to make possible easy communication and to give unity and cohesion to the society. American history is a required subject in most states. Civics courses which have to do with democratic citizenship are standard in high schools or in upper elementary grades. Finally, in a democratic society, wide participation of parent groups, teachers, and other leaders and followers in the democratic processes is urged. Attempts are made to develop institutional governing bodies that represent broad membership of institutions rather than majority groups or vested interests. In keeping with the emphasis placed upon individuality and the respect for it, much attention is given to individual development and achievement.

In a totalitarian nation-state, a different cultural emphasis is reflected in the schools. The end product is to fashion a functioning, useful citizen for life in a totalitarian society, while in our society it is to develop a useful citizen for life in a democratic society.

Collective functions of institutions

Institutions serve *survival* needs. This is an important function of the family as it ministers to the care of the young, but survival functions are also shared by other institutions. All institutions are

203

culture-bearers. Culture-bearing is a major function of family, school, and church.

Institutions have *control* functions. While formal control functions are heavily vested in government and law and in the regulations and norms of all institutions, informal controls based on the sharing and respect for norms and value systems, respect for others, and tolerance for different points of view are major responsibilities of the family, school, and church.

Because of both their nature and their functions, all institutions contribute to social *integration* within the institutional structures themselves as well as in the larger society where institutions provide the framework for societal growth and development.

Institutions facilitate *communication*. The mass media of communication are well institutionalized. Language training is an important function of family and school. The school gives much attention to the communicative expression, not only in the languages but also in art, music, and the dance. The church is interested in communicating to its followers a body of beliefs, doctrines, and theology. Science develops its own technical vocabularies and symbols of communication and is also concerned with public knowledge of its work. The American public school system was well founded on principles enunciated by Thomas Jefferson, an important one being that basic literacy is essential to an effective communicating process, for participating in a free society, and for understanding the principles of democratic government.

The essentiality of institutions does not mean that they do not have problems. The very nature of institutions tends to develop within and for them certain problems. Being configurations of culture, people, and behavior which have continuity, institutions tend to become rigid and formal. They tend to become "cultural deposits." Within formal institutions there are, of course, informal social structures ranging from cliques to coffee breaks. These form through *interaction* and *association* and are broken through *dissociation*.

Institutions tend to become big and bureaucratic, bureaucracy being a necessity in complex organizations. Hierarchies of statuses and roles and of functionaries and divisions tend to develop within them. Bureaucratic organizations tend to become heavily loaded with paraphernalia and red tape. The energies of the institution are often absorbed in keeping the institutional machinery going. Institutions do not adjust easily to change. New people entering the institution may either succumb to the frustration of institutional pressures or become disgusted and leave. Lags in both perspectives and programs become a generalized condition; and a state of status quo and stagnation plagues the structure and its clientele until a set of new leaders, sometimes a new generation, develops.

Learning, education, and socialization

These three important processes are closely tied together in the educational process. *Learning* may be defined simply as the way we organize our responses into new behaviors. Other concepts of learning are: (1) it is mental activity that affects subsequent mental activity; (2) it is the product of acquiring tendencies to behavior with which we were not born; and (3) it is the individual's acquired tendencies as revealed in behavior, knowledge, skills, and attitudes.

Education may best be thought of as the process of directing learning. Education is more directed than out-of-school learning, which is largely trial and error. Education is much more purposeful, having starting points and objectives, or goals. The directing of learning is, first of all, by the teacher, but also by the learner, text, and study program. All education involves learning but all learning is not education. Both are important in socialization.

Socialization is the learning of a culture—the learning of roles and statuses and the norms and behaviors appropriate to the roles and statuses. There is adult socialization as well as childhood and youth socialization. The child develops into a socially conscious, socially sensitive and socially responsive human being as a result of socialization. One learns not only what the status positions are, and who fills them, but also social roles and who fills them also. One learns also the relationships between statuses and roles. The child learns how to fill a role and how a status is achieved and ascribed. One also learns the rewards which accompany the fulfillment of roles and statuses and the penalties which result from nonfulfillment. Socialization inculcates discipline in the individual; it also develops aspiration as well as a knowledge of the rewards for conformity and the penalties for nonconformity.[17]

Socialization is more than adaptation to a social system or to a

[17] For more on socialization see Frederick Elkin, *The Child and Society* (New York: Random House, 1960); and Jean Piaget, *The Moral Judgment of the Child* (New York: Collier Books, 1962).

culture. The individual is not born with human attributes other than body form and potentiality for development. He becomes human as a result of the interaction of the socialization process and of maturation. When the individual is socialized, he incorporates parts of his cultural environment into his own thinking and into his own behavior. He internalizes the norms of the culture and its role expectations for different occasions and for different age and sex groupings. Under normal development, he becomes a supporter of the value system. Socialization requires constant dynamic adjustment to new conditions, new relationships, and new forms and values.

The social systems having parts or roles in the socialization process are numerous. The national, state and community cultures pose requirements and needs which are usually first met by the child in his family. The family takes these requirements and needs and seeks to shield the child against some and to encourage the development of others. The family leaves its own socialization stamp on the child—the stamp of class, attitudes, education, occupation, religion, politics; and the stamp of quality of interpersonal relationships within the family, whether happy, rivalrous, antagonistic, or cooperative and supportive. The peer group and youth subcultures play an important part in socialization. The school, however, socializes in a more formal manner, as may the church or government.

Discipline is one of the requirements of the socialization process. Discipline is also essential in education. For socialization to be successful, and the results permanent, discipline must shift from external controls to internal controls, or from externally imposed discipline to self-discipline. One of the requirements of any social system is a certain amount of discipline from its members. In large-scale organizations, what Max Weber termed *bureaucratic discipline* becomes necessary.[18] This perhaps reaches its greatest manifestations in military organizations. Weber [19] phrased the nature of social discipline in the following language:

The content of discipline is nothing but the consistently rationalized, methodically trained, and exact execution of the received order, in which

[18] See Max Weber, *Essays in Sociology,* trans. and ed. H. H. Gerth and C. W. Mills (New York: Oxford Univ. Press, 1946), Chapter 10, "The Meaning of Discipline."
[19] *Ibid.,* p. 253.

all personal criticism is unconditionally suspended and the actor is un-swerving and exclusively set for carrying out the command.

From Weber's statement we see that social or organizational discipline is necessary in school and classroom; and parents might well lay the foundation in the home for such discipline patterns, emphasizing the necessity for organizational discipline and some-thing of its nature and requirements. Self-discipline on the part of the learner is also necessary in the learning process. At all levels, being a pupil requires self-control, application, the allocation of time, the establishing of a system of time and behavior priorities, the set-ting of routines and obedience to the authority of text, teacher, laboratory, library, and other established methods of study and in-vestigation.[20]

Processes of social interaction in classroom and school

The characteristic forms which interaction takes between persons in a social system are what the sociologist calls "social processes." The master social process is "interaction," that is, the way in which the behavior of one person stimulates and influences the behavior of another. Interaction in the school is perhaps at its best in the give and take between a responsive class and a responsive teacher, or in the relationship between members of a class perhaps breaking up into small groups to work intensively on projects and assignments.

There is no single method of classifying social processes. Perhaps the best method in social studies instruction is to classify them along a tension continuum. Such a classification starts with cooperation on the low-tension end of the continuum and ends with conflict at the high-tension end. In between are found assimilation, accommoda-tion, and competition.

Cooperation is the quest for identical ends or goals by two or more persons working together. In cooperation there is a synthesis of goals and, to some extent, a synthesis of thought and a synthesis of effort. There is substantial experimental evidence that coopera-tion encourages greater effort on the part of participants than does

[20] For more on socialization see Harry C. Bredemeier and Richard M. Stephenson, *op. cit.,* Chapter 3, "The Process of Socialization," and Chapter 4, "The Structure of Socialization."

competition, that the collective results are greater than in highly competitive situations, and that the participants enjoy the effort more in cooperative situations.[21]

Assimilation is highly important in learning. It involves the internalization of knowledge, attitudes, norms, statuses, and roles. One internalizes a lesson on the role of a participant in group discussion and utilizes it as his own. One assimilates a foreign language and uses it in communication. One develops a value system which he learns largely from others. The term assimilation was long applied to immigrants who came to America and who were assimilated into the ways of life of the nation. They came to our land as strangers and by degrees assimilated the culture. Native peoples also learned from the immigrant. The process of assimilation is found in many forms in the school. The child, as a newcomer to the school and its ways, is gradually assimilated to a point where he no longer feels strange. In the process he assimilates behavior patterns as he interacts with others in school, and others assimilate behavior patterns as they interact with him.

Accommodation is the process of adjustment to situations and conditions which we cannot change and which, in varying degrees, may be unsatisfactory to the persons involved in an interaction process. For example, the school has to strike a happy medium in many matters to serve the greatest needs of the greatest number. The individual student may find some things unsatisfactory, annoying, and distasteful, but he cannot change the system. He simply must learn to discipline and accommodate himself to it. He must learn to tolerate fellow students whose skin color, tastes, and values are different from his. Tolerance is a form of accommodation and adjustment. Therefore, accommodation is a necessity in any system of human relations.

Competition is the quest for identical ends or values by two or more persons competing with each other. Basically, competition arises because there are only limited quantities of things people want—goods, position, money, land, jobs, and status. American society places much value upon achievement through the competitive process and tends to institutionalize competition. The general belief is that competition produces the strongest motivation, the best

[21] See Bernard Berelson and G. A. Steiner, *Human Behavior: An Inventory of Scientific Findings* (New York: Harcourt, Brace & World, 1964).

effort, and the best product at the cheapest possible price. Some of these assumptions are doubtful because competition has both commendable and bad features.

Competition is emphasized in the educational process. There are times when perhaps it is overemphasized. The winners are starred, publicized, feted, applauded, and otherwise heralded. Inadequate concern is often manifested for those who lose out in the competitive process. At times, also, competitors may become unfair and unethical in the competitive process. Frequently, the much lauded end results are not as good as when persons cooperate to reach the goals they desire. In competition the emotional emphasis is upon winning; in cooperation it is upon getting the job done.

Conflict is the effort of competitors to gain identical ends or different goals by eliminating competitors, or by placing competitors in an unfair position. Conflict is emotional. It is likely to be destructive of goodwill, cooperation, and mutual helpfulness. It can disrupt the stability, organization, and continuity of a school, an athletic team, a family, or a community.

Social processes are not separate and distinct in operation. They are intertwined with each other. For example, cooperation may give rise to accommodation, and competition may lead to cooperation, as may conflict. Two or more processes may be operative in any given interactional situation. The theory of schism as to how conflict develops appears to be a sound one.[22]

Education and the sociology of change

Change is a deviation from the past that may be characterized in two ways. *Culture change* is a change from the past in culture traits, complexes, values, attitudes, and behaviors. *Social change* is a deviation in the structure, function, and relationships of social systems. As such, social change is only one aspect of the total configuration of culture change.

There are many ways in which education contributes to change. It begins simply. A young child enters school. He learns new words, new number concepts, and new facts about his country.

[22] Jessie Lee Bernard, *American Community Behavior*, rev. ed. (New York: Holt, Rinehart, and Winston, 1962), Chapter 6, "The Nature of Conflict."

The process of his own change thus becomes evident in the learning of content and skills that are new to him. Here, however, we are concerned with how education *in toto* contributes to change.

Education tries to promote learning and to direct study in situations conducive to the discovery of new attitudes, new knowledge, and new habits and skills. A static society is likely to be one in which there is fear of change. Education in a dynamic society seeks to remove the fear of change. Education widens the range of alternatives open to a person or a group. Educated people are more willing to weigh facts and assess the alternatives than are the unschooled. On the whole, they are more tolerant of new ideas than are uneducated people. Education is highly selective. It helps the learner to select from the total culture those features which are of greatest social significance—the best in knowledge, art, music, science, and literature.

Education changes the horizons and perspectives of people. It changes value systems. As a result of new knowledge, one may become dissatisfied with the existing state of his knowledge, the conditions under which he lives, his present condition of life, and the goals which have previously motivated him. He may become dissatisfied with the conditions in his community. He perhaps is dissatisfied with the means for achieving the goals open to him and others at the time. Finally, at the higher levels, education seeks to extend knowledge through investigation and research and its application. In extending knowledge, the bases for change may also be initiated. A good illustration is found in the control and development of atomic energy.

Another way in which education contributes to social change is through its contribution to the social mobility of the learner—the movement up and down a social scale from one social class or status hierarchy to another. One of the increasingly important functions of the school is the provision of the means of social mobility. To take children from lower- and middle-class homes and prepare them for places in the increasingly complex, industrial, technologically urbanized cultures of today means that they may move from one social class to another. They are prepared for career mobility within occupations, career mobility being a form of social mobility. The current age of technology has also made possible unprecedented social and occupational mobility by creating more jobs and diverse social class levels for people. Lower-class people may move into middle classes and middle-class people into upper classes as a result of education.

The rapidity of all changes imposes upon educational systems another obligation, that of providing for continuing education.[23] The current technological revolution not only requires more education and education in specific fields, it also provides new operations in the educational process, including the preservation and reproduction of records and documents, the use of mass media in teaching, and machine programming for learning. It has also made available opportunities to apply learning to a larger degree in old occupations, as well as creating a variety of new opportunities in electronics, computer operations, space engineering, metallurgy, city planning, atomic energy research, and the application of atomic energy research to agriculture, health, and nuclear power.

Every age from the Old Stone Age down to the present has had its technology, requiring of its people different skills and imposing upon them different requirements and conditions. No age before our own has possessed the scientific technologies that could wipe a population from the earth. We live in an age of crisis and change, with a new patent issued every ten minutes in the United States. The challenge of education in crisis and change was never so great or its opportunities greater than at the present time. Through the social studies, students should see the challenge and develop a desire to meet it.

Methodology in Sociology

Because of the diverse interests of sociologists, one can find a variety of methods of sociological inquiry, ranging from historical methods on the one hand to highly developed, organized, and controlled experimental methods on the other.

Emphasis in present-day sociology in America is theoretical and

[23] For some basic influences on cultural and social change see Wilbert E. Moore, *Social Change* (Englewood Cliffs, N.J.: Prentice-Hall, 1963); Julian H. Stewart, *Theory of Cultural Change* (Urbana: Univ. of Illinois Press, 1955); Everett Hogen, *On the Theory of Social Change* (New York: Dorsey Press, 1962); and William F. Ogburn, *Social Change* (New York: Viking Press, 1927).

empirical, empirical data being used to test theories, illustrate them, or extend them. The approach is definitely scientific, even though sociological research presents difficulties not found in the fields outside the social sciences. Johnson [24] has pointed out that sociology has the following characteristics of a science:

1. It is *empirical,* that is, it is based on observation and reasoning, not on supernatural revelation, and its results are not speculative. In the early stages of their creative work, all scientists speculate, of course, but, ideally at least, they submit their speculations to the test of fact before announcing them as scientific discoveries.
2. It is *theoretical,* that is, it attempts to summarize complex observations in abstract, logically related propositions which purport to explain causal relationships in the subject matter.
3. It is *cumulative,* that is, sociological theories build upon one another, new theories correcting, extending and refining the older ones.
4. It is *nonethical,* that is, sociologists do not ask whether particular social actions are good or bad; they seek merely to explain them.

Sociology thus seeks to apply the methods of science to the study of man in his social systems.

One of the hallmarks of a science is whether or not the phenomena within a discipline can be studied with the usual methods available for scientific inquiry. Sociological phenomena may be studied by one or more of the following methods of study:

1. Observation.
2. The case-study method.
3. Statistical method.
4. The laboratory method.
5. Logical inquiry.[25]

The above methods are precisely those used in all the sciences. The laboratory method, so common in the natural sciences, is perhaps the rarest method of study in sociology. Perhaps the chief reason is that laboratory studies, under controlled conditions, are not easy to establish in sociology. However, small group laboratories are common and there are controlled laboratory and experimental studies in juvenile delinquency and other forms of deviant behavior. Deviants are often compared to nondeviants.

Coefficients of correlation in sociology have been used since 1920. Tests of significance, such as chi-square, are newer. Inter-

[24] Harry M. Johnson, *op. cit.,* p. 2.
[25] Cole, *op. cit.,* pp. 9–12.

viewing and polling techniques are common and are not new, although methods of sampling are newer. Scales are often devised for measuring standards of living, social participation, social distance, attitudes and values, and degrees of deprivation. Some of these have become standardized. Sociometric techniques have been used to reveal group configurations in social systems, especially communities, schools, and classrooms. Multivariant analysis has been aided greatly by the development of computers. Repetitive studies in different situations have given repetitive results which have been a first step in the establishment of an empirical sociology.[26]

Sociologists, like other scientists, make use of models. These are mental constructs of how a social system is constructed or how and why social behavior takes place. The germ theory of disease is a generalized model in bacteriology, public health, and medicine. Reckless has developed a "new theory" of delinquency around the models of inner and outer containment.[27] He explains each as follows, and they are given at this point because of their significance to teachers and to education:

Inner containment consists mainly of self components, such as self-control, good self-concept, ego strength, well-developed superego, high frustration tolerance, high resistance to diversions, high sense of responsibility, goal orientation, ability to find substitute satisfactions, tension-reducing rationalizations, and so on. These are the inner regulators.

Outer containment represents the structural buffer in the person's immediate social world which is able to hold him within bounds. It consists of such items as a presentation of a consistent moral front to the person, institutional reinforcement of his norms, goals, and expectations, the existence of a reasonable set of social expectations, effective supervision and discipline (social controls), provision for reasonable scope of activity (including limits and responsibilities) as well as for alternatives and safety-valves, opportunity for acceptance, identity, and belongingness. Such structural ingredients help the family and other supportive groups contain the individual.

The structure-function model is a common one used in sociological research and in teaching. Social disorganization usually is explained on the basis of either an equilibrium vs. conflict model or an equilibrium vs. disorganization model, although students of dis-

---

[26] For a good story of the growth of a science, in this case rural sociology, loosely defined, see: Edmund deS. Brunner, *The Growth of a Science* (New York: Harper & Row, 1957).

[27] Walter C. Reckless, "A New Theory of Delinquency and Crime," *Federal Probation*, 25:42–46 (December), 1961.

organization may use a social change or change of values model. Many mathematical models are used by statistical and mathematical sociologists.[28]

As another illustration, Bernard uses the schism model to explain the development of community conflict (see Figure A).[29]

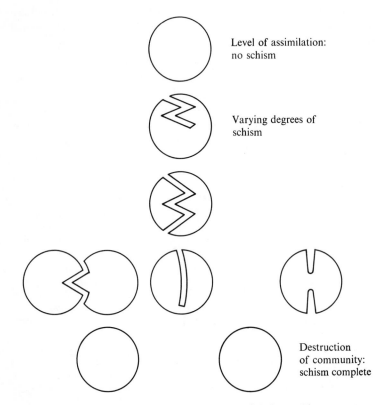

Level of assimilation: no schism

Varying degrees of schism

Destruction of community: schism complete

FIGURE A   *Schematic Representation of Schism Cleavages in Community Conflict*

The size of the sample or universe with which the sociologist works in his research may be large or small. Small group research is

28 For more on models see Inkeles, *op. cit.*, Chapter 3, "Models of Society in Sociological Analysis."
29 Bernard, *op. cit.*, p. 88.

with small universes.[30]   The group study universe is usually a microscopic one.   Regional research is usually macroscopic in scope.[31] Both have their place in sociology.

There is currently some danger that sociological research on a macroscopic scale, such as the continental, national, and regional, is being neglected for the more microscopic studies in which the universe of study is a small, carefully selected sample, or unit, of social study or behavior.

Sociology in the School Curriculum

Sociology as a college subject is so well established and is so thoroughly accepted that there is little need to consider its significance at this point.   Certainly, there are many unsolved problems in the teaching of sociology in colleges.

While the author is a strong advocate for sociology as a special subject in high school, say in either the junior or senior year, there are those who are equally as strong in the viewpoint that at the high school level a fused social science program is preferable.   Out of his experience in writing high school texts, the author developed the following outline for a text, which appears to be both interesting and functional:

OUTLINE OF ONE-SEMESTER COURSE IN SOCIOLOGY [32]

Introduction. Fundamental Social Concepts
Part I. Historical, Cultural, and Biological Backgrounds of Society
    Chapter   1. Our Ties With the Past
    Chapter   2. The Revolution in Our Culture
    Chapter   3. Biological Foundations in Our Social Development
Part II. Our Social Roles and Our Social Worlds
    Chapter   4. Developing Our Personalities and Our Roles
    Chapter   5. Living Effectively in Our Families
    Chapter   6. Living Effectively With Groups of Our Own Age
    Chapter   7. Working Effectively on the Job
    Chapter   8. Living Effectively as a Consumer
    Chapter   9. Citizen Roles

[30] For example, Paul Hare, Edgar F. Borgatta, and Robert F. Bales, *Small Groups* (New York: Alfred A. Knopf, 1955).
[31] Thomas R. Ford, ed., *The Southern Appalachian Region* (Lexington: Univ. of Kentucky Press, 1962).
[32] Used in William E. Cole and C. S. Montgomery, *High School Sociology* (Boston: Allyn and Bacon, 1963), pp. vii–viii.

Some years ago the writer attempted to state what he believed high school students should learn about their society.[33] The more important categories of knowledge were:

1. Something of the past.
2. Behavior in the present.
3. The trilogy of ideologies—fascism, Communism, and democracy.
4. The great interdependencies.
5. Social relations in local settings.
6. Change and progress.
7. Relations with all these other people.

Rather than to try to indicate in great detail what should be taught in sociology at either the elementary or high school level, it is perhaps best to indicate only the nature of a society and some of its prerequisites, because of lack of space and the fact that other aspects of this book bear upon the topic.

In an interesting, thought provoking, and well-written article on "The Functional Prerequisites of a Society," Aberle and others [34] de-

[33] William E. Cole, "What High School Seniors Should Know About Their Society," *The High School Journal*, 37:33–37 (November), 1953.

[34] D. F. Aberle, A. K. Cohen, A. K. Davis, M. J. Levy, Jr., and F. X. Sutton, "The Functional Prerequisites of a Society," *Ethics*, 60:100–111 (January), 1950. The quotation is from p. 101.

fine a society as follows: "A society is a group of human beings sharing a self-sufficient system of action which is capable of existing
longer than the life-span of an individual, the group being recruited
at least in part by the sexual reproduction of the members."

Aberle and others then proceed to set forth the functional prerequisites of a society in some detail:

1. Provision for adequate relationship to the environment and for sexual recruitment.
2. Role differentiation and role assignment.
3. Communication.
4. Shared cognitive orientations.
5. A shared, articulated set of goals.
6. The normative regulation of means for achieving goals.
7. The regulation of effective expression.
8. Socialization.
9. The effective control of disruptive forms of behavior.[35]

Aberle and others also set forth four conditions which will
terminate the existence of a society, although not necessarily the
existence of its members:

1. The biological extinction or dispersion of the members.
2. Apathy of the members.
3. The war of all against war.
4. The absorption of the society into another society.[36]

In an excellent article on some social requisites of a democracy,
Lipset [37] presents in a diagram (see Figure B) some of the conditions
associated with the emergence of a democracy as well as some of the
consequences of the democratic system.

Perhaps, in the light of the previous analysis the teacher of
social science can best see the significance of what she is trying to do
and how best to do it. It is important that the data and discoveries
of sociology find a significant, meaningful place in the integrated
social science offerings of the elementary school; either in the
separate or fused courses at the high school level; and in the distinctive subject and departmental offerings of the college curriculum.
Sociology thus can make a significant contribution both to the art

[35] *Ibid.,* pp. 104–111.
[36] *Ibid.*
[37] Seymour Martin Lipset, "Some Social Requisites of Democracy: Economic Development and Political Legitimacy," *American Political Science
Review,* 53:69–105 (March), 1959. The diagram is from p. 105.

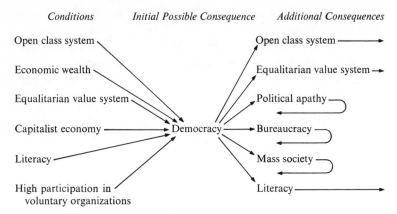

FIGURE B   *Requisites and Consequences of Democracy*

and content of teaching, to the understanding of the students taught, and to an understanding of the social systems in which both student and teacher work and live.

SUGGESTED READINGS

Bales, Ernest E., *Democratic Educational Theory* (New York: Harper & Row, 1960).   Educational theory in its democratic traditions.

Berelson, Bernard, ed., *The Behavioral Sciences Today* (New York: Basic Books, 1963).   Chapter 5, "Sociology: Its Present Interests."

Berelson, Bernard and Gary A. Steiner, *Human Behavior: An Inventory of Scientific Findings* (New York: Harcourt, Brace & World, 1964).   Chapters 7–16.   A good documentation of research and conclusions on many aspects of human behavior.

Berger, P. L., *Invitation to Sociology* (New York: Doubleday, 1963).   Paperback.

Bohlke, Robert H., "The Teaching of Sociology in Secondary Schools: Problems and Prospects," *Social Trends*, 42: 363–374 (March), 1964.   Some of the problems and prospects of high school sociology.

Bredemeier, Harry C., and Richard M. Stephenson, *Analysis of Social Systems* (New York: Holt, Rinehart and Winston, 1962).   A generalized, advanced-level introductory text utilizing the social systems approach.

Brookover, W. A., *A Sociology of Education* (New York: American Book Co., 1964).   A basic text in educational sociology.

CHAMBLISS, ROLLIN, *Social Thought* (New York: Dryden Press, 1954). A comprehensive volume on social thought and social theory, starting with the ancient societies and continuing through the period of Auguste Comte.

COLE, WILLIAM E., *Introductory Sociology* (New York: David McKay Co., 1962). A college text using a social systems approach.

COLE, WILLIAM E. AND C. S. MONTGOMERY, *High School Sociology*, rev. ed. (Boston: Allyn and Bacon, 1963). A high school sociology text built around the social systems concept.

GORDON, MILTON, *Assimilation in American Life* (New York: Oxford Univ. Press, 1964). Full-scale analogies of assimilation of racial, religious, and nationality groups in the United States.

HOUSE, FLOYD NELSON, *The Development of Sociology* (New York: McGraw-Hill, 1936). Much material on the beginnings of sociology in the world, and particularly in the United States.

MERTON, ROBERT K., LEONARD BROOM, AND LEONARD S. COTTRELL, JR., *Sociology Today* (New York: Basic Books, 1960). Problems and prospects of sociology around mid-century.

MOORE, CLYDE B., AND WILLIAM E. COLE, *Sociology in Educational Practice* (Boston: Houghton Mifflin, 1952). An attempt to relate sociology to the process and problems of education.

NIMKOFF, M. F., "Anthropology, Sociology, and Social Psychology," Chapter 2 in *High School Social Studies Perspectives* (Boston: Houghton Mifflin, 1962). A summary of key ideas from the behavioral sciences.

PARSONS, TALCOTT, ed., *Theories of Society* (New York: Free Press of Glencoe, 1961). Two volumes of rich source materials on sociology, including especially good sections on factors and patterns of social change and stabilization and change.

SIBLEY, ELBRIDGE, *The Education of Sociologists in the United States* (New York: Russell Sage Foundation, 1963). An appraisal of the training of American sociologists.

The Social Studies and the Social Sciences (New York: Harcourt, Brace & World, 1962). A series of articles on the content and teaching of the social studies, sponsored by the American Council of Learned Societies and the National Council of the Social Studies.

SYKES, G. M., "Sociology," in *The Social Studies and the Social Sciences* (New York: Harcourt, Brace & World, 1962). A summary of key ideas from sociology.

ZOLLOCHAN, GEORGE K., AND WALTER HIRSCH, eds., *Explorations in Social Change* (Boston: Houghton Mifflin, 1964). Some ideas on the contribution of education to change.

8   Psychology

E. Ohmer Milton
Department of Psychology
University of Tennessee

As a college professor with some fifteen years' experience in attempting to impart certain principles from academic psychology to young adults, I must confess that I am genuinely puzzled about the matter of introducing the subject in a somewhat formal manner into the social studies portion of the curriculum, grades one through twelve. Some consolation is provided, however, by the fact that I need not be concerned in too great detail with the "how" of accomplishment; this must be left to others. Moreover, judging by the fact that, throughout its history as a specific discipline, there has been little attention to the introduction of psychology into the elementary grades particularly, almost all psychologists must have some reservations. For the most part and for reasons which are not clear, psychology has been a college subject, although in the past few years it has gained increasing favor in secondary schools as an elective subject.

I do not presume to speak for my colleagues; any one or all of the 23,000 American psychologists might emphasize different portions of our field;[1] a complete presentation of our views and activities would require several volumes.

[1] For example, see W. J. McKeachie, "Psychology" in *The Social Studies and the Social Sciences* (New York: Harcourt, Brace & World, 1962), pp. 171–190.

The Field of Psychology

All through the ages man has sought to understand himself and the world about him—especially the latter. Perhaps this has been a dominant urge because man can reflect upon the past, take account of the present, and contemplate the future. Until very recently, however, his own behavior has largely been thought to be the result of, or explained by, forces beyond his own control—divine intervention, magic, instinct, and heredity. Indeed, belief in such forces seems to persist for the great majority of persons. Favorite topics for both high school and college students are hypnosis and extrasensory perception. We may have held tenaciously to mysterious "explanations" about human behavior as ways of relieving ourselves of responsibility for our eccentricities and shortcomings. Mother undoubtedly comforts herself about her role in little Joe's inadequate school performance when she says (after reluctantly deciding his teacher is not to blame): "His father's folks were just the same." Yet all of us are interested in varying degrees in finding out what is true about human behavior—at least as the "truths" apply to the *other fellow*.

Now it seems safe to assert that truth about human behavior is the most elusive of all truths. Partly for this reason, psychologists' aspirations in discovering truth are rather modest ones. Most of our efforts are directed toward discovering those things about human behavior which appear to be true at the moment—our methods of investigation require this. For the most part, we leave the task of adding together tiny increments of truth which may lead to ultimate truth to the philosophers and historians. Also, since the discipline is so young, there has not been sufficient time to permit the bringing together of many diverse points of view and apparently isolated findings.

Though our goals about truth are limited, as one examines reports of psychologists on behavior it is evident that psychology in the 1960's is an extensive field. During its history of only seventy-five years, with the greatest growth occurring since World War II, its concerns have broadened from those of observing the rather simple problems of differences in reaction-time among people to the social issues of the moment to the behavior of man in space. With all these complex problems and many others, the experimental method, with special attention to the unique problems which are created when man studies man, has been viewed as the ideal means of studying behavior. It is also evident that the boundaries of psychological knowledge are no longer clear-cut and distinct from those of many other fields. Today there is much overlap with such areas as biology, anthropology, sociology, psychiatry, physiology, and physics.

Almost all aspects of behavior are studied by psychologists. One way of gaining some indication of the areas of special interest in the field is by examining the titles or names of the Divisions of the American Psychological Association:

General Psychology / Consulting Psychology
The Teaching of Psychology / Industrial Psychology
Experimental Psychology / Educational Psychology
Evaluation and Measurement / School Psychologists
Developmental Psychology / Counseling Psychology
Esthetics / Military Psychology
Clinical Psychology / Maturity and Old Age
Consumer Psychology
National Council on Psychological Aspects of Disability
The Society of Engineering Psychologists
Personality and Social Psychology
The Society for the Psychological Study of Social Issues
Psychologists in Public Service

The Importance of Learning

If there is any single message which psychology has to convey at the moment, it is that of the tremendous role which learning plays in determining the behavior of man, rather than that of forces beyond his control. Psychologists are not noted for agreement about specifics in scientific affairs, but they do agree about the overshadowing importance of learning as the major determinant of human behavior. Perhaps the earlier this message is brought to children in a manner they can grasp, the better for us all.

George Miller of the Harvard Center for Cognitive Studies summarizes the magnitude and profundity of the learning issue in this manner: [2]

[2] George A. Miller, *Psychology: The Science of Mental Life* (New York: Harper & Row, 1962), p. 212.

Our entire way of life is predicated upon our ability to learn. Not only do we rely on learning to give us the basic skills with which we earn our daily bread, but also to educate our children for citizenship in a free society. It is a solid axiom of the great liberal tradition in England and America that education is the best tool for social progress. We believe that people learn their system of values, learn to love themselves and others, learn to channel their biological drives, even learn to be mentally ill. When we begin to analyze the learning process, therefore, we are probing the ultimate source of our humanity. . . .

This view notwithstanding, there is a tenacity with which people hold to false explanations about humans; such tenacity is reflected in this comment attributed to George Bernard Shaw (source unknown):

There is no harder scientific fact in the world than the fact that belief can be produced in practically unlimited quantity and intensity, without observation or reasoning, and even in defiance of both by the simple desire to believe founded on a strong interest in believing. Everybody recognizes this in the case of amatory infatuation of the adolescents who see angels and heroes in obviously (to others) commonplace or even objectionable maidens and youths. But it holds good over the entire field of human activity.

To our great advantage as educators and teachers, of course, is the fact that beliefs are also learned. In the past, beliefs about magical and other mysterious forces have been learned by successive generations of children; to a large extent, this appears to continue for the great bulk of the population. Currently, though, information is available from which sounder understanding of the determinants of behavior can be learned.

The importance of learning in man's behavior is far more than an academic matter. If we fully accept it as being true, then we must also accept the responsibility for improving man's lot that accompanies it.

Concepts and Generalizations

There are several concepts and generalizations from psychology that well may be given attention in the social studies. The following generalizations about man (detailed at greater length in the Psychology section of the Appendix) seem to have special relevance to instruction at all levels:

Behavior is caused . . . . Each form of behavior exhibited by the individual has a pattern of causes which are multiple, complex, and interrelated . . . .

Human behavior is purposive and goal-directed. The individual may not always be aware of basic purposes and underlying needs that are influencing his behavior . . . .

Behavior results from the interaction of genetic and environmental factors . . . .

As a biologic organism the individual possesses at birth certain physiological needs, but the methods of satisfying these needs and their subsequent development are to a great extent socially determined by a particular subcultural unit.

Through the interaction of genetic and social and physical environmental factors the individual develops a pattern of personality characteristics.

Individuals differ from one another in personal values, attitudes, personalities, and roles; yet at the same time the members of a group must possess certain common values and characteristics.

Each of the social groups to which an individual belongs helps shape his behavior . . . . The behavior of any individual reflects in many ways the influences of group pressures.

Socialization processes (for example, child-rearing practices) differ markedly in different social classes, groups, and societies. Personality structure and behavior are largely influenced by these practices.

Other especially important generalizations for educators are: (1) Since perception is selective, each person not only tends to see the world differently, but each tends to interpret and react to stimuli differently (one reason for confusion in knowledge). (2) Motivation is primarily a function of social learning. Middle-class children, for example, are motivated for academic achievement, while lower-class children are not. (3) Intelligence levels, as measured by tests, are not fixed and static. That is, for a given child, I.Q. scores can vary considerably over a period of time. (4) The first few years of life are of profound importance in determining a child's later adjustment.

Again, the importance of learning should be noted in each of the above generalizations. Research during the past few years has suggested that learning may possibly occur in the human organism even prior to birth.

Methods of Inquiry

Prediction as a goal

Cause and effect. One of the most important attributes of psychology is the emphasis on the scientific study of behavior. One way of thinking about science is that its pursuit leads to an understanding of natural events—an understanding which is based upon rational, demonstrable cause-effect relationships. This type of understanding can lead to predictions about the future course of those events, for example, the weather, and on the basis of the predictions there can be some control over them; there is less damage now than formerly from severe storms because precautions can be taken ahead of time.

In a like vein, psychology seeks to understand human behavior on the basis of rational, demonstrable cause-effect relationships; the preferred method of inquiry is experimentation. Admittedly, there is a long way to go in the attainment of that ideal. Actually, the choice of weather as an example was no accident. On the one hand, the weatherman's predictions seem grossly inaccurate much of the time; but, on the other hand, when one considers the hundreds of factors and forces which produce the weather in a given locale, remarkable progress has been made in understanding climate. Similarly, psychology's pronouncements, or what we have to offer, about some of the basic human issues are woefully inadequate. Yet, the Project Talent search, which began a few years ago and will continue many more, will surely benefit many young people (as well as our nation). Project Talent, involving the evaluation of approximately 400,000 youngsters, is largely the result of many years of research into human behavior. It almost goes without saying that man's behavior is exceptionally complex; that inescapable fact combined with methods of investigation which require further refinement and improvement lead to understanding which is far from perfect.

As far as the pursuit of truth and knowledge of the world are concerned, the field of psychology strives toward a rather unique concept of "understanding." In this respect, we have an advantage over such fields as history and political science in that we can manipulate subjects more freely, since in many instances individuals are studied singly or in small groups and for short periods of time. Some psychologists feel that understanding may be thought to have been attained to the degree to which our own behavior or the behavior of others can be predicted and controlled. Many individuals have not thought of their everyday actions in this context, but most of us are constantly making predictions about our influences upon others as we seek control. Our adult roles usually require this. To use rather commonplace illustrations:

1. When a mother spanks her three-year-old for playing in the street, she is *predicting* that the infliction of pain and/or her disapproval will cause the child to cease and desist in the future.
2. When the teen-age female behaves in a certain coquettish manner, she is *predicting* that a male or males will respond in a particular manner. (As this is being written, a sixteen-year-old young lady is calculatingly raking the autumn leaves in the full sight of a group of interested males.)
3. When a teacher uses a given technique of instruction she is *making the prediction* that its use will result in learning by her students.

In each of those cases, manipulation or control is being sought.

Prediction and probability. Now it is abundantly clear that those predictions and many others are not always correct ones—especially those that teachers make about the teaching-learning situation. It is probably safe to say that our predictions will never attain 100 percent accuracy. If this is true, it is both possible and desirable to state them in terms of probabilities. This is the reason that psychologists so freely use such qualifying terms as "perhaps," "maybe," "in most cases," and other similar expressions (to the chagrin of students).

Thus, if utilization of a given set of principles for predicting future events results in 75 percent accuracy, whereas another set results in only 25 percent, then the former is based upon a greater degree of "understanding." In this connection, a youngster who can use a mathematical formula appropriately in several situations can be said to understand it better than does a youngster who can apply it correctly in only one situation. When we as adults provide conditions which we hope will promote learning by children, in a sense, we are attempting to control their behavior.

It is usually easy to "explain" behavior after the fact and thereby exhibit so-called "understanding." Notable in this regard are the explanations of many experts as to why many children have not learned to read—yet if the nationwide statistics are correct, something is awry about our understanding of the reading process.

This type of formulation of understanding enables us, too, to help children come to grips at early ages with the fact that understanding is a probability and not a certainty and perhaps in turn to live more comfortably in a world of ambiguities. Major decisions which all people make about a great variety of both personal and other issues are matters of playing the odds. The majority of students seem to be looking for certainties in their courses and in their personal choices about careers because, in part, they have not been taught earlier about this being an uncertain world. They are distinctly uncomfortable in the face of inevitable ambiguities, uncertainties, and probabilities.

It is for these reasons and others that psychologists place so much emphasis upon methodology in their college courses. The answers to problems and questions are highly dependent upon the measures or procedures which have been used to obtain them. Many of our seeming contradictions about knowledge in many fields result from the fact that different procedures were used in obtaining the data upon which knowledge is based. Some readers will more than likely recall the demise of the old *Literary Digest* magazine. It went out of business because the method of sampling voters prior to the 1936 presidential election left much to be desired and grossly incorrect predictions were made; poor methodology led to the wrong answers. Predictions about election returns or the behavior of voters now tend to be exceptionally accurate as the result of improved methodology. In like manner and more recently, psychologists and educators arrived at some false conclusions about programmed learning materials because of flaws in the methodology of evaluating them.

Control of behavior

Generally speaking, reference to "control of human behavior" and to efforts to discover ways of improving that control arouse fears in many people. There seems to be the lurking suspicion that success in such pursuits will result eventually in man becoming a sort of automated robot—his "will" will be of little use in his personal affairs. Unfortunately, popular accounts about such psychological techniques as brain-washing exacerbate these concerns. Sober reflection should suggest that the possibility of man being unduly manipulated to his detriment is remote indeed. In the first place, it is not the technique, or procedure, or device which is dangerous in itself. Surgery, for example, is being improved every day and mankind is benefiting, despite the fact that surgery was used exploitatively by the Nazis. In the second place, because of the complexity of man's behavior it appears that many, many years will elapse before psychological techniques are refined to the point of constituting any threat. In the third place, and most importantly, *ignorant* people can be manipulated or controlled far more readily than can educated ones; Hitler burned books as one of his first steps of control.

Thus, as we attempt to improve conditions for learning (control it)—the major concern of psychologists—and more children learn to read better, the *less* we have to fear about control in any undesirable sense. You may be sure that the future behavior of the eighth-grade drop-outs can be predicted much more accurately than can the future behavior of college graduates. In other words, since the limits to the economic and social behavior of nongraduates as a group are much more restricted than those of graduates, we can state with greater certainty what those of the former group will be doing ten years from now.

Moreover, emphasis upon methodology in producing knowledge is useful in preventing undesirable control. A few years ago the public became alarmed about "subliminal perception" and the fact that presumably a technique was available by which people could be influenced to buy goods and products without being aware of the manipulation. Popular accounts had it that advertisements could be flashed on television and movie screens below levels of perception and that such ads would be instrumental in stimulating viewers to purchase various objects. Highly educated people were upset and thought they were being manipulated against their wills. If people had known just a little about perception and the methods of its study in the laboratory, the furore would not have developed.

Animal research

As most readers of this chapter have been informed in introductory courses, psychology is the study of behavior of all organisms, but particularly that of humans. The word "behavior" is used in a very broad sense: as any observable activity. It includes the obvious such as walking and the not so obvious such as blood pressure. Throughout our work, attempts are made to employ the rules and procedures of science.

It may be helpful to clarify certain features of psychology which are not always clear to nonpsychologists. One of these is the necessity for animal research. A major reason that we study lower animals is for the light that can be shed indirectly upon human behavior by such pursuits. Judging by the groans of college students and the rather wry comments in the press about "rat psychology," we have not made our position sufficiently or properly clear in this regard. Perhaps two illustrations may help to clarify the necessity of lower animal experimentation in psychology.

In recent years, teaching machines, or programmed learning, or programmed instruction has been introduced on the American educational scene. This technique for promoting the learning of subject matter came about almost entirely as the result of years of investigating the environmental *conditions* under which lowly white rats and pigeons *learn* that which the experimenters desired them to learn. There is here, of course, a striking parallel with much of formal education: children are required to learn those things which our society has decreed they must learn, for example, to read, spell, and write and speak our language according to certain rules. Seemingly we often lose sight of these *impositions,* yet in many cases, what is to be learned by children is even written into laws (control of behavior).

Over the years investigators were able to identify several external or environmental conditions which promoted learning or the desired performance by the animals. In about 1958 these conditions for learning were incorporated into devices for use by children. The fact that teaching machines have been misused in some classrooms and that many questions about learning remain unanswered should not obscure the ultimate contributions which may accrue from our study of learning in lower animals. It is my impression that many of us are now asking more straightforward questions (and hence questions more likely to be answered) about classroom learning, largely as a result of the impact of teaching machines: Under what conditions in the classroom will children learn these aspects of subject X? rather than, How do children learn subject X? The first question lends itself much more readily to investigation than does the second. This is not to say that we should not be interested in "how children learn"; actually psychologists spend large amounts of time and energy pursuing the "how" of learning. But the "how" suggests activity in and of the nervous system—something which cannot be studied in the classroom; nor can educators wait for those answers to come. Perhaps the major contribution of all the lower animal research has been that of generating and stimulating comparable investigations into human learning. At the same time, and perhaps more importantly, it has provided models and directions for experimentation. Quite disconcertingly, "learning curves" of white rats are remarkably similar in shape to some of the "learning curves" of college sophomores.

Still another illustration of the value of psychological research on lower animals is the work of Harry F. Harlow in his studies of the factors and forces in the environment which contribute to the development of affection (or lack of it) in monkeys. Certainly no brief needs to be made for the necessity of studying that topic. He has found striking relationships between the early infantile experiences of monkeys and their later adult behavior. It goes without saying that the procedures used initially with the monkeys, as efforts were made to identify significant forces, could not have been used with humans. Just how we can utilize these findings with respect to man has not yet been determined, but certainly sometime in the future ways will be found to do so.

When one contemplates the complexity of human behavior and the myriad forces which contribute to it, one hardly knows where to begin in an effort to isolate and study it. The use of animals assists in these tasks. This complexity may be another reason for our proclivity in turning to the mysterious. Around 1920 some psychologists had identified as many as 1,800 instincts. By the late 1930's, many of those presumed instincts had come to be called "needs" with the implication that the needs were innate. Lower animal research has not only enabled us to explode the existence of all those instincts, but it has also led to better formulations of the origins of many needs. It may result in the identification of better ways of promoting the development (learning) of the needs which our society deems to be desirable ones.

Experimental and other scientific methods

In such studies and in others which they undertake, psychologists strive to employ generally accepted experimental procedures, known in some circles as *the* scientific method. If, however, psychologists have learned anything within recent years, it is the notion that there is *no one* scientific method. The rules of science are man-made and, as such, are subject to error in the first place and to modification in the second. Scientific procedures and methods of investigation are being altered as more and more is being learned about the complexity of human behavior. At one time, efforts were almost exclusively those of attempting to isolate various facets of behavior as though each one were independent of all others. And whereas there is still some necessity for that approach, procedures currently deal with how various facets *interact* with each other. Recent developments in the field of statistics and the creation of electronic computers are of immeasurable benefit in studying interactions.

In this connection, not too many years ago studies showed that particular methods of classroom instruction seemed to be uncorrelated with student performance; that is, students seemed to learn in spite of our efforts, not because of them. Nevertheless, current studies utilizing more appropriate methodology are revealing that methods of instruction are related to performance; more specifically, students react differentially to specific procedures. For example, there are suggestions from research that bright youngsters require teaching techniques different from those required by youngsters of average ability. In other words, there is interaction between level of ability and method of instruction. These findings, of course, should have profound impacts upon classroom arrangements. To put it another way, in education it has been maintained for years that the number of students per class was the important variable. It seems now that this is not the case (studies at the college level have shown no correlation between number of students per class and achievement); other factors are of greater significance. Thus it appears that decisions about the problem of homogenous-heterogeneous grouping, to mention one educational issue, can be based upon something other than mere opinion or belief.

So rather than attempting to describe *a* scientific method which psychologists employ, it seems more appropriate and meaningful to identify a common attitude which reflects the manner in which psychologists pursue "truth." Independent of interest in a special area of the field—clinical, comparative, social, developmental, experimental, physiological—psychologists share an attitude of seeking demonstrable cause-effect relationships for human behavior. The preferred method, as has already been mentioned, is that of experimentation. It should be obvious that experimentation is not always possible for all problems in the field, either at the moment or in the foreseeable future. Moreover, such an attitude is an ideal to be pursued rather than a reality which has been attained. This attitude seems to be reflected most often in our query, What is the evidence? when a particular pronouncement has been uttered. We like to *believe* (shades of Bernard Shaw), incidentally, that this attitude develops as a *result* of our graduate training. To my knowledge, such has not been demonstrated, although you can be sure that we are seeking evidence to confirm it.

Psychologists strive to heed the following words that have been attributed to Francis Bacon and seek to avoid the path to "truth" which he described: [3]

In the year of our Lord 1432, there arose a grievous quarrel among the brethren over the number of teeth in the mouth of a horse. For 13 days the disputation raged without ceasing. All the ancient books and chronicles were fetched out, and wonderful and ponderous erudition, such as was never before heard of in this region, was made manifest. At the beginning of the 14th day, a youthful friar of goodly bearing asked his learned superiors for permission to add a word, and straightaway, to the wonderment of the disputants, whose deep wisdom he sore vexed, he beseeched them to unbend in a manner coarse and unheard-of, and to look in the open mouth of a horse and find answer to their questionings. At this, their dignity being grievously hurt, they waxed exceedingly wroth; and, joining in a mighty uproar, they flew upon him and smote him hip and thigh, and cast him out forthwith. For, said they, surely Satan hath tempted this bold neophyte to declare unholy and unheard-of ways of finding truth contrary to the teachings of the fathers. After many days more of grievous strife the dove of peace sat on the assembly, and they as one man, declaring the problem to be an everlasting mystery because of a grievous dearth of historical and theological evidence thereof, so ordered the same writ down.

[3] Norman L. Munn, *Introduction to Psychology* (Boston: Houghton Mifflin, 1962), p. 4.

It is indeed heartening that to an increasing extent psychologists and educators are looking into the "open mouth of the horse" in the classroom. Surely this will lead to progress in education, namely, better and more efficient learning for more children (control of behavior).

Of course, many of the problems which require investigation are not amenable to experimentation. The great variety of other procedures can perhaps be grouped into two types: the sample survey and the case method. An illustration of the former is the Project Talent study, while the latter is often used in attempting to understand and help emotionally disturbed children.

Observer bias. In the pursuit of the goal of seeking demonstrable cause-effect evidence psychologists face special difficulties. In many instances we are both the "observer and the observed"—another feature of psychology and other behavioral sciences which requires clarification. This means, first, that special precautions must be taken in research so that we do not observe or find what we *believe* or *want* to be true. There are many subtle ways of influencing human subjects to respond or behave in a certain desired fashion. For example, opinion questionnaires must be worded carefully so that the respondent will give his own feelings or opinions rather than those he thinks the interviewer is seeking. Second, it means that the procedure or process of observation during research sometimes affects in an untoward fashion those who are being observed or studied. Thus, not only are our endeavors complicated by this phenomenon, but it often promotes misleading and false interpretations of cause-effect relationships.

Little needs to be said about the first part of the problem, namely, the danger of observing what we believe, other than to declare that elaborate precautions are utilized in our experimental designs to guard against those possibilities. Something needs to be said, however, about the fact that the behavior of the observed persons (or subjects) is often affected substantially by the mere act of observation, if for no other reason than the fact that nonpsychologists (especially educators) need and use psychological data.

Hawthorne Effect. One kind of effect of the observations upon those being observed goes under the name of the "Hawthorne Effect," the name having been derived from the place where the effects were first clearly recognized—the Hawthorne Plant of the Western Electric Company. A study was conducted around 1930 to determine or identify the working conditions which influenced the employees in their assembly of certain component parts of telephones. A group of young women was subjected over a period of time to both positive and negative working arrangements; for example, frequent rest periods and no rest periods. The number of components they assembled was found to be unrelated to the conditions under which they worked; that is, they assembled as many under adverse circumstances as under favorable ones and, furthermore, maintained production that was considerably above the average for the plant. It was finally realized that the major determining factor in their performance or behavior was the fact that they were being observed. To put it another way, their work rate was more influenced by the attention of the investigators than by those factors which were believed to be significant.

In recent years, false hopes were raised for the mentally ill when tranquilizers were first introduced and the benefits therefrom were strikingly favorable. Then, too, the first few groups of youngsters who used programmed learning materials learned exceptionally well and at almost unbelievable speeds. In both those instances, however, the initial successes were not repeated in other groups, for the "Hawthorne Effect" had been operating rather than the determinants which were believed to be the significant ones. If allowances are not made for the "Hawthorne Effect" in the investigation of human behavior, such oversight can result in many false notions; it produces false "truths."

Psychology in the Social Studies

I cannot overlook this opportunity of having a very few words about the "how" of introducing psychology into the elementary and secondary curricula. It seems that many of the generalizations which have been mentioned and the difficulties of experimental investigation could be introduced as early as the primary grades. At least one study has shown that children at that level are seeking psychological information (page 236). An especially effective vehicle for the introduction might well be much of the work that has been undertaken in perception. Excellent discussions can be found in almost all introductory textbooks. Furthermore, illustrations of simple and easy-to-make materials for demonstrations and experiments are contained in those sources. "Seeing is not believing," or selective perception would be a helpful truth to convey. Also certain principles of learning could be introduced via "how to train pets."

There have been at least two recent reported instances of the subject having been taught in a more or less deliberate fashion in two elementary grades. Reactions and comments of those youngsters should provide instructive guidelines for all those individuals who are thinking about and planning further development of the social studies portion of the primary curriculum.

In 1956 a formal course was offered—two terms in length—to a group of eighth graders.[4] One of the questions asked of the students was, What do you expect to accomplish in this course? A preponderance of the replies indicated concern about "why people act as they do," for example:

. . . to try to find out about myself and why I do the things I do . . .

. . . to find out why some people are nice and why some are hotheads . . .

I want to learn how to get along with people.

I think I may be able to overcome some of my problems by knowing more about them, such as, when I get up in front of a group I get very nervous.

I hope to find out what makes people have the emotions they have, such as being angry, doing things they know they shouldn't do, etc.

. . . to find out why people behave in a certain way, why there are personality clashes and restlessness in class.

Further, some of their questions reflected interest in the sorts of problems with which psychology has been most concerned traditionally:

. . . to try to find out why people are different from each other.

. . . to find out why some are musically inclined and some can't even read music.

[4] Joseph B. Patti, "Elementary Psychology for Eighth Graders," *American Psychologist,* 11:194–196 (April), 1956.

Recently a school psychologist was asked to talk to a fourth grade class on "Psychology as a Science" as part of a unit in science.[5] Reception of the presentation was exceptionally enthusiastic and led to a return engagement for the speaker later in the year. Whereas these children's questions were much broader in scope than those of the eighth graders (at age ten or so children haven't learned about the artificial boundaries of knowledge), their concerns were also mostly about "why people act as they do"; by way of illustration and *uncontaminated* by grammatical corrections:

Why does my brother tease me.
Why does father yell at you.
Whey is my sister a peast.
What makes a chiled winey in the morning.
How come boys and girls when they go into the first grade think they are jerks?
Why do people fight?
How come a man is King of the family.

These children also exhibited some interest in the more traditional aspects of the field:

Why do cat's eyes get bigger when it is dark.
How come some people are smart and some arn't.
I stepped on a nail and it didn't hurt why didn't it hurt.
What part of the head lets you see.
What makes people go to sleep?
Could you kid become a genus after she or he has have many years of college?

Perhaps the most obvious conclusion to be drawn from the queries and reactions of the children in these two grades is that primary youngsters do have important questions and exhibit curiosity about matters for which the field of psychology may have something to offer. The observation that children are curious about causation in human affairs will certainly come as neither a surprise nor as any enlightenment to teachers or to others who have worked extensively with them. An interesting paradox about formal education, however, is brought into sharp focus: throughout the public school era children are taught forthrightly about all aspects of the world—geography, history, mathematics, language, and so on. But

[5] Robert Belenky, "Psychology in a Suburban School System," *American Psychologist,* 18:669–670 (October), 1963.

they are not taught directly about human behavior. Yet, in the final analysis, man's behavior is the basis of all other subject matter. Mathematics, to mention only one discipline, is nothing more than a series of abstractions which man has devised for his convenience in dealing with the world. In view of the fact that mathematics is often referred to as the "exact science" (somewhat incorrectly) it is interesting that man has changed it so much in the past few years.

Role of Psychology

There is no intended implication here that other disciplines have nothing to contribute with respect to understanding man, but rather only the emphasis that psychology is the one field in which understanding of behavior is the prime concern. Of some importance, too, is the fact that the interests of children in many facets of behavior have been disregarded, at least in the early grades.

It would appear likely, also, that children "know," in a sense, a great deal about psychology. After all, most of them have been exposed to radio and television and all of them have had contact with at least a few people—such experiences having led them to form judgments and opinions about human behavior in general. Regrettably, popularized presentations of subject matter are not always the best, and contact with a few persons in a limited number of situations does not usually give a proper basis for broad valid generalizations. Thus it seems reasonable to suppose that adults have brought from childhood many false notions and distortions about human behavior (if college students are any sort of representative sample, that is more than supposition). Not long ago a woman asked a newspaper columnist: Can mental illness be caused by sleeping in metal hair curlers? Not only does that question reflect gross ignorance about psychology but about anatomy and physiology as well. Many of us can attest to the difficulties encountered in attempting to alter many of the incorrect ideas of college students as well as those of older adults.

Finally, in view of the fact that the boundaries of all knowledge are becoming less distinct, psychology should not be introduced in separate units. Instead, there should be combination and integration with material from other subject matter areas. It has always seemed strange to me that, on the one hand, throughout formal education we beseech students to integrate subject matter from various sources; while on the other hand, we create conditions for learning which seem to hamper or prevent integration—namely, the presentation of information in neat and discrete, but artificial, parcels. This, of course, should not preclude the offering of an elective course in psychology in high schools as a capstone to the many important concepts and generalizations that have been introduced earlier in the program.

SUGGESTED READINGS

Berelson, Bernard and Gary A. Steiner, *Human Behavior: An Inventory of Scientific Findings* (New York: Harcourt, Brace & World, 1964). A very careful evaluation of psychological literature in an effort to list generalizations about behavior for which there is agreement and support from research data.

Engle, T. L., *Psychology: Its Principles and Applications,* 4th ed. (New York: Harcourt, Brace & World, 1964). A new general text in psychology for high school students. Emphasis upon methods of inquiry. Also contains material on "perception" which can be adapted to other grade levels.

Engle, T. L., Leonard West, and Ohmer Milton, *Record of Activities and Experiments, with Programed Units* (New York: Harcourt, Brace & World, 1964). (For use with *Psychology: Its Principles and Applications,* 4th ed.). A workbook to accompany Engle's text. Important points and ideas are programmed. Contains experiments which students can conduct which require little or no equipment.

Hilgard, Ernest R., *Introduction to Psychology,* 3d ed. (New York: Harcourt, Brace & World, 1962). A text for the first college course.

Holland, James G. and B. F. Skinner, *A Program for Self-Instruction: Analysis of Behavior* (New York: McGraw-Hill, 1961). A programmed presentation of B. F. Skinner's basic ideas about "operant conditioning."

Miller, George A., *Psychology: The Science of Mental Life* (New York: Harper & Row, 1962). A history of the development of the field of psychology. A high school teacher can obtain many ideas to enliven the course.

Russell, Roger W., *Frontiers in Psychology* (Chicago: Scott, Foresman and Company, 1964). A book of readings designed to acquaint students with the newest developments in the field. Also contains an examination of the philosophical assumptions underlying psychology.

SHOBEN, EDWARD J. AND FLOYD L. RUCH, *Perspectives in Psychology* (Chicago: Scott, Foresman and Company, 1963). Via selected journal articles, a major purpose of this book is to acquaint the student with sources of the wide range of differences among psychologists as they attack the human puzzle.

9   Philosophy

John W. Davis
Department of Philosophy
University of Tennessee

WHEN I WAS FIRST ASKED TO PREPARE THIS ESSAY ON THE NATURE OF philosophy and its role in the social studies program, my first reaction was the same as that of my colleagues in philosophy with whom I later discussed the topic: If by "role" is meant its contribution as a subject matter, philosophy has no role in the school curriculum. As a colleague put it, "How can you expect to teach philosophy to grade school pupils and high school students, when we can hardly teach it to college students?"

As I say, this was my first reaction, for I now believe that the conclusion that philosophy has no role in the elementary and secondary schools is a mistake. Later I shall examine some of the reasons for this mistake and point out some specific contributions that philosophy may make to the social studies program. But first I should like to explain what philosophy is by (1) briefly describing the historical relation between philosophy and the sciences; (2) examining some of the changing conceptions of philosophy; (3) pointing out basic problems that define the various subdivisions within the field and stating some of the solutions that have been proposed to these problems; and (4) examining some of the basic differences between philosophy and the other disciplines, the social sciences, from which the teacher draws in developing a social studies program.

What Is Philosophy?

The word "philosophy" is derived from the Greek word *philosophia,* meaning "the love of knowledge and wisdom." The word "love" may here be interpreted as meaning a kind of aspiration, hence the philosopher is one who aspires to knowledge and wisdom. The emphasis appears to be upon the seeking, rather than upon the knowledge and wisdom sought. But philosophers have usually regarded philosophy as both the seeking, or philosophizing, and the truths sought.

The sciences may, however, also be described as a seeking and as truths sought. Should we, therefore, identify philosophy with science? The *Dictionary of Philosophy* describes philosophy as "the most general science," and states that originally philosophy was defined as "the rational explanation of anything; the general principles under which all facts could be explained; in this sense, indistinguishable from science." [1] Perhaps an examination of the historical relation between philosophy and science will permit us to describe and distinguish more precisely the seeking and the truths sought by each.

The historical relation between philosophy and the sciences

Originally science and philosophy, and religion as well, were one. As a matter of fact, all of these had their beginning in mythology, which has been described as "the primitive attempt to understand the world." The creators of Western philosophy and science were a succession of wise men, "professors of wisdom," who appeared in the sixth and fifth centuries B.C., and who were keenly aware of the inadequacies of myth. We shall return to these wise men later.

According to Zeller,[2] the complete fusion of philosophy and science distinguishes this early period of the history of knowledge. No distinction was made between speculation and empirical re-

[1] Dagobert D. Runes, ed., *Dictionary of Philosophy* (New York: Philosophical Library, 1942), p. 235.
[2] Eduard Zeller, *Outlines of the History of Greek Philosophy* (Cleveland: Meridian Books, World Publishing Co., 1955), p. 39.

search. In the beginning, all branches of natural knowledge, astronomy, mathematics, and even medicine, were included in the scope of philosophy. Only *historie,* the combination of history and geography, stood apart; but even here the line of separation is vague. Medicine, as a practical *tēchnē,* was the first science to separate itself. Logic, mathematics, and astronomy were early recognized as special disciplines, although, unlike the other two, logic has remained within the family of philosophy. Later, during the Middle Ages, it was customary to divide philosophy into several major areas, two of which were natural and moral. As new methods for gaining knowledge were discovered and more and more hypotheses were systematized, natural philosophy (physics, chemistry, geology, and biology) was gradually recognized as an independent discipline distinct from philosophy. What are now called social sciences, the moral philosophies, were rather late in separating. Anthropology, sociology, political science, economics, and psychology are the later offspring, and some of them may not even now have broken all the ties that bind them to the family of philosophy, for their scientific status is still being debated.

Philosophy—mother of sciences, servant of sciences, or the science of sciences?

This brief outline of the history of knowledge suggests that rather than being a science herself, philosophy should be described as the mother of the sciences, for she has mothered or helped mother one offspring after another. And as these offspring have been fed by the new discoveries made by individuals who have specialized in serving their growth, they have separated from their parent.

Assuming that philosophy is a mother, her offspring are infrequent and somewhat unpredictable, for not every philosopher is a Newton; very few are originators of new sciences. Most philosophers must settle for a less honored position, but a nonetheless necessary one. Their job is to keep her alive and fertile, to keep her in good health until she is ready to give birth again. Philosophical discussions and arguments serve to keep her spirit aflame, and the sciences with their new knowledge provide nourishment for her body.

To be sure, not all of her offspring have been so distinguished as today's natural and social sciences. Metaphysical and ethical systems, for example, are regarded by some critics as her feeble-minded, if not psychotic, children, as we shall see. She has also had a few miscarriages and given birth to not a few monstrosities. And while she is a grand old lady, she has not been above having a bastard or two. In this country, dialectical materialism is usually placed in this category. There are a few other candidates as well.

But even if the sciences can be described as offspring that have separated from philosophy, most philosophers believe that the separation can never be complete, for there are important benefits which each provides for the other. On the one hand, philosophy needs the information furnished by the sciences, for traditionally at least some philosophers have been concerned with giving an account of man and the universe which draws upon the whole of man's scientific knowledge. Thus, E. S. Ames defines philosophy as "the endeavor to achieve a comprehensive view of life and its meaning, upon the basis of the results of the various sciences." [3]

A science may be described in general as systematized knowledge of some particular field, but the field of philosophy is broad and inclusive. It is, some say, the most comprehensive of endeavors: an attempt to discover the whole truth about everything. It is the one discipline that attempts a synthesis of all of man's knowledge and experience. This being the case, philosophy is dependent not only upon the sciences but upon art and religion as well. Hence a better definition than the one above is that of J. A. Leighton who writes, "a complete philosophy includes a world view, or reasoned conception of the whole cosmos, and a life-view, or doctrine of the values, meanings, and purposes of human life." [4]

This conception of philosophy has generally been held by the majority of the great philosophers, men like Plato, Aristotle, Thomas Aquinas, Descartes, Spinoza, Leibniz, Locke, Kant, Hegel, and Schopenhauer, to mention only a few before the twentieth century. These men developed comprehensive systems of thought which provided answers to most of the perennial problems of mankind, problems like: What is the meaning of life? Is man an end in himself? What is the difference between right and wrong? Is there

[3] Quoted by H. H. Titus in *Living Issues in Philosophy,* 3d ed. (New York: American Book Co., 1959), p. 10.
[4] *Ibid.*

243

some overall plan or purpose being realized in history? What is beauty? What are time and space? Is it possible to prove that God exists? Is there really such a thing as an objective truth or is truth just a matter of personal opinion?

Of course, the answers of one philosopher have not always agreed with the answers of another, but most philosophers will have relied to some extent upon the results of science, art, and religion in formulating their answers, and, moreover, many of their answers strongly influence the answers given to similar questions by philosophers and laymen today.

On the other hand, some contemporary philosophers assign to philosophy a much more modest role. They are skeptical regarding the value of such comprehensive philosophical systems. They emphasize that philosophy should serve rather than be served by the sciences. For example, some of them stress the "synthesizing role" which philosophy may play within the scientific domain. Thus Charles Frankel describes philosophy as growing "out of blocks and discordancies within and between our systems of belief." "Its task," he says, "is the integration of belief." One way that philosophy accomplishes this task is to resolve the conflict between concepts, those like "freedom" and "causation," through analysis, clarification, and redefinition; another way, one based on modern symbolic logic, is to "create artificial languages through which our beliefs can be rationally reconstructed and the paradoxes and difficulties that set the inquiry in motion eliminated."

Frankel also describes the synthesizing role which philosophy can serve with respect to the social sciences.

These sciences contain a variety of freely floating terms—"motivation," "attitude," "welfare," "the public interest"—which are imperfectly understood. By clarifying the meaning and interconnections of these and other basic concepts, philosophers can serve to indicate the places at which the different social sciences may meet, and the uses to which results in one domain may be put to enrich inquiry in another.[5]

Perhaps these different conceptions of philosophy are not mutually exclusive, for definitions have been given which express philosophy's role in relation to science as both served and servant.

[5] Charles Frankel, "Philosophy and the Social Sciences," in *Both Human and Humane,* ed. C. E. Boewe and R. F. Nichols (Philadelphia: Univ. of Pennsylvania, 1960), pp. 116–117.

The *Dictionary of Philosophy,* for example, defines technical philosophy today as "the science of sciences, the criticism and systematization or organization of all knowledge, drawn from empirical science, rational learning, common experience, or wherever." [6]

In short, philosophy and science serve each other—as do philosophy and religion, and philosophy and art. Consequently, philosophy may be to some extent all of these: mother of sciences, servant of sciences, and science of sciences. We shall return to this problem later, but now we need to see what philosophy is as a subject matter in our colleges and universities.

Perennial Problems of Philosophy

As we have seen, there is no definition of philosophy which is accepted by all philosophers, but there is general agreement that certain questions or problems are philosophical. There are, it appears to me, three sets of questions that are the peculiar concern of the philosopher: questions relating to the nature of (1) basic reality, (2) value, and (3) knowledge. What fundamentally is? What ought to be? What are the nature and sources of knowledge? These questions define the three major fields of philosophy—metaphysics, axiology, and epistemology. They are *the* philosophical questions. With the exception of logic, all the other areas or divisions within the field of philosophy are but attempts to relate these basic problems to specific subject matters or disciplines, as we shall see.

These questions are not new; they are as old as philosophy. One might say that they are as old as man, but perhaps it would be more correct to say that they are the questions of the mature man. They are the questions which man confronted when he came of age. They are the questions that must be answered if man is to give a thorough account of his experience. Moreover, they are the questions whose answers are presupposed by both our beliefs and our behavior. A major purpose of education in philosophy is to make us sensitive to these questions, and to make us see that we cannot avoid philosophical commitments of one sort or another. The an-

[6] Runes, *op. cit.*

swers to these questions make it possible for us to tie some of the loose ends of experience together. Our philosophical commitments are essential parts of life's jigsaw puzzle. And it is the nature of man to work at the puzzle. Perhaps man is the creature who is destined to be forever working puzzles, for there appears to be no one correct way to fit the pieces together, although some ways appear to be better than others.

The problem of reality: metaphysics

The fathers of our Western philosophy were primarily metaphysicians; theirs was the first question, that of the basic substance underlying all things. But like their later brothers, they failed to reach agreement. Thales suggested that the basic stuff was water, but Anaximander proposed the Boundless, Anaximenes argued for air, or "breath," and the Pythagoreans spoke for number. Other early philosophers were impressed by a different but related problem, that of change. Thus, for Heraclitus increasing change is the dominant characteristic of things. "One can never step twice into the same river, for fresh waters are ever flowing in upon you." But, not so, says Parmenides. Change, plurality, and motion are unthinkable. There is only uncreated, indestructible, indivisible Being. "Only Being is, not-being is not and cannot be thought." Some of the later Greek philosophers developed median positions. There are unchanging things, but change results when these things are combined or separated. Empedocles lists the unchanging things as the qualitatively different elements—fire, air, water, and earth —and declares that change results when these are combined or separated by love and hate. Anaxagoras disagrees. Our world is composed of innumerable substances, the seeds of gold, flesh, hair, silver, and so forth, and change is the combining and separating of these by "mind." But, according to Democritus, they are both mistaken; the unchanging things are atoms which differ from each other only in size and shape, and change is to be explained by the natural motion of the atoms as they fall through empty space.

The distinctive feature of these and other early attempts to solve the metaphysical problems of the nature of reality and change is the obvious lack of agreement among the proposed solutions. This is not, however, a defect that is peculiar to early philosophers, for this is still a distinguishing feature of metaphysical speculation. There are still no answers acceptable to all metaphysicians. Actually these early Greeks were men of great genius, for while their conclusions, especially those of the earliest ones, appear to us as belonging to naive and unlearned men, they did discover many of the basic questions and some of the possible answers to them. Later philosophers have refined and elaborated many of their conclusions. The result has been the development of various world views and schools of philosophy like realism (abstract terms, or universals, are as real as, if not more real than, actual physical particulars), idealism (reality is the nature of ideas, mind, or selves), materialism (matter alone is real), pantheism (all is God), pluralism (reality is many rather than one or two basic stuffs), naturalism (nature is the whole of reality), and mechanism (the universe is mechanistic in nature and is to be explained on the basis of its analogy to a machine).

Metaphysics is usually divided into *ontology,* the study of being qua being, and *cosmology,* the study of the origin, development, and structure of the universe. The natural sciences, which at one time were indistinguishable from metaphysics, had their origin when philosophers began to make inquiry into particular forms of being as contrasted with being itself. It was discovered that while there could be little agreement concerning the nature of being itself and the structure of the universe, as we have seen, there could be much agreement concerning the nature and relations of particular forms of being; the results of the latter inquiry, natural philosophy, being open to public verification. And as knowledge was systematized and accumulated, the natural philosophies became the natural sciences.

The problem of value: axiology

Philosophers are not apt to be merely metaphysicians. They are usually concerned with problems relating to value and knowledge as well, for the answers given in one area may be decisive for problems in another.

The failure of metaphysicians to discover an answer acceptable to all led some philosophers to abandon metaphysical speculation, and to shift attention from nature to man and to problems of a more practical kind, especially to problems relating to the good for man.

The result was moral philosophy, which was a jumble of studies relating to both value and man, a mixture of what are now called ethics, political science, aesthetics, psychology, sociology, and philosophy of religion, to mention but a few.

The central moral problems for the early philosophers were those of the nature of the good life and ideal human character. What is the good life, and what must I do to attain it? Is it a life of pleasure, of knowledge, of virtue, of honor, of wealth, or of what? Can I obtain it by being dutiful, by living according to custom, by following reason, or by some other means? Here, as in metaphysical inquiry, there was no lack of answers. While some of the sophists, professional teachers in ancient Greece, insisted that conformity to customs and traditions is the one indispensable condition for the good life, other less conservative sophists were equally outspoken for a life of fulfilled desires. While Socrates and Plato argued for a harmony of soul which reflects the Good, Aristotle spoke for the happiness, or well-being, resulting from the realization of the form proper to man, the "rational soul." While Aristippus championed the vigorous life of the most intense sensual pleasure of the moment, and Epicurus the serene life of *ataraxia,* freedom from pain in the body and trouble in the mind, Antisthenes thought otherwise: "I had rather go mad," he says, "than to experience the first drop of pleasure." And while the Stoics did not go this far, they too proclaimed the life of virtue, of indifference to fortune, and of apathy, which they regarded as harmony with the divine reason, or God.

Just as in the case of metaphysics, this early abundance of opinion is suggestive of the diversity in later moral philosophy, for there is no agreement today among philosophers concerning the good and the right. And here again we find that the history of the discipline has been to a great extent an elaboration and refinement of earlier answers, for many, if not all, of our major contemporary theories have their origin in Greek, Roman, and Hebrew thought. Moreover, today's problems are about the same as those of yesterday. A glance at the table of contents in any standard contemporary ethics text will reveal that the problems treated today are, in general, those discussed by Plato, Aristotle, and other early philosophers. There are chapters which describe the major types of ethical theories, for example, theories based on custom, theology, conscience, duty, pleasure, happiness, self-realization, interest, nature, and intuition;

and there are discussions of metaphysical and epistemological problems relating to ethics, for example, the problems of psychological egoism (Are all of our motives selfish?), cultural relativism (Are there universally valid moral standards?), and determinism (Are men capable of voluntary acts?).

There may also be, however, at least in the up-to-date text, in contrast to these discussions "in" ethics, discussions "about" ethics, discussions about the language and logic of morals and of value in general which today's philosopher calls *metaethics* and *axiology*. And this may be the major point of difference between earlier and contemporary moral philosophy. Axiology (Gr. *axios,* of like value, worthy; and *logos,* account, reason, theory) is a modern term for theory of value. But while the term may not have been used until the twentieth century, the general inquiry into the nature of value can be traced at least back to Plato and the "idea" or form of the Good.

In early philosophy, as we saw, there was no sharp separation between the problem of value and the problem of man. This is to be expected, for in ethics, which has traditionally been the dominant type of inquiry in moral philosophy, the two problems are fused together into the one problem of human worth; ethics being defined as a critical study of good and bad, right and wrong, in human conduct. But as emphasis was given to one problem rather than the other, two different areas of study have developed: on the one hand, the general theory of value, with ethics being regarded as the study of only one type of value, namely, moral; on the other hand, the various descriptive studies relating specifically to man and his activities, studies which are included in the school program as social studies, or social sciences, but which might also be called anthropological sciences, to contrast them with the natural sciences.

Axiology as a modern study developed when philosophers began to speculate concerning the problem of what all values have in common. An ice cream sundae, a good milch cow, the love of God and of one's country, a beautiful painting, a good hanging, and a good rat poison all apparently have something to do with value, but as to exactly what this common thing is (pleasure, desire, approval, an indefinable property, or something else), philosophers have been unable to agree, and they may never agree.

My own opinion is that the most fruitful approach to this problem lies in recent attempts to develop a logic for value. Robert S. Hartman,[7] for instance, gives a logical definition of value in terms of concept fulfillment: a thing is valuable to the degree that it posses- ses the properties of its concept. A horse, for example, is good as a horse if it has all the properties of its class, say, mane, flank, shank, haunch, and withers—to name but five of the forty-seven external parts of a horse. Hartman treats this definition of value as an axiom, upon which he has erected an extremely elaborate and rig- orous system of formal axiology, a scientific system concerned with the study of the logic of value, or the *pure form* of value. Thus Hartman's formal axiology is a science of the possible with respect to value. Through an analysis and enumeration of the types of value, the forms of value combinations, and the forms of value propositions, the logic of value provides an inventory of possibilities for use by the social sciences, which are regarded as specific value sciences.

Hartman argues that rather than treat axiology as a sister to metaphysics, it should be regarded as analogous to mathematics, and both mathematics and axiology considered as species of logic and as formal frames of reference for sciences; mathematics, the logic of number, providing the formal frame of reference for the natural sciences, and axiology, the logic of value, providing an analogous overarching formal system for social and philosophical sciences, each of which may be regarded as an application of a specific category of value to a specific type of subject matter. For example, psychology, sociology, and economics are interpreted as applications of the cat- egory of *extrinsic* value (the value of a thing as measured in terms of the properties it shares with other members of a specific class, as in the example of the horse above) to individual persons, groups of persons, and individual things, respectively. On the other hand, ethics, political science, and aesthetics are seen as applications of the category of *intrinsic* value (the value of a thing considered as unique) to individual persons, groups of persons, and individual things.

Hartman's theory, being of recent development, has not found much acceptance among philosophers. But we must not make the mistake, as some contemporary philosophers have, of thinking that because philosophers have been unable to agree on solutions to

[7] Robert S. Hartman, "Value Theory as a Formal System," *Kant-Studien,* Vol. 50, No. 3, 1958–1959; and "The Logic of Value," *The Review of Meta- physics,* Vol. 14, No. 3 (March), 1961.

axiological problems that such problems and the answers given to them are unimportant. They are tremendously important. Answers to such questions lie at the very heart of our culture. They furnish us with the cloud of aspirations which ennoble the human heart. They provide the lure which is gradually drawing man to richer and deeper levels of life. They provide us with the vision of human dignity, the idea of the worth of man, which becomes a reality under its own inspiration. One of the principal duties of the philosopher is to make us aware of these assumptions and aspirations, to make them clear to us, and to point out their relations and implications.

The problem of knowledge: epistemology

But the problem of lack of agreement remains. Very early in history philosophers were led to speculate concerning the reason why they were unable to agree, and the result of these speculations is our third philosophical subdivision, epistemology, or theory of knowledge. Three basic problems were recognized early: (1) What is the object of knowledge? (2) What is the source of knowledge? (3) What is the test for truth?

Again, basic answers were not long in coming. Concerning the object of knowledge, some philosophers (e.g., common sense realists), took the common sense view that when one knows a real object, say, an apple, he knows the external, concrete apple just as it is in all of its hardness or softness, redness or greenness, sweetness or sourness, and so on. He knows it immediately. Other philosophers (e.g., sensationalists and phenomenalists), argued that what one knows is not the external thing but our impressions or sensations of it. Our knowledge of the apple is not immediate but mediated by sensations which are copies of the properties of the apple. We can never get beyond our sensations to the apple itself. This led some philosophers (e.g., subjective idealists), to conclude that the apple really was not there, as a physical thing at least. Our sensations are the apple, they said, and since sensations exist only when sensed, apples and other supposedly material things exist only in mind. To be is to be perceived, or to perceive, says George Berkeley. Another group (e.g., platonic realists), argued that all these philosophers share the common mistake of thinking that knowledge is

251

of sensible things. But true knowledge has its ground neither in sensation nor in the material objects some persons think they copy. Knowledge is of intelligible objects, the ideas, or forms, which can be grasped only by reason. Our knowledge of mathematics is a good example. A circle is something that can be grasped only by the intellect, for there are no true circles—plane, closed curves equidistant from a center—in the sensible world. And if "apple" is an object of knowledge, it is not this or that physical apple but that which all particular apples have in common, the idea, or form, apple, which is an intelligible and not a sensible object.

These answers, and others of a similar sort, obviously influenced the answers given to the questions concerning the methods for obtaining knowledge and the tests for truth, for the philosophers who argued for sensations and/or sensible objects generally proclaimed sense experience as the source and criterion of knowledge. They are called *empiricists*. We know what we have sensed, they say; our experiences of hearing, seeing, touching, smelling, and tasting constitute our knowledge. On the other hand, those who argued for intelligible objects and perfect forms generally have emphasized the importance of reason, and are called *rationalists*. Others have championed intuition, and are called *intuitionists*. The exact relation of reason and intuition is not clear. Some persons think that intuition is a way of knowing distinct from reason and the senses, and that it furnishes us with an insight into a supernatural reality which is inaccessible to both reason and the senses. Others think of intuition as a supplement to both, a kind of funding of one's past experience and thinking.

The method of authority is usually listed as a fourth solution to the problem of the source of knowledge, but with reliance on authority the basic problem remains, for the authority must have used one of the other methods in gaining his knowledge.

There are related theories of the test of truth. I shall mention three: the correspondence, coherence, and pragmatic theories. The empiricist who claims that all knowledge is derived from the senses is apt to say that statements are true when they correspond with the facts. Thus the statement, "The apple is sweet," is true, if the apple in fact is sweet, as this is determined by sense experience. On the other hand, the rationalist who claims that the mind has the ability to discover truth by itself is apt to claim that a statement is true if it is consistent with other statements that are accepted as true.

Hence Descartes, an important seventeenth-century rationalist, says that knowledge is a coherent system of ideas whose relations are so clear and distinct that they cannot be doubted.

More recently, the pragmatists, a group of American philosophers led by Charles Peirce, William James, and John Dewey, have proclaimed utility, workability, or satisfactory consequences as the test of truth. A true idea is one that works. I may believe, for example, that a particular apple will serve as a good desert for my lunch, but if, when biting into it, I find that worms by a kind of "biter's rights" have pre-empted my claim, then my belief has not led to satisfactory results and is therefore false.

These various philosophical solutions to the problems of the source of knowledge and the test for truth have been incorporated in the methods of modern science: observation, intelligent trial and error, controlled experimentation, statistical and sampling methods, etc. Modern science, like all good thinking, treats the various methods and tests as complementary, for in the formulation and testing of hypotheses, which is often described as *the* method of science, and which appears to be a synthesis of the scientific methods mentioned above, the scientist must rely not only on sense experience but, because of the absence of some relevant experience, upon authority, reason, and intuition as well. This can be illustrated by relating these more philosophical methods to the scientific method as described in terms of the steps in its application, the pattern of scientific investigation, which John Dewey described as steps in reflective thinking. The first four steps, the awareness of the problem, the observation of the facts relevant to the problem, the use of previous knowledge, and the organization of data, depend primarily on sense experience and less on reason and authority. The fifth step, the formulation of the hypothesis, appears to be mainly an intuitive function with some assistance from reason. The sixth step, the deduction of the implications of the hypothesis, is clearly a function of reason, and finally, the seventh step, the testing of the hypothesis, may make use of all of the traditional methods.

It is in the testing of the hypothesis that the various tests for truth are employed. Correspondence, coherence, and utility are all incorporated in the modern criteria for hypotheses: (1) testability, (2) compatibility with previously well-established hypotheses, (3) predictive or explanatory power, and (4) simplicity.

In short, not only do today's natural and social sciences have their origin in natural and moral philosophy, but the methods which these sciences employ are a synthesis of the findings of philosophers working in our third subdivision of philosophy, theory of knowledge, or epistemology.

The other philosophical subdivisions

Metaphysics, axiology, and epistemology are, then, the three basic areas of philosophical investigation; investigation relating to three different types of things: reality, values, and knowledge. But what about logic and the other traditional philosophical subdivisions like aesthetics, philosophy of history, philosophy of religion, and philosophy of science?

Logic. Concerning logic, I should like to argue that, except for the fact that logic has traditionally been taught by philosophers, there is no more reason for regarding it as a part of philosophy than there is for treating mathematics, history, or psychology as parts of philosophy. Logic was recognized, as was mathematics, very early in the history of knowledge to be a specific discipline. Unlike the other areas of philosophy, in logic there has been a gradual development of an acceptable body of knowledge. In this one area, philosophers have built upon the work of their predecessors.

The study of logic is the study of the methods and principles used in distinguishing correct from incorrect reasoning. It is usually divided into two major areas, according to the type of reasoning or argument studied: deductive, or formal, logic on the one hand, and inductive, or material, logic on the other. Deductive logic is in turn divided into traditional logic, which is mainly a study of Aristotelian syllogistic logic, and symbolic logic, which is a modern effort to avoid the ambiguities and inadequacies of ordinary language by the development of a logical language or calculus through the use of symbols. Deductive logic is concerned with arguments whose premises claim to provide proof for their conclusions, as in the following *syllogism*: No cats are dogs, and all collies are dogs, therefore no collies are cats. Inductive logic, in contrast, is an examination of the nature and problems of arguments whose premises claim to furnish not proof but some evidence of their conclusion, as in the following *argument by analogy*: Jones', Smith's, and Young's cars are all 1965 Fords of the same body weight and horsepower. Jones and Smith get about twenty miles to the gallon with their cars. Therefore, it is very probable that Young's car will also give good mileage.

Both of the arguments given as examples are good arguments. This is to say that the deductive argument is *valid* and the inductive argument has a high degree of probability. The first argument is valid because the conclusion necessarily follows from the premises. If the premises are true, the conclusion must be true. The argument has proper form or structure (algebraically expressed as $PM = O$, $SM = O$ ∴ $SP = O$), and any argument which has the same form, regardless of its content, will be valid. The deductive logician has developed several methods for testing arguments in terms of their form. The second argument, on the other hand, is not evaluated so much in terms of form as in terms of content, although specific criteria are applicable to arguments by analogy and other inductive arguments, for instance, the number of entities involved, the number of similarities and differences among the entities, and so on.

In addition to developing criteria for arguments of this sort, the inductive logician attempts, among other things, to determine the elements of scientific method and statistical inference, and to classify specific types of informal fallacies, for example, the various types of fallacies of relevance and ambiguity. The following is a good example of a fallacy of relevance of the type *argumentum ad hominem*, argument directed to the man: We can ignore what the teachers say about the importance of higher salaries for teachers, for as teachers they would naturally be in favor of increasing teachers' pay. The premise is *logically irrelevant,* but *seems* relevant, to the conclusion, hence the fallacy. An equally fallacious argument is the following example of the fallacy of ambiguity, which in this case arises through an equivocation of terms: Secretaries are long-legged African birds, Miss Jones is a secretary, therefore Miss Jones is a long-legged African bird. The shift in meaning with respect to "secretary" is obvious, but changes in meaning are frequently much more subtle, and must be guarded against.

The discipline of logic is indispensable for all sciences and philosophy, for both the scientist and the philosopher are dependent on clear and accurate reasoning. Just as there is, strictly speaking, no one scientific method by means of which scientists get scientific knowledge, so there is no one philosophical method by means of which philosophers get something called philosophical knowledge. As we have seen, philosophers differ in the extent to which they stress, and accept or reject, the methods of sense experience, reason, intuition, and authority. But philosophers, whether they emphasize the analysis of ideas or their synthesis, must, like scientists, try to be careful and accurate thinkers; hence logic is the basic discipline for the philosopher, as it should be for the scientist.

Other subdivisions. All the other traditional subdivisions of philosophy are attempts to relate metaphysics, axiology, and epistemology to specific subject matters or sciences, and there can be as many subdivisions as there are specific subject matters. In the catalogs of today's colleges and universities, courses are listed in the philosophy of history, art, science, religion, education, language, law, economics, politics, civilization, and morals, or ethics. But it also makes sense to talk of philosophies of society, man, mind, recreation, logic, mathematics, sex, and agriculture.

Obviously, in some of these areas attention will be given more to one basic type of problem than to another. For example, in aesthetics, ethics, and political philosophy the problem of value is central; in philosophy of science and philosophy of logic epistemological problems are basic. However, in philosophy of history and philosophy of religion metaphysical, axiological, and epistemological problems appear to be of equal importance.

Let us take philosophy of history as an example. Philosophy of history has two different aspects, speculative and critical. Speculative philosophy of history is mainly a metaphysical and axiological inquiry concerned with interpreting the meaning of history. Are ends achieved and values created? Are things getting better or worse? Is there some pattern, plot, or theme which we can perceive? Is there one causative factor or many at work? There are, of course, many theories. The general public is daily reminded of the clash between two of today's dominant philosophies: on the one hand, the Hebrew-Christian providential view, which sees history and civilization as controlled by a divine purpose; and on the other, the Communistic view of history, dialectical materialism, which emphasizes economic factors as central in determining human history.

Critical philosophy of history is primarily an epistemological inquiry dealing with problems relevant to historical knowledge. Is history a theoretical rather than merely descriptive study? Is history a science? What is the role of hypothesis in the historian's method? What is a historical fact? You will find some of these questions discussed in greater detail in Dr. Ralph Haskins' chapter on history elsewhere in this book.

It should also be pointed out that metaphysics, axiology, and epistemology are not unrelated, for there are, obviously, axiological and epistemological problems in metaphysics, metaphysical and epistemological problems in axiology, and metaphysical and axiological problems in epistemology.

The Continuing Disagreement Concerning the Nature of Philosophy

Having summarized various problems and divisions of philosophy briefly, we need to return to our earlier discussion concerning the conflicting conceptions of philosophy.

A major quarrel among philosophers today concerns the general worth of philosophy. On the one hand are those philosophers who belittle most of the traditional types of philosophy: logical empiricists and many linguistic analysts regard logic and perhaps philosophy of science as the only philosophical disciplines worthy of attention, and argue that metaphysical, axiological, and epistemological discussions regarding reality, value, and truth are a waste of time, mere quibbling over words, arguments about nonsense. Many of these philosophers adopt the position that there are only two kinds of meaningful statements: *empirical* statements like "It is snowing outside," and "Mary has on a red dress," which can be verified by sense experience; and *analytic* statements like "All spinsters are unmarried women," and "No circle is a square," whose truth or falsehood is established by an examination of the definitions of their terms. These critics argue that since traditional philosophical statements, for example, "The sensible world is unreal," "The universe is rational," and "God is good," are neither empirical nor analytic, they are nonsense. Such statements, they say, have no literal significance. Consequently, these philosophers believe that rather than learning philosophy, students should be taught *not* to philosophize, for most traditional types of philosophical inquiry are a kind of intellectual sickness resulting from linguistic confusions, hence rather than promote the discipline one should teach the nature and cure of the disease.[8] Most philosophy has arisen because of a failure to analyze correctly sentences like the ones above, and because of a failure to refrain from drawing conclusions which only *seem* to follow from them. Hence, of traditional philosophy, only logic is deserving of respect and ought to be taught in the schools, for training in logic should improve both the clarity and the consistency of the student's thinking and thus help him to avoid linguistic confusions and perhaps to develop an immunity to the disease of philosophy.

On the other hand are the defenders of traditional philosophy who accuse positivistic and analytic critics of a type of psychological projection; it is the critics who are in need of therapy; their nihilism is itself a kind of intellectual sickness. To be sure, says the spokesman for traditional philosophy, there have been mistakes in philosophy, and some can be traced to linguistic confusions, but only a sick mind would fail to see the great value of the more traditional types of philosophy. There are certain questions, religious, metaphysical, moral, and so on, which the sciences cannot answer, and which may never be adequately answered, but which are yet worth thinking about. No one science claims to give us the whole truth about anything, for the sciences furnish limited views. Philosophy alone tries to collect the findings of all the sciences, tie them together, and present a meaningful picture. Man as scientist, it is said, is but a fraction of man; only man as philosopher is a whole man.

Perhaps the fact of the quarrel itself is the best evidence of the vitality of philosophy.

Some Differences Between Philosophy and the Sciences

It should be obvious by now that if philosophy is a science, it is not a science in exactly the same sense as are the natural and social sciences. There are, undoubtedly, many differences between philosophy and these sciences. An examination of some of these differences should make the nature of philosophy clearer. In the first

---

[8] For a more detailed discussion of this controversy see John W. Davis, "Is Philosophy a Sickness or a Therapy?" *The Antioch Review*, Vol. 23, No. 1 (Spring), 1963.

place, whereas the sciences include bodies of knowledge whose content has been from the simple to the complex,[9] one scientist building upon the work of another, there has been no comparable growth in the history of philosophy. It is true that later philosophers have been influenced by earlier ones, but with a few exceptions instead of accepting the findings of earlier thinkers and building upon them, later philosophers have mostly reacted to them by suggesting a different perspective, a new solution, or even other problems.

This is not to say that no progress has been made in philosophy, for an examination of the history of philosophy will show that philosophers have succeeded in pointing out the inadequacies and mistakes of their colleagues. They have succeeded in revealing each other's fallacies, in uncovering elusive psychological confusions and semantic ambiguities. Philosophers do generally agree that certain theories are mistakes. For example, most philosophers agree in rejecting the epistemological theory that there are innate or inborn ideas, and in rejecting psychological hedonism, the theory that all desire is for pleasure and the avoidance of pain. There are many dead-ends and ancient fallacies which a knowledge of the history of philosophy will help the student to avoid. Hence today's student can profit from the mistakes of earlier philosophers.

Moreover, the great philosophical world views, the enduring metaphysical, ethical, and epistemological points of view, which have been hammered and tempered in the fire of philosophical criticism, do provide intellectually satisfying accounts of man's experience, and on occasion offer satisfactory moral guidance. This is the position which T. V. Smith, a well-known contemporary philosopher, developed regarding ethics:

> Any ethical doctrine (or religious, for that matter) which has stood the test of time, and has been seasoned by historic testing, is legitimate and, in general, is as good as any other. . . . They are all *equally* good, and all *very* good. Truth to tell, each great doctrine borrows from all others until nothing is left out of use. . . . No great system leaves out much, if anything, which any other system contains.[10]

[9] One might just as well say "from the complex to the simple," since the axioms of advanced science contain in germ the whole of the scientific systems which are descriptive of the complex phenomena of the natural world.

[10] T. V. Smith, *A Non-Existent Man, an Autobiography* (Austin: Univ. of Texas Press, 1962), p. 137.

In the second place, philosophy is not a systematized body of knowledge in the same sense that sciences like physics and chemistry, or even psychology and political science, are systematized bodies of knowledge. Philosophy today, except in the case of logic, as we have seen, is a more or less unorganized mixture of somewhat systematic reflections concerning problems which have not as yet, and may never have, an empirical solution. There are in philosophy many "systems" of thought—as there appear to be in some social sciences—but none of these has the degree of *systematization* that characterizes the texts of modern physics and other more exact natural sciences, although some of them "are more systematic than some sciences, e.g., Spinoza's *Ethics* in contrast to anthropology," [11] political science, and just about any social science. Moreover, as Robert S. Hartman points out,[12] these philosophical "systems" are unique and independent of each other—again, as they appear to be in some social sciences—for the knowledge of one philosopher's "system" does not essentially help us to understand another. We do not need to know Kant's system, for example, in order to understand that of Hegel. But in order to understand the texts of more exact natural science there is one absolutely indispensable system which we must know, namely, the system of mathematics, a superstructure overarching all the natural sciences.

This points to an important differences between the social and the natural sciences. The social sciences do not have the same scientific status as these older sciences, for they do not have the same high degree of systematization. Many social scientists believe that the best way to correct this deficiency is to make mathematics the formal frame of reference for the social sciences as it is for the natural. And it is true that mathematical methods are beginning to play a significant role in such areas as econometrics, psychometrics, and sociometrics, segments of economics, psychology, and sociology, respectively; but these areas, while growing, are still relatively small, and there are many large segments in these sciences which are not

[11] Comment on a previous draft of this essay by my friend and colleague Professor Merritt H. Moore, to whom I am greatly indebted for much helpful criticism and many valuable suggestions too numerous to mention.

[12] Robert S. Hartman, "The Logical Difference Between Philosophy and Science," *Philosophy and Phenomenological Research*, Vol. 23, No. 3 (March 1963), pp. 354–355.

yet, and may never be, amenable to fruitful mathematical analysis.[13] Because of this, some philosophers argue, as we have seen,[14] that the social sciences are primarily value sciences and that rather than depend on mathematics a new overarching superstructure based on a logic of value must be created for them.

In the third place, philosophical knowledge may not be knowledge in the same sense as scientific knowledge. Critics of philosophy are fond of pointing out that philosophical knowledge seems to "make no difference to anything or to anybody but the philosopher himself." The sole function of his philosophy, as Schiller expresses it, "seems to be to make the philosopher himself feel happy and superior to anybody who does not understand his philosophy enough to enter into it, that is, to everybody else in the world." [15] It is often said that the essence of a scientific statement is that it can be empirically tested either directly or indirectly. Thus scientific knowledge is knowledge about the world, descriptions about matters of fact, predictions, that can be tested in experience. But it is a matter of debate among philosophers as to whether philosophical statements are to be given this distinction. Some naturalists, John Dewey, for example, and others appear to believe that philosophical statements are to be tested just as scientific statements are, and, indeed, that philosophy is to be made scientific simply by using the methods of the natural sciences. Others disagree. Bertrand Russell, who is probably the most well-known philosopher alive today, says that philosophical statements must both "be applicable to everything that exists or may exist" and "be such as can be neither proved nor disproved by empirical evidence." [16] Hence, according to Russell, scientific philosophy is indistinguishable from logic.

Finally, in the fourth place, whenever philosophers have begun to deal with problems that could be empirically solved, and one thinker has built on the work of another, philosophers have begun to regard themselves as scientists and to regard their field of inquiry as distinct

[13] For an interesting discussion of recent developments, see S. S. Wilks, "Mathematics and the Social Sciences," in C. E. Boewe and R. F. Nichols, *op. cit.,* pp. 66–80.

[14] Cf. Hartman, page 250 in this chapter.

[15] F. C. S Schiller, *Humanism* (London: Macmillan, 1912), p. 351.

[16] Bertrand Russell, *Mysticism and Logic, and Other Essays* (London: Norton, 1917), pp. 110–111.

from philosophy. And this, as we have seen, describes the history of knowledge, for in the beginning no distinction was made between philosophy and science.

Are Elementary and Secondary Students Too Immature for Philosophy?

Before we examine specifically the role which philosophy may play in the social studies program, we should take cognizance of an objection to the teaching of philosophy in the elementary and secondary schools.

A few years ago the Committee on Philosophy in Education of the American Philosophical Association made a study of the teaching of philosophy in American high schools. The Committee's report contains much information that is relevant to our present inquiry. It was discovered, for example, that "courses in philosophy have been taught on the secondary-high school level for centuries. They form a recognized and required part of the curriculum in dozens of countries around the world." [17] In the light of this, it is surprising that in the United States philosophy is taught in only a few high schools, and there it is apt to be treated as an honors course with the enrollment limited to a few of the brighter students. The teaching of philosophy courses in the elementary schools is, of course, nonexistent, but here, as in many high schools, some of the teachers of other subjects introduce philosophical considerations into their respective subject matters.

The Committee found that those who oppose the teaching of philosophy in the high schools usually base their arguments on the intellectual immaturity of the pupils. "Boys and girls of fifteen, sixteen, and seventeen are intellectually too immature to understand and profit from the study of philosophy." And some opponents want to include eighteen- and nineteen-year-old college students as well, for in some colleges and universities freshmen and sophomores are discouraged from taking introductory courses in philosophy.

[17] "The Teaching of Philosophy in American High Schools," *Proceedings and Addresses of the American Philosophical Association,* 1958–1959, p. 92. See also Merritt H. Moore, "The Teaching of Philosophy in the United States," *The Teaching of Philosophy* (Paris: UNESCO, 1953), pp. 144–157.

This type of opposition has a long and respected history. Plato, for instance, argued that young men and women should not be taught philosophy until they have reached the age of thirty, for until then they are not mature enough to be aware of the seriousness of critically analyzing ideas. Young people, he said, merely play at philosophy. They argue for the fun of it, and they have no respect for the truth. They are like puppy-dogs who rejoice in pulling and tearing everything apart.

Now since there is this kind of opposition to the teaching of philosophy to young men and women, one can only imagine the critic's shock at the suggestion that philosophy be taught beginning in the elementary school.

The objection is based at least in part, it seems to me, on two confusions, one concerning the nature of intellectual immaturity and the other the maturity required for philosophy. Concerning the former, it should be pointed out that in one sense the child of age twelve may be intellectually mature, for with the exception of vocabulary there may be little additional growth on the part of his basic intelligence components. Consequently, except for difficulties arising out of vocabulary limitations, the child at twelve should have little more difficulty with philosophy than he will have at eighteen or twenty; indeed, in some cases he may even have less, for reasons which I shall give later.

Intellectual maturity and immaturity, as these terms are ordinarily used, are relative matters. Thus in comparison with a person who possesses the required background knowledge of American government and politics, the person who is completely lacking in such knowledge is intellectually immature for an advanced course in American constitutional law. He is intellectually immature in the sense that he is intellectually unprepared to take advanced work in political science. Again, some American parents are amazed to learn that in some schools boys and girls of eight and nine are taught to read and speak French or German. These parents may regard their own children of a similar age as too immature for such instruction; yet, strangely enough, they do not find it unusual that their children began speaking English—recognized by linguists to be a most difficult language—by the age of two.

Concerning the maturity required for philosophy, then, while pupils may not be ready for a serious, detailed presentation and just appraisal of elaborate philosophical systems, they may be ready for a more elementary critical analysis of basic philosophical problems. No one is suggesting that Kant's *Critique of Pure Reason* or Spinoza's *Ethics Demonstrated in the Geometric Manner* be required reading for fifth- or sixth-grade pupils, for works of this sort presuppose some acquaintance with other philosophical writings, and are difficult even for professional philosophers. But why should it be assumed that until a student is ready to cope with the most complex of philosophies he is not ready for any philosophy? No one makes this assumption concerning other areas of study. The student does not begin his study of history with European historiography or the diplomatic history of the United States, nor does he begin his study of psychology with a course in physiological psychology or advanced psychometrics.

It is sometimes argued that the learning process in philosophy is different from that in other disciplines. The pupils' learning in the sciences, for example, is said to be analogous to their learning to swim. They play along the shore in shallow water and are not permitted into deeper water until they have learned to swim. Their grade school days, then, are a playing along scientific shores, a getting used to scientific waters. In the high school they are given a chance to swim, but only in shallow waters, and not without the close supervision of the teacher. Only in college do the students ever really get the chance to venture into the deeper waters of any science and swim on their own. To be sure, some pupils never go beyond the getting used to the water, for they never succeed in swimming in the science; they never cease crawling along the bottom, and so they never get into the theoretical structure of science. Some, of course, get in over their heads and drown. Consequently, the teacher must be both life guard and swimming instructor. The pupils must be kept close to the shore, and on occasion rescued from deeper waters, until they have learned to swim.

Now the difference between science and philosophy, it is said, is that in learning philosophy there can be no playing in shallow waters. The student cannot wade gradually into deeper and deeper waters, for there is a sharp drop off at the water's edge. There is no getting used to the water here; when the pupil jumps in he is immediately over his head and must swim or drown. Very few high school students are mentally tall enough to have both their head above the water and their feet touching bottom, and to toss a grade school pupil into such water is almost surely to invite a drowning.

Therefore, some persons would have us erect signs around philosophy, signs reading "Danger, Deep Water," "Danger, Tricky Currents," or "Beware of the Undertow." Now it may be that all of these signs have their place, not only beside philosophy, but around scientific waters as well. However, the opponent of philosophy commits the logical fallacy of composition; he mistakenly attributes the characteristics of a part of philosophy to the whole. He sees only the deep end and overlooks the shallow end of the pool. I should like to argue that there can be a "kiddies' pool" in philosophy just as there is in other disciplines. There can be a getting used to abstractions, philosophical ideas and critical analysis; there is an important elementary training period here as in the sciences.

The Role of Philosophy in the
Social Studies Program

There is no reason why the beginning student must jump into philosophy by way of either a specific philosophical system or courses that have as prerequisites an advanced knowledge of both philosophy and some other subject matter. The proper place to begin is with the basic philosophical problems, and these can be treated on an elementary level. Moreover, they can be related to topics in ethics, religion, aesthetics, and the social sciences with which pupils are already familiar; for example, the difference between right and wrong, the meaning of freedom, the existence of God, the censorship of art, the source of human dignity, the role of authorities in a democratic society, and the difference between truth and falsehood.

Logic also can be introduced on every level. Even grade school pupils can be taught to distinguish between correct and incorrect patterns of deductive and inductive reasoning in the social studies as they do in mathematics and science education. They need to recognize the simpler types of formal and informal fallacies such as the syllogistic (formal) fallacies of the undistributed middle term, of drawing an affirmative conclusion from a negative premise, and of exclusive premises, and the informal fallacies of appeal to force, of argument from ignorance, of argument directed to the man, of appeal to pity, of appeal to the people, of false cause, of amphiboly, of accent, of division, and others that are discussed in the standard introductory texts to logic.

Perhaps a few examples will make it clear that an understanding of these fallacies is not beyond the grasp of young boys and girls. The following is an example of the fallacy of the undistributed middle term:

> All Communists are persons who criticize our present foreign policy.
> All demopublicans are persons who criticize our present foreign policy.
> Therefore, all demopublicans are Communists.

Notice that in both premises the term, "persons who criticize our foreign policy," which provides the link between "demopublicans" and "Communists," is undistributed in that in neither premise are we talking about *all* persons who criticize our present foreign policy. One might just as well argue that since all dogs are animals, and all cats are animals, then all dogs are cats. Both arguments have the same form. Obviously, the conclusion does not follow. Our next example is an instance of the fallacy of appeal to force:

> It should be obvious to you, Mrs. Brown, that it is your turn to stay after school today. I say that it is, and I am the principal. You want to stay on here next year don't you?

In this argument the conclusion is not proved by the premises, because the premises are logically irrelevant to the truth of the conclusion. But because of the threat of force the conclusion may be accepted. As in all fallacies of relevance, the argument gets its persuasiveness from the psychological, rather than logical, connection between the premises and the conclusion. Our final example illustrates the fallacy of division:

> Dogs have been hunters for thousands of years, so my dog Spot should really catch lots of rabbits.

Quite the contrary, Spot couldn't care less for rabbits. There is an ambiguity here; the properties of a class, dogs, have been identified with the properties of a member of the class, Spot, but the class may have characteristics which its members do not possess. As in all

266

fallacies of ambiguity, the force of the argument is dependent upon our inattention to subject matter, our carelessness.

The teacher will find that most elementary logic texts contain explanations and examples of each of the specific types of formal and informal fallacies.

That our schools will turn out full-fledged philosophers is not to be expected—nor will essays of this sort produce professional teachers of philosophy. The most that we can hope for is that the students will gain an awareness of and appreciation for philosophical problems and be more careful and accurate in their thinking, arguing, and decision-making.

It is a mistake to assume that philosophies and philosophical problems are found only in philosophy classes, for philosophies are not something given to students by teachers of philosophy. By the time the child has reached the sixth grade he has at least the beginning of a philosophical point of view, and by the time he has reached the senior year of high school or the freshman year of college what was earlier a flexible philosophical outlook has pretty well solidified into dogmatism. As a matter of fact, the average sixth grader is closer to being a true philosopher than is the college freshman,[18] for the sixth grader has a more open mind, his point of view has not crystallized; at least the crust is easier to break. Philosophies are things neither given to, nor forced upon, students by teachers of philosophy; they belong to the cultural inheritance of the student. Ideas concerning the good and the bad, the real and the unreal, the true and the false, the nature of man and God, are absorbed by the student long before he gets into his first philosophy course. The unfortunate thing is that by this time he may be unable to philosophize; his natural curiosity for diverse philosophical points of view has died as the dominant beliefs which he acquires from his society—and which that society tends to require of him—have become fixed. The task of the teacher is to make the pupil aware "that there really are many different, defensible answers to many

[18] Cf. Clifton Fadiman's statement in *The Instructor,* 66:42 (Jan.), 1957, p. 42: "I should like to set before you what may seem a crackpot notion. The notion is that the best place to teach philosophy is not the university but the elementary school; and that the ideal student of philosophy is the child from eight to twelve."

different, important, intelligible questions; that the world in which he lives is not a single, one-dimensional object, toward which one simple-minded, clear-cut and culturally ordained attitude alone is appropriate." [19] That this comes as a staggering discovery to many college students is a discredit to our elementary and secondary schools.

Strangely enough, such staggering experiences are sometimes given as a reason why courses in philosophy should not be taught even to college freshmen, let alone high school students. Not only are such students intellectually too immature for philosophy, says the opponent, they are apt to be emotionally immature as well. Philosophy courses do prove unsettling to some students, even to some graduate students, but this is because they have learned not to be philosophers; at an early age they ceased to philosophize, and so it comes as a shattering experience to them to learn that there are respectable answers in disagreement with theirs to problems which they have ceased to regard as problems. They need to be roused from their complacency. As Joseph Wood Krutch says, "Unless education to some extent maladjusts the educated man to life as it is lead [sic] it can neither improve anything nor even change anything." [20]

Rather than being a reason for postponing the teaching of philosophy, emotional immaturity should be a reason for introducing pupils to it early. The sixth grader will not be at all disturbed at finding that there are really many different, defensible points of view concerning the good, the true, and the real. He may, indeed, find the whole affair charming, but if he has to wait six or seven years, the discovery may have traumatic effect.

Apart from the influence of logic in helping the student to think clearly and correctly, the most important contribution that philosophy can make to the social studies program is to help the student to become aware, if not to appreciate, that there are diverse philosophical points of view on the nature of truth, freedom of will, the existence of universal moral laws, the nature of man, and so on. The role of the teacher is not to give the student a philosophy, but

[19] "The Teaching of Philosophy in American High Schools," *op. cit.*, p. 93.

[20] Joseph Wood Krutch, *More Lives Than One* (New York: William Sloane Associates, 1962), p. 340.

to keep him from developing a narrow philosophical provincialism, to keep his philosophical outlook flexible.

The normal child is not only curious but also, I think, inclined to dogmatism. His attitude is not to take the answers given to his questions as tentative and provisional but as absolute, ultimate, and final. For the very young child the mere fact that a statement has been made is enough to make it true, the mere fact that something is done is enough to make it right. And when such statements are made by those in authority, parents, ministers, and teachers, they are beyond question, beyond review, absolutely true. The student cannot help but feel uneasy and dissatisfied when he is later asked to mistrust "absolute truths" and to accept all explanations as hypotheses, as tentative solutions to problems.

I suggest that the teacher's role is to lead his pupils away from dogmatism to thoughtful open-mindedness. Dogmatism is a form of arrogance and pride, a vice, concerning knowledge claims. Thoughtful open-mindedness, on the other hand, is a healthy skepticism, a form of humility; it is modesty with respect to knowledge claims. Such an approach is not only Christian—since humility is a Christian virtue and pride a vice—but democratic as well, for the dogmatist is not likely to be tolerant and respectful concerning the beliefs of others, while the thoughtful skeptic in being humble cannot help but be tolerant and appreciative of the beliefs of others, even though he is not persuaded to accept and adopt them. Religiously, humility is the feeling one has when he sees his place in the Universe as a whole, only one of the many children of God. Politically, it is the feeling of the democrat who is aware that his voice and his demands are those of only one citizen among the many within the state. In contrast, the dogmatist is one who arrogantly asserts that he is first among the children of God and demands that his voice alone be heard within the state.

Thus with respect to its role in the school, philosophy may be defined as the attempt to introduce the virtue of humility into pupils whose normal curiosity tends to be smothered by the vice of dogmatism. And now a word of warning: when dogmatism has been destroyed, nihilism rather than open-mindedness may take its place. The student may foolishly conclude that it really does not matter what one believes: a person may be an idealist and believe that reality is of the nature of mind, or he may be a materialist and believe that reality is matter; he may be a hedonist and believe that good is pleasure, or he may be a logical empiricist and believe that all ethical judgments are mere expressions of emotion; he may be a pantheist and believe that all things are a part of God, or he may be an atheist and believe that there is no God; he may be a democrat and believe that human dignity is best achieved in the state wherein the people are given freedom to govern themselves, or he may be a totalitarian and believe that the state is supreme and that man's sole purpose is to serve the state. Some may feel that it really makes no difference which side one takes or whether he even takes a side, for there is no objective or real ground of truth and of moral principles. Thus the student may think that the reason he should tolerate other beliefs is that beliefs are not important enough to disagree with.

The point is that beliefs matter very much! Beliefs of others are to be tolerated not because they are unimportant but because they are important; and they are imporant because they may contain aspects of the truth. There may be infallible truths, but fallible human beings select them and interpret them; so we cannot be absolutely sure regarding any belief, although we can be more sure of some than of others. The teacher's task is to help the student explore the reasons for accepting various philosophical beliefs, to discover their hidden assumptions and implications for action, and to ascertain their compatibility with other beliefs that are accepted as true. Thus the teacher's task is two-fold, to help the student see that there may be good reasons for each of the diverse philosophical positions, but that this is *not* itself a good reason for refusing to take any position at all.

It is to be expected that pupils will accept the skeptical attitude with more grace than will many of their parents in discovering that their children have been led to develop it. Parents are notoriously dogmatic and are rather sensitive to "dangerous" doctrines and free thinking. Some demand the democratic right to deny their children the right to think for themselves! Because of this, some teachers will prefer to let sleeping dogs lie, and in this case, let sleeping pupils sleep; there will, however, be less growling from dogmatists and less danger of being bitten by them, if philosophical considerations are introduced on the elementary level rather than waiting for high school and college. The emotional immaturity of parents may not be challenged unless the child becomes emotionally disturbed, and this is less likely if the child is introduced to philosophy early.

The teacher's position is not an easy one. He has a duty not only to parents but also to his students and his state. As a teacher his first duty is to his student. He must assist in the growth of his pupil, and this is to say that he must help the pupil to become a free, responsible human being, to realize his dignity as a rational individual. And in a democracy this is precisely the teacher's duty to the state.

In a healthy, growing society differences of opinion are to be expected and even encouraged. In a democratic society it should be no disgrace that one's beliefs are in disagreement with those of his neighbor, but it should be a cause of alarm if such disagreement were discouraged. Controversy ought to be encouraged,[21] for our "social truths" are hammered out and continuously tested in controversy. In the conflict of open discussion our democratic ideals are given renewed life, and we as a people are strengthened through a renewed commitment to them. Without such free and open discussion our ideals become mere empty platitudes having no influence on our behavior either as individuals or as a people and may soon be forgotten.

If philosophy serves no other purpose than that it stimulates thoughtful controversy, this would be enough to warrant its inclusion in the social studies program, for in such controversy not only are ideas tested but the conditions are provided for the growth of young, curious minds. The basic test of any school is that the students should leave with as much curiosity as, and considerably less inclination toward dogmatic authoritarianism than, they began with, and philosophy should help the school to meet this test.

SUGGESTED READINGS

PHILOSOPHICAL DICTIONARIES, ENCYCLOPEDIAS, AND HISTORIES

BALDWIN, JAMES M., ed., *Dictionary of Philosophy and Psychology* (New York: Peter Smith, 1960).

[21] See Robert L. Brackenbury's "A Case for Controversy," in *The National Elementary Principal*, 42:14–19 (April), 1963.

Blau, Joseph L., *Men and Movements in American Philosophy* (Englewood Cliffs, N.J.: Prentice-Hall, 1952).

Hastings, James, ed., *Encyclopedia of Religion and Ethics,* 6 vols. and Index (New York: Charles Scribner's Sons, 1951).

Runes, Dagobert D., ed., *Dictionary of Philosophy* (New York: Philosophical Library, 1942; a later edition published by Littlefield, Adams, 1961).

Thilly, Frank and Ledger Wood, *A History of Philosophy,* 3d ed. (New York: Henry Holt & Co., 1957). A good history of Western philosophy—Greek, medieval, modern, and recent.

AESTHETICS

Jarrett, James L., *The Quest for Beauty* (Englewood Cliffs, N.J.: Prentice-Hall, 1957). A survey of the problems and theories of aesthetics with illustrative material drawn from all of the arts.

Rader, Melvin, *A Modern Book of Aesthetics* (New York: Henry Holt & Co., 1935). A good anthology.

Santayana, George, *The Sense of Beauty: Being the Outline of Aesthetic Theory* (New York: Dover Publications, 1955). One of the best books on aesthetics ever written.

AXIOLOGY AND ETHICS

Albert, Ethel M., and others, *Great Traditions in Ethics* (New York: American Book Co., 1953). A book of readings from the history of moral philosophy. Introductory and summary statements help the reader to interpret the selections.

Frankena, William K., *Ethics* (Englewood Cliffs, N.J.: Prentice-Hall, 1963). A brief, clear introduction to the problems and positions of moral philosophy with some philosophizing on the part of the author.

Hill, Thomas E., *Contemporary Ethical Theories* (New York: Macmillan, 1950). A comprehensive survey of axiological and ethical theories of the present century.

Garvin, Lucius, *A Modern Introduction to Ethics* (Boston: Houghton Mifflin, 1953). A popular textbook which deals with the theories of morality and many of the present-day problems of personal and social morality.

Toulmin, Stephen E., *An Examination of the Place of Reason in Ethics* (New York: Cambridge Univ. Press, 1950). An important paperback which is a good example of the more recent meta-ethical discussion found in British and American ethical theory.

EPISTEMOLOGY AND METAPHYSICS

Ayer, A. J., *Language, Truth and Logic,* 2d rev. ed. (London: Victor Gollancz, 1946). A good explanation of logical positivism by one of its most outstanding defenders.

CANFIELD, JOHN V. AND FRANKLIN H. DONNELL, JR., *Readings in the Theory of Knowledge* (New York: Appleton-Century-Crofts, 1964). A good anthology.

DEWEY, JOHN, *Reconstruction in Philosophy,* rev. ed (Boston: Beacon Press, 1948). The defects of traditional philosophy are pointed out from the point of view of Dewey's instrumentalism.

HARTSHORNE, CHARLES, *The Logic of Perfection and Other Essays in Neoclassical Metaphysics* (Lasalle, Ill.: Open Court Publishing Co., 1962). Excellent essays on the metaphysics of becoming or creativity by an outstanding contemporary metaphysician who believes that "Metaphysics is essentially a question of the logical structure of concepts."

HOCKING, WILLIAM E., *Types of Philosophy,* 3d ed. (New York: Charles Scribner's Sons, 1958). An introduction to epistemology and metaphysics written by one of America's most distinguished idealists.

KAUFMANN, WALTER, *Existentialism from Dostoevsky to Sartre* (New York: Meridian Books, 1956). An excellent selection of writings from authors who share the attitude and outlook that stress the predicament and existence of man.

INTRODUCTION TO PHILOSOPHY

HOSPERS, JOHN, *An Introduction to Philosophical Analysis* (Englewood Cliffs, N.J.: Prentice-Hall, 1953). An introductory text written from the point of view of linguistic analysis.

KAPLAN, ABRAHAM, *The New World of Philosophy* (New York: Random House, 1961). Good lectures introducing the general public to the contemporary world philosophies of both the East and the West.

TITUS, HAROLD H., *Living Issues in Philosophy,* 3d ed. (New York: American Book Co., 1959). A very popular text for the beginner who wants a comprehensive introduction to the problems and types of contemporary philosophy.

LOGIC AND PHILOSOPHY OF SCIENCE

COHEN, MORRIS R. AND ERNEST NAGEL, *An Introduction to Logic and Scientific Method* (New York: Harcourt, Brace & World, 1934). A very good general text on logic for the mature student.

CONANT, JAMES B., *On Understanding Science* (New York: Mentor Books, 1951). A lucid explanation of the nature of science.

COPI, IRVING M., *Introduction to Logic,* 2d ed. (New York: Macmillan, 1961). A popular, recent text designed for the beginner.

HULLFISH, HENRY GORDON AND PHILIP G. SMITH, *Reflective Thinking: The Method of Education* (New York: Dodd, Mead, 1961). Examples of logical processes applied to the teaching of topics in the schools.

WERKMEISTER, WILLIAM H., *A Philosophy of Science* (New York: Harper & Row, 1940). An outstanding introduction to philosophy of science and the philosophical implications of modern science.

PHILOSOPHY OF HISTORY AND PHILOSOPHY OF RELIGION

BRIGHTMAN, EDGAR S., *A Philosophy of Religion* (Englewood Cliffs, N.J.: Prentice-Hall, 1940). One of the best general introductions to philosophy of religion and written by an outstanding personal idealist.

BURTT, EDWIN A., *Types of Religious Philosophy,* rev. ed. (New York: Harper & Row, 1951). An excellent introduction to the major types of Western religious philosophy, but not an easy book for the beginner.

MOURANT, JOHN A., *Readings in the Philosophy of Religion* (New York: Thomas Y. Crowell, 1954). Selections from ancient and modern religious classics.

WALSH, W. H., *Philosophy of History* (New York: Harper Torchbooks, 1960). A clear exposition of the basic problems in the philosophy of history.

10 A review of new curriculum developments and projects

~~~~~~

John U. Michaelis
School of Education
University of California, Berkeley

THE PURPOSE OF THIS CHAPTER IS TO GIVE A BIBLIOGRAPHIC REVIEW of new curriculum developments in current social studies projects, guides, and textbooks. Examples are given of developments that illustrate ways in which the social studies are being grounded in the social sciences. In some instances, examples have been chosen from recently published textbooks, units of instruction, and courses of study. Attention is again called to the Appendix, which contains a summary of social science generalizations from a recently prepared framework for planning the social studies; this is an example of a new development that is typical of many new projects.

The presentation of new curriculum developments follows the same order as the preceding chapters, beginning with history. This plan was selected to show direct relationships between current developments and the different disciplines. In each section, specific reference is made to developments in elementary schools and secondary schools. Although an effort was made to identify all current projects in the social studies, undoubtedly there are some that have been overlooked.

275

History

History has been a mainstay of the social studies program down through the years. Local, state, and early American history have been included in the elementary grades in many school systems. American history and world history are the two most prevalent social studies courses in secondary schools.[1]   In line with recommendations of an influential committee report, many school systems provide instruction of American history in the middle, upper, and high school grades, thus assuring a minimum of three years of historical study centered on our country.[2]

Elementary schools

As recommended in Chapter 2, some schools include in the primary grades a study of the history of the community and surrounding area—township, county, and region.   Specific attention may be given to history of schools, transportation, communication, changes in housing, early settlers, Indian life, landmarks, local festivals, origins of special days, holidays, famous men and women, and related topics.[3] Units on state and national history, and content dealing with the history of Canada, Latin America, and Old World backgrounds of American history may be found in grades four through seven. Although little attention is given to firsthand experience in historical methods of inquiry, visits to landmarks and restorations, interviews of oldtimers, and the use of such sources as letters, diaries, and old newspapers are a part of the program in some classrooms.

Among the new developments in social studies projects are the

[1] For a detailed report, see: S. B. Anderson, and others, *Social Studies in Secondary Schools: A Survey of Courses and Practices* (Princeton, N.J.: Educational Testing Service, 1964).   Also see: Bertram A. Masia, *Profile of the Current Social Studies Curriculum in North Central Association Schools* (Chicago: North Central Association, 1963); W. D. Moreland, "Curriculum Trends in Social Studies," *Social Education*, 26:73–76 (February), 1962.

[2] Edgar B. Wesley (Director), *American History in the Schools* (New York: Macmillan, 1944).

[3] For a more complete listing, see: John Jarolimek, *Social Studies in Elementary Education* (New York: Macmillan, 1963), pp. 304–305; and Ralph C. Preston, *Teaching Social Studies in the Elementary Schools* (New York: Holt, Rinehart and Winston, 1958), pp. 113–114.

preparation of primary reading materials on famous people,[4] the study of American society in grades five through twelve,[5] the development of major social science concepts in grades five, eight, and eleven,[6] and the publication of a background paper on state and local history.[7] History is included with other social sciences in a comprehensive project that embraces kindergarten through grade fourteen and is focusing on key concepts, generalizations, and methods of inquiry.[8] Some recently published textbooks are including material contributed by historians and addressed directly to teachers.[9]

Secondary schools

There are several projects which deal with history as either a separate subject or a part of other courses in the program of instruction in secondary schools. In addition to those directed by McClendon, Price, and West, as noted previously, are three other projects supported by the Cooperative Research Branch of the United States Office of Education. Leppert is working with a group on three basic courses that will be a part of a five-year sequence on the structure of man's social order, the dynamic nature of societies, and the role of social change.[10] Working with teachers of able students, Fenton is preparing materials that will include key concepts and methods of inquiry from history and other disciplines.[11] Michaelis

[4] Greater Cleveland Social Science Program (Cleveland: Educational Research Council, 1964).

[5] Jonathon C. McClendon, *New Approaches to and Materials for a Sequential Curriculum on American Society for Grades Five to Twelve* (Evanston, Ill.: Department of Education, Northwestern Univ., 1963).

[6] Roy A. Price (Director), *Identification of Major Concepts from the Social Sciences* (Syracuse: Department of Education, Syracuse Univ., 1963).

[7] Philip D. Jordan, *The Nature and Practice of State and Local History* (New York: Macmillan, 1958).

[8] Edith West (Director), *Social Studies Curriculum Guides and Materials for Grades K-14* (Minneapolis: Department of Education, Univ. of Minnesota, 1963).

[9] For a good example, see: Paul Hanna, and others, *Beyond the Americas,* Teacher's ed. (Chicago: Scott, Foresman, 1964), pp. 17–19.

[10] Ella C. Leppert (Director), *The First Three Courses in a Sequential Social Studies Program for Secondary Schools* (Urbana, Ill.: Department of Education, Univ. of Illinois, 1963).

[11] Edwin Fenton (Director), *A High School Social Studies Program for Able Students* (Pittsburgh: Carnegie Institute of Technology, 1963).

is directing an Asian studies project in which guides and materials including historical material on Asian counties wll be prepared.[12]

A comprehensive project, The Social Studies and Humanities Project, will include history along with sociology, anthropology, and political science.[13] The position is taken that the foregoing disciplines deal with one topic—the behavior of men in society. Hence the program to be developed will be unitary in nature. Emphasis is to be given to the Western tradition with some reference to the non-Western tradition. In grades seven through nine the theme of "man in community" will be developed in relation to emergence of the Western world beginning in Greece (grade seven), the shift from subject to citizen in the seventeenth and eighteenth centuries (grade eight), and selected case studies of larger communities in modern society (grade nine). The program for senior high school is currently being outlined.

Two projects are giving direct attention to key concepts, use of original source materials, and processes of historical interpretation. Roswenc is chairman of a group which has prepared short booklets dealing with such concepts as conflict and consensus and liberty, power, presidential power, and status.[14] In each booklet, the selected concepts are defined; a main problem and related questions are presented; and original statements of such men as Randolph, Hamilton, and Madison are presented for critical study. After analyzing the statements in light of specific questions, students are asked to write a paper on a broad question designed to organize what they have learned from the source materials. A short list of additional sources is included at the end of each booklet. The second project dealing directly with methods of inquiry is directed by Halsey.[15] The purpose of this project is to prepare units in which historiography is stressed. Unit booklets for students contain primary

[12] John U. Michaelis (Director), *Preparation of Teaching Guides and Materials on Asian Countries for Use in Grades I–XII* (Berkeley: Department of Education, Univ. of California, 1964).

[13] Elting E. Morison (Chairman), *A Program of Curriculum Development in the Social Studies and the Humanities* (Cambridge: Massachusetts Institute of Technology).

[14] Edwin C. Roswenc (Chairman), *Basic Concepts in History and Social Science* (Amherst: Department of American Studies, Amherst College, 1962). Published booklets are available from D. C. Heath, Boston.

[15] Van R. Halsey (Director), *American History—A High School Course* (Amherst: Amherst College, 1962).

and secondary sources which are to be analyzed and interpreted in the light of critical questions.[16]

An increasing emphasis on the interpretation of original source materials is also evident in texts for students. For example, Fenton has compiled a collection of source readings and interpretations for use in world history.[17] After an introduction entitled "What Is History?" which is designed to help students understand the nature of history, a series of problems is presented. Each problem is preceded by placing it in a setting and by raising questions that students should keep in mind as they read the following source material. The problems range from "The Importance of the Neolithic Revolution" to "The United States in the World Community." Included among the sources are excerpts from the Code of Hammurabi, the Old Testament, and writings of Machiavelli, Marx, Beveridge, Commager, and other well-known individuals. Many of the methods of inquiry discussed in Chapter 2 are brought into play as the sources are analyzed in relation to selected issues, concepts, and problems.

Dealing with a variety of historical topics are the pamphlets prepared under the direction of the Service Center of the American Historical Association.[18] Ranging from *A Style of History for Beginners* and *State and Local History* to *American Intellectual History* and the *History of India,* around sixty pamphlets have been published. They are excellent sources of information on reference materials, diverse points of view, and historical interpretation.

Two volumes on world history have been produced under the leadership of Stavrianos, Director of the World History Project.[19] One volume is a basic textbook and the other is a book of readings in which a variety of source materials have been organized to supplement the textbook. The pattern of organization of areas selected for study in depth is illustrative of how one group has met the problem of defining a structure for studying culture regions. Each of seven

[16] Available from D. C. Heath, Boston.

[17] Edwin Fenton, 32 *Problems in World History* (Chicago: Scott, Foresman, 1964).

[18] Walter Rundell, Jr. (Director), Service Center for Teachers of History, American Historical Association, Washington, D.C. Pamphlets are available from Macmillan, New York.

[19] L. S. Stavrianos, and others, *A Global History of Man,* and *Readings in World History* (Boston: Allyn and Bacon, 1962).

major culture regions is presented under the four main headings of basic facts, politics, economics, and culture. The following example illustrates the main points considered under each heading:

THE UNITED STATES

Basic Facts: "A Wide, Untried Domain Awaits"
> *Geography:* area and importance; physical features; natural divisions; Appalachian region; agricultural interior; mountainous West; influence of mountains; rivers; resources
> *People:* race and religion; growth; mobility
> *Historical Periods:* 1607–1815; 1815–1890; 1890-present; establishing a national identity; involvement and leadership

Politics: "From Consent of the Governed"
> *Present State:* the essential balance; the role of the voter; pressure groups; conflict and compromise
> *Historical Origins:* new challenge; new response; the Revolution; the Constitution; more direct participation; "little" government, "big" problems; government's growing scope; the progressive movement; rejecting crank or radical solutions; the government grows; New Deal; World War II; the limits on bigness; world impact (effects on other countries, appeal of American democracy)

Economics: "Nothing Succeeds Like Success"
> *Present State:* freedom with limits; more money for more people
> *Historical Origins:* regional differences; English response; economic restrictions; results of the Revolution; the Constitution; to regulate or not to regulate; the boom begins; it grows too fast; foreign trade; the "spend-more" theory; Great Depression; remedies; the war boom; result: optimism; mass production; American loans; lend-lease programs; aid programs; Soviet challenge

Culture: "Something for Everyone"
> *Present State:* cultural fusion; the arts; education; the uses of science; religion
> *Historical Origins:* the wilderness; industrialization; reform; art and inventions; the widening middle class
> *Global Impact:* Benjamin Franklin; a cultural desert; flood tide of influence; the dilemma of mass culture

Two volumes addressed to the question of what should be included in the secondary social studies programs contain chapters which deal specially with history.[20] In each volume historians and area studies specialists have outlined themes, main ideas, and specific

[20] *High School Social Studies Perspectives* (Boston: Houghton Mifflin, 1962); and *The Social Studies and the Social Sciences* (New York: Harcourt, Brace & World, 1962).

information that they believe to be of greatest importance in American history, Western civilization, world history, and selected area studies. A third volume addressed to the question of what should be included in the curriculum in the schools contains a brief statement on history.[21] The related chapters in these three volumes should be compared with those contained in this book.

Geography

Geography, like history, has been a mainstay of the social studies program. However, primary attention is given to geography in elementary schools rather than in secondary schools. For example, the program of instruction in elementary schools includes geography in all grades with a heavy emphasis in grades four through seven. In contrast, although a course in world geography is offered in over half of the secondary schools,[22] only a small proportion of students elect it.

Elementary schools

Although no projects deal exclusively with geography in elementary schools, several of them include geography along with other disciplines,[23] and one deals with geography in both elementary and secondary schools.[24] The emphasis in these projects is on the identification of key concepts and generalizations with some attention to methods of inquiry.

The report issued by the National Council for Geographic Education deals with geography in all grades, stresses the unity of physical and cultural geography, and suggests nine basic concepts that should be incorporated in the structure of the program: globalism, the round earth on flat paper, the life-layer, areal distinctions,

---

[21] *The Scholars Look at the Schools.* A Report of the Disciplines Seminar. NEA Project on Instruction (Washington, D.C.: National Education Association, 1962), pp. 38–40.

[22] Anderson, *op. cit.*

[23] For example, see those cited in footnotes 4, 5, 6, 8, 12.

[24] Wilhelmina Hill, ed., *Curriculum Guide for Geographic Education* (Normal, Ill.: National Council for Geographic Education, Illinois State Normal Univ., 1963). (Paperback ed., 1964.)

differences and likenesses, the region (and regionalizing) resources culturally defined, man the chooser, spatial interaction, and perpetual transformation.[25]   The discussion of these nine key concepts is one way of viewing structure in the curriculum; it should be compared with the statement of generalizations in the Appendix and with the discussion of concepts and generalizations presented in Chapter 3.

Instead of recommending a single sequence, the NCGE Committee recommended two or more sequences for each grade so that schools would have an opportunity to make choices among them.[26] The sequences in the primary grade go beyond the immediate environment to include the home and away, the local neighborhood, and different communities and their environments.   The sequences for grades four through eight range from the hot-wet land type studies and state studies to studies of the Eastern Hemisphere and topical studies of the United States.   Globe and map concepts are a part of the sequence at all levels and special emphasis is given to the development of geography skills and techniques.   Included in the skills are those involved in field studies, interpreting pictures and photographs, making and interpreting maps and globes, identifying specimens and constructing scenes, using atlases, and geography report writing. The many concrete suggestions for developing skills [27] should prove helpful in acquainting pupils with the methods of inquiry used by geographers, as suggested in Chapter 3.

Recently published textbooks and courses of study reflect an increasing emphasis on key concepts, generalizations, and methods of inquiry.   In a statement addressed to teachers, for example, Kohn suggests a model for studying cultural areas in terms of the distribution and interrelation of natural features, population, human activities, and elements fostering changes in human activities.[28]   The Illinois social studies guide outlines concepts and generalizations for the primary and intermediate grades; these may be used as tools of inquiry.

Secondary schools

The NCGE report suggests several possible sequences for each grade in secondary schools, recommending that a minimum of one year of

[25] *Ibid.*, pp. 14–22.
[26] *Ibid.*, pp. 32–42.
[27] *Ibid.*, pp. 51–71.
[28] In Hanna, *op. cit.*, p. 16.

geography be required of all secondary students.[29] The required course should develop "increased power with geography tools and habits of research," [30] a recommendation in keeping with the current trend to stress methods of inquiry. The suggested sequences include economic or commercial geography, historical geography, world cultures, political geography, and geography of current world problems.

The High School Geography Project has been set up under the auspices of the Association of American Geographers and the National Council for Geographic Education to develop one or more high school courses.[31] In their first report, attention is given to problem solving, illustrative classroom experiences, a unit in physical geography, a regional approach, and the structure of geography.[32]

Geography is being given attention in the projects sponsored by the U.S. Office of Education.[33] Whether or not separate courses or units will be developed is not clear at this time. However, the proposals for various projects do include activities aimed at identifying concepts, generalizations, and methods of inquiry that can be incorporated in the instructional program.

Specific recommendations for geography instruction in secondary schools are included in *The Social Studies and the Social Sciences*,[34] and in *High School Social Studies Perspectives*.[35] In the first of these, James outlines objectives, concepts, the use of the culture concept in geography, and major culture regions which he believes should constitute the basic structure of the program. In the second volume, Cressey stresses the importance of techniques such as cartography, an understanding of physical and cultural phenomena, and detailed familarity with one region as essential backgrounds for teachers. Believing that regional geography is the "climax of the field," Cressey discusses the importance of population distribution,

[29] *Op. cit.*, p. 44.

[30] *Ibid.*, p. 45.

[31] Gilbert White (Chairman), High School Geography Project, Joint Committee of the Association of American Geographers and the National Council for Geographic Education, 1785 Massachusetts Ave., Washington, D.C.

[32] Clyde Kohn, ed., *Selected Classroom Experiences: High School Geography Project* (Normal, Ill.: National Council for Geographic Education, Illinois State Normal Univ., 1964).

[33] Cited in footnotes 5, 6, 8, 10, 11, 12.

[34] *Op. cit.*, pp. 42–87.

[35] *Op. cit.*, pp. 81–87.

patterns of land use, and location of mineral resources as three key elements in the structure of regional studies.[36]   Listed as important techniques of inquiry are mapping, interpretation of photographs, statistical analysis, field observation and survey, and analysis of documents.[37]

Economics

There appear to be more curriculum activity and more funds for projects in economic education than in any other area of the social studies.   There are projects and activities at all grade levels in which efforts are being made to incorporate economic concepts in the social studies program and to develop units of instruction which focus directly on economics as an area of study.   A variety of teaching units, source materials, outlines of economic concepts classified by grade levels, and other curriculum materials are available from the Joint Council on Economic Education, which has set up centers of economic education throughout the country.[38]

Elementary schools

Of the many projects and activities underway, two have been selected to illustrate how the structure of economics may be defined for the purposes of curriculum planning.   In the program instituted at Elkhart, Indiana, Senesh defined structure in terms of "fundamental idea relationships of economics" including the following key concepts:

1. The conflict between unlimited wants and limited resources.
2. The division of labor that has resulted in attempting to lessen the gap between wants and resources.
3. The increasing interdependence resulting from division of labor and leading to the necessity for trading.
4. The development of monetary systems and methods of transportation to facilitate trading.
5. The development of methods for deciding what to produce, how

---

[36] *Op. cit.*, p. 85.
[37] *Op. cit.*, pp. 82–83.
[38] Checklists of materials and newsletters may be obtained from the Joint Council on Economic Education, 2 West 46th Street, New York 36, N.Y.

much to produce, how to produce, and who will receive what is produced.

6. The development of the market as a means of bringing producers and consumers together, resulting in decisions as to what and how much to produce.

7. The modification of the market by the government to promote economic growth, stability, security, freedom, and justice.[39]

These relationships should be kept in mind by teachers as they develop principles and concepts through directed activities in which children deal with economic situations meaningful to them. In the materials for grade one, for example, specific concepts such as producers and consumers, goods and services, tools and machines, buying and saving, and dividing the work are developed in the context of stories and activities. Children put the concepts to use in analyzing and discussing how families decide what to buy in terms of what they have, how division of labor is used to produce clothing and other goods more efficiently, what is needed to start a business, what happens when people do (and do not) buy all that is produced, and similar economic situations. The art of making choices is stressed and children are guided to consider reasons for choices, various alternatives, and the consequences of different alternatives.

The second project selected to illustrate structure in curriculum planning is built on economic relationships that include the following concepts and principles related to processes of consumption and production:

1. The problem of scarcity: unlimited wants in relation to limited resources make it necessary to decide how productive resources will be used.

2. How Americans deal with the problem of scarcity: people work to obtain and produce goods and services; money received for work is used for buying and saving; what is produced is based largely on consumer preferences; efficient production results from an effective combination of labor, materials, and equipment.

3. The market: the interaction of consumers who buy goods and services with producers who supply goods and services results in the setting of prices; money is exchanged for goods and services.[40]

[39] Adapted from Lawrence Senesh, *Our Working World.* A Resource Unit on Families at Work (Chicago: Science Research Associates, 1963), pp. 2–4.

[40] Adapted from: Robert Lee (Director), *Elementary School Economics,* Part I (Units One–Six) (Chicago: Industrial Relations Center, Univ. of Chicago, 1961), p. 8.

In six units for use in grades four and five detailed attention is given to the development of an understanding of how Americans obtain goods and services. The first unit deals with the problem of scarcity, how all nations face the problem in making choices as to what and how to produce, and how scarcity affects families. The second unit deals with wants, the priority of human wants, why all wants cannot be satisfied, and why families must make choices. Units three through five are centered on the second aspect of structure noted above (how Americans deal with the problem of scarcity) in the following order: relationships among wants, work, and money; evolution of our exchange system, and functions of money; the importance of consumer choices, and why people save money. The sixth unit summarizes relationships among wants, work, money, and consumption and savings.

In each unit care is taken to develop the meaning of economic terms so that pupils will use them with precision in formulating key ideas and principles. For example, work is defined as the "use of physical and mental energy to produce goods and services." The difference between goods and services is clarified and producers of goods and services are identified. The meaning of *division of labor* is developed in the context of work at home, in school, in adult activities, and in the production of both goods and services. Tests, review exercises, matching games, and other activities are provided to evaluate children's understanding of key concepts.[41]

Certain key assumptions underlie this program and other programs of economic education in the elementary school. The first is that children have adequate backgrounds of experience to deal with economic concepts. The second is that there will be progressive growth in understanding throughout the grades. The third is that instruction in economics will strengthen learning in other areas of the social studies.[42]

A major three-year project that will encompass thirty school systems, with three serving as model systems, has been instituted by the Joint Council on Economic Education.[43] Resources will be

[41] Jeremiah German, and others, *How Americans Obtain Goods and Services* (Chicago: Industrial Relations Center, Univ. of Chicago, 1961).

[42] Robert Lee, *op. cit.*

[43] M. L. Frankel (Director), Joint Council on Economic Education, New York.

focused on curriculum development, teacher education, and study materials in elementary and secondary schools.

Secondary schools

There has been an increase in interest in the teaching of economics in secondary schools and an increase in the offering of courses in economics.[44] Many projects have been launched, and diversified materials have been produced for both teachers and students.

A key report addressed to school personnel has been prepared by a task force composed of five economists and two secondary school educators.[45] A highlight of their report is the recommendation that a rational way of thinking about economic problems replace emotional and unreasoned judgments. In the four stages proposed by the task force we have a model for considering methods of inquiry in economic analysis. The four stages are: [46]

1. Define the problem, considering facts, issues, and "where we are in relation to where we want to go."
2. Clarify goals and order them in rough priority.
3. Consider alternative means of achieving goals.
4. Analyze consequences of various alternatives, choosing the "best" in terms of achieving the most important goals.

In order to apply these four stages to the analysis of an economic problem, students must have a grasp of key concepts, data, and principles from economics. In other words, as noted in preceding chapters, techniques of inquiry become useful when the inquirer has the conceptual backgrounds essential to an understanding of the domain of study.

In dealing with substantive portions of economics, the task force

[44] Anderson, *op. cit.*, p. 12.

[45] National Task Force on Economic Education, *Economic Education in the Schools* (New York: Committee on Economic Development, 1961). (Available from the Joint Council on Economic Education, 2 West 46 Street, New York 36, N.Y.)

[46] *Ibid.*, p. 15. For good examples of economic analysis and applications of economic concepts in units and courses grades one through twelve, see: M. L. Frankel, ed., *Teachers Guide to Developmental Economic Education Program, Part Two, Suggestions for Grade Placement and Development of Economic Ideas and Concepts* (New York: Joint Council on Economic Education, 1964).

outlined the content needed to understand the economy under the following headings:

1. Essential analysis, facts, and institutions.
2. How the economic system uses productive resources in satisfying competing wants.
3. Economic growth and stability.
4. The distribution of income.
5. Communism, socialism, capitalism.[47]

The report has been used extensively in curriculum revision and has influenced textbook writers.[48]

Helpful in extending economic understanding and giving insights into methods of inquiry are the 162 references listed in reports of the Materials Evaluation Committee of the Committee for Economic Development.[49] Pamphlets, leaflets, monographs, and other items which can be used to enrich textbooks and units of study are annotated and listed under headings that indicate major topics with which they deal.

Illustrative of the many booklets available on economic topics are those produced in a project sponsored by the Council for the Advancement of Secondary Education.[50] Major topics treated in the booklets are capitalism, other economic systems, money and banking, and business enterprise. A fifth booklet consists of a collection of readings on economics.

One project has been set up to plan a course in economics and to prepare related materials.[51] The course is to be a model of a grade nine through twelve sequence that is based exclusively on separate disciplines as follows: economics in grade nine, history in

[47] Ibid., pp. 22–60. For a good elaboration of the concepts, see: James D. Calderwood, Teachers Guide to Developmental Economic Education Program, Part One, Economic Ideas and Concepts (New York: Joint Council on Economic Education, 1964).

[48] For example, see: Stanley P. Wronski, and others, Modern Economics (Boston: Allyn and Bacon, 1964).

[49] Study Materials for Economic Education in the Schools. Reports of Materials Evaluation Committees, Supplementary Paper No. 12, Committee for Economic Development (New York: Joint Council on Economic Education, 1963).

[50] Galen Jones (Director), Economic Literacy Series (Washington, D.C.: Council for the Advancement of Secondary Education, 1961). (Booklets are available from McGraw-Hill.)

[51] Edward J. Furst (Director), Development of Economic Curricular Materials for Secondary Schools (Columbus: Ohio State Univ., 1963).

ten, psychology and sociology in eleven (one term each), and geography and political science in twelve (one term each). The rationale is that economic problems underlie contemporary problems, human behavior must be understood by students, and central issues are political. Hence, the sequence begins with economics and ends with political science.

Political Science

Although no major projects dealing exclusively with political science have been instituted, many current projects are giving attention to the place of political science in the social studies.[52] In addition, political scientists have made proposals regarding instruction in both elementary and secondary schools.

Elementary schools

A strong plea has been made for basic instruction in government and politics in the elementary school.[53] The plea is based on a study of political socialization which revealed that children develop some political understandings and attitudes early in their lives. Yet central concepts such as politics, politicians, parties, and pressure groups are grasped by only a few children below grade six, there is over-idealization of certain political figures, and there is a lack of awareness of power relationships among varied interests and groups.[54]

In a statement addressed to teachers in a recently published textbook for children, a professor of political science has outlined fundamental concepts and ideas that well may be included in elementary social studies.[55] Among the basic concepts are the nature of political power, the ethical basis of political power, the structure and process of government (including bureaucracy, parliamentary

---

[52] See references cited in footnotes, 4, 5, 6, 8, 10, 11, 12, and 13. Also see: Henry Toy, *Civic Education Project* (New York: American Heritage Foundation, 1964).

[53] David Easton, "Political Science," in *The Scholars Look at the Schools* (Washington, D.C.: National Education Association, 1962), pp. 41–44.

[54] David Easton and Robert D. Hess, "The Child's Political World," *Midwest Journal of Political Science,* 6:229–246 (August), 1962.

[55] In Hanna, and others, *op. cit.,* pp. 31–34.

systems, unitary and federal systems, and party systems), and scope of political power. This statement illustrates ways in which many of the concepts and ideas presented in Chapter 4 can be developed in elementary schools.

Secondary schools

The essays on political science in *The Social Studies and the Social Sciences*[56] and in *High School Social Studies Perspectives*[57] contain a variety of helpful suggestions, recommendations, and points of view on topics that range from major objectives to techniques of inquiry. In the first volume, specific contributions of political science are discussed in terms of critical understandings, appreciations, skills, and the application of philosophical and scientific analysis to the process of politics. Specific suggestions are made in regard to ways in which the methods and perspectives of political science can be applied to the interpretation of history. In the second volume, the creation of citizens is rejected as an objective, and insightful points are made about the "molding of citizens" and requirements for "citizenship in a democracy." Branches of political science are outlined and approaches and methods of study are discussed: historical, analytical, prescriptive, descriptive-taxonomic, and political behavior. It is recommended that high school teachers use case studies to illustrate subject matter, modes of inquiry, and the nature of research findings.

An example of structure based on twenty-four main ideas or generalizations drawn from political science and history is contained in a teaching guide designed for use in grade eight.[58] Seven of the main ideas were formulated and used as foci for the organization of content, learning activities, and instructional materials in a unit on "The Structure and Functions of United States Government":

Written in a spirit of compromise, the Constitution provided a basis for a republican form of government, with a large measure of popular control, limited government, and separation of powers.
The Constitution provided for flexibility to meet changing conditions.
The Bill of Rights provided essential guarantees of freedom.

[56] *Op. cit.*, pp. 88–105.
[57] *Op. cit.*, pp. 99–126.
[58] Alameda County School Department, *Social Studies, Grade Eight.* (Hayward, Calif.: County Superintendent of Schools, 1964).

Differing political views resulted in the emergence of organized political parties.

The national government provides services which are essential to the public interest.

State and local governments provide parallel, not duplicate, services which are essential to the public interest.

Practical instructional materials have been produced in projects sponsored by The Lincoln Filene Center for Citizenship and Public Affairs at Tufts University. A resource unit on "Ideology and World Affairs" outlines key understandings, learning experiences, key terms, and instructional resources for fifteen topics related to democracy, Communism, foreign policy, totalitarianism, authoritarianism, and future prospects.[59] A guide to *Practical Political Action* is designed to equip students for active participation in the grass-roots political process.[60]

One project has been set up to prepare a set of materials for teaching political science in high schools. A textbook, *Problems and Promise in American Politics,* has been produced, and a book of readings is being prepared.[61]

The American Political Science Association has sponsored a variety of activities related to the teaching of government in high schools during the past sixty years,[62] but it is not currently involved in a major curriculum development project.

Anthropology

Anthropology has had a minor place in the social studies during the past, but there is increasing recognition of its importance in the social studies in particular and to education in general.[63] In the

[59] Earl Latham and George Goodwin, Jr., *Ideology and World Affairs* (Medford, Mass.: The Lincoln Filene Center for Citizenship and Public Affairs, Tufts University, 1963).

[60] Franklin Patterson, ed., *Practical Political Action* (Boston: Houghton Mifflin, 1962).

[61] Donald H. Riddle (Director), Secondary School Project, Eagleton Institute of Politics, Rutgers Univ., Douglass College, New Brunswick, N.J. (Available from McGraw-Hill.)

[62] Cora Prifold, *A History of the American Political Science Association's Activities in the Field of Secondary Education in Government 1906–1962* (Washington, D.C.: The Association, 1962).

[63] George Spindler, ed., *Education and Culture* (New York: Holt, Rinehart and Winston, 1963).

elementary schools, attention has been given to content drawn from anthropology in units of study dealing with American Indians, Eskimos, life in the Congo, prehistoric peoples, and other groups. A few high schools have offered a course in anthropology, and anthropological content has been included in world history and sociology courses.[64]   Recently, there has been an upsurge of interest that is reflected in three current projects.

Elementary schools

The elementary school portion of The Social Studies and Humanities Project is based primarily on anthropology.[65]   Anthropologists are doing field work to prepare film ethnologies and other resources which will be used in the following sequence: I—The Netsilik Eskimo, II—Aborigines and Bushmen, III—Evolution, IV—The Origins of Husbandry, V—The Origins of Urban Life, VI—The Origins of the Western Tradition.[66]   Pupils will be given opportunities to develop understandings of the methods of inquiry used by archaeologists and cultural anthropologists as well as to develop key concepts and generalizations.   Units of study are now being tried out in the schools.

A project focused exclusively on the elementary school (grades one through seven) has been initiated to prepare "instructional materials logically organized according to the discipline of anthropology." [67]   Curriculum materials will be prepared and used by two groups of cooperating teachers.   One group of teachers will receive systematic instruction in anthropology.   Suitability of materials for general use will be checked by comparing the achievement of pupils being taught by the "trained" and "untrained" teachers.

Illustrative of how anthropological material is being incorporated in some social studies programs is an introductory unit on Hispanic

[64] Harold Hofenbacher, *Putting Concepts from Anthropology into the Secondary School Program* (Dearborn, Mich.: Dearborn Public Schools, 1954); Robert L. Schell, *Cultural Anthropology* (Abington, Pa.: Abington High School, 1962). Jack L. Ellison, *Syllabus for the First Semester of Twelfth Grade Social Studies* (Chicago: Francis Parker School, 1961); and W. J. Pickett, Jr., *A One Semester Course in the Humanities* (Flagstaff: Flagstaff High School, 1963).

[65] *Op. cit.*

[66] *ESI Quarterly Report* (fall–winter), 1963, pp. 22–23.

[67] Wilfrid C. Bailey and Marion J. Rice, *Development of a Sequential Curriculum in Anthropology for Grades 1–7* (Athens: Univ. of Georgia, 1964).

America for use in grade six.[68]   The unit is centered on Muquiyauyo, a village in the highlands of Peru. Methods of inquiry used by cultural anthropologists are studied in detail and put to actual use by the pupils in making observations in different classrooms. Ethnographic materials on Muquiyauyo have been compiled in a booklet that accompanies the unit.[69]

A stimulating essay containing key concepts from anthropology and comments on their significance in the study of other peoples is in the teacher's edition of a recently published textbook for children. [70] Attention is given to races of mankind, migration and adjustment, the value of racial differences, cultural adaptation, and adjustment by education.

Secondary schools

In addition to the comprehensive projects which are including anthropology along with other social sciences as a basis for curriculum planning,[71] and the essays that deal with anthropology in secondary schools,[72] there is one project that is focusing exclusively on anthropology in secondary schools.[73]   Two primary purposes of the Anthropology Curriculum Study Project are to identify significant knowledge within anthropology and to develop practical ways of introducing this knowledge into high school instruction.[74]   Two sets of material have been prepared for experimental use in high schools. The first, entitled *The Emergence of Civilization,* is not a study of civilizations per se.   Rather, the emphasis is on the process of culture change which resulted in "the dramatic crossing of a cultural threshold" in Mesopotamia, Egypt, India, China, Middle America, and South America.[75]   Theories of the emergence of civilization are in-

[68] Palo Alto Unified School District, *Hispanic America,* Part I: With a Beginning Emphasis on an Anthropological Study of a Small Community in Peru (Palo Alto, Calif.: The District, 1962).

[69] Palo Alto Unified School District, *Muquiyauyo* (Palo Alto, Calif.: The District, 1962).

[70] In Hanna, *op. cit.*

[71] Cited in footnotes 4, 5, 6, 8, 10, 11, 12.

[72] *The Social Studies and the Social Sciences, op. cit.,* pp. 136–155; and *High School Social Studies Perspectives, op. cit.,* pp. 29–51.

[73] Malcolm Collier (Director), Anthropology Curriculum Study Project, Univ. of Chicago.

[74] *Anthropology Curriculum Study Project,* a brief report (fall), 1963.

[75] Jack Ellison, *The Emergence of Civilization* (Chicago: Anthropology Curriculum Study Project, Univ. of Chicago, 1963).

troduced and followed by case studies which students use to test the theories. *The Idea of Liberty in American Culture* is a teaching unit that brings together readings from different disciplines and suggests how analytic concepts may be used to analyze and interpret source readings.[76]   A primary purpose is to demonstrate that students can study their own culture in a scholarly way without losing faith in it or becoming cynical.   These two units are designed to be used in existing courses—world history, and American history or government. Other materials now in preparation will treat such topics as early man and capacity for culture, language and culture, background to slavery, methods of studying society and culture, three cultures in New York, American Indians and European colonization, and the peopling of the New World.   Four area studies are being prepared: African Life-Ways, Indian Civilization, Middle Eastern Peoples, and Latin American Communities.

Two recently published volumes on anthropology in colleges and universities should prove to be helpful to those interested in planning high school courses.[77]

Sociology

Sociology is a part of the social studies in many ways.   History and geography units and textbooks are replete with the sociologist's terminology and descriptions of social processes and institutions.[78] Some programs of instruction emphasize basic human activities similar to those outlined by a sociologist: meeting needs for food, shelter, and clothing the family as a social group; socialization through group life and education; producing and distributing goods and services; social control through informal and formal means; religions, ethics, and the arts.[79]   Although no major projects are dealing exclusively with

[76] Robert Hanvey, *The Idea of Liberty in American Culture* (Chicago: Anthropology Curriculum Study Project, Univ. of Chicago, 1964).

[77] D. G. Mandelbaum, and others, *The Teaching of Anthropology* and *Resources for Teaching Anthropology* (Berkeley: Univ. of California Press, 1963).

[78] For example, see: John Palmer, "History Textbooks and Social Change," *Social Education*, 25:135–136 (March), 1961.

[79] Gresham M. Sykes, "Sociology," in *The Scholars Look at the Schools, op. cit.*, pp. 30–31.

sociology, many of those cited earlier are including sociology as a foundation discipline along with other social sciences.[80]

Elementary schools

The program advocated by Hanna incorporates content from the social sciences and organizes it around such basic human activities as transportation, communication, education, production and distribution, recreation, government, and esthetic expression.[81] The sequence is defined in terms of expanding communities of men, beginning with the family and school and moving outward to the world community. Both the scope and sequence reveal a strong linkage to sociology even though the program draws the bulk of its content from other social sciences.

Direct use has been made of concepts and strategies from sociology in a study based on a structural approach to curriculum development.[82] Four concepts (norms, sanctions, values, and roles) were selected, introduced to children, and put to use in finding examples of behavior related to each concept. Guiding questions were used to help children find observable forms of each concept. Among the different forms observed and reported by children were: norms such as playing fair and joining in games; sanctions as shown in smiling, frowning, and being rewarded; values such as cleanliness and friendliness; and roles of policemen, women, and others in the community. The authors suggest that the procedure might well be used in studying different groups, thus developing children's ability to make comparisons in much the same way that sociologists do.

In an essay directed to elementary school teachers, a sociologist has suggested ways in which sociology may contribute to the social studies.[83] The suggestions are related to such fundamental concepts as social interaction and social structures, social change, and

[80] See footnotes 4, 5, 6, 8, 12.

[81] Paul R. Hanna, "The Social Studies Program in the Elementary School in the Twentieth Century," in Wesley Sowards, ed., *The Social Studies: Curriculum Proposals for the Future* (Chicago: Scott, Foresman, 1963), pp. 42–78.

[82] Bruce Joyce and Carl Weinberg, "Using the Strategies of Sociology in Social Education," *Elementary School Journal,* 64:265–272 (February), 1964.

[83] In Hanna, *Beyond the Americas, op. cit.,* pp. 24–26.

world community. For example, teachers are urged to guide children to search for explanations of behavior in the interactions of the parts of a social system rather than in racial characteristics or other insignificant information. There are additional examples directly relatable to the discussion of social systems and other concepts in Chapter 7 of this volume.

Secondary schools

One major project specifically focused on sociology has been initiated to plan teaching units, a high school course, teacher education materials, a study of the feasibility of an introductory course in the social sciences, and a survey of social studies programs in secondary schools.[84]

The essays on sociology in *The Social Studies and the Social Sciences* [85] and *High School Social Studies Perspectives* [86] contain many teachable concepts and ideas. Considered together, they provide a summary of concepts, generalizations, and methods of inquiry that can be used to outline the structure of a basic course that would highlight relationships among anthropology, sociology and social psychology. The author of the essay in the second volume noted above does in fact discuss concepts drawn from all three disciplines.

The offering of a high school course in sociology has been a practice in large high schools for many years. A significant change in recent years has been to place greater emphasis on sociology as sociology rather than on problem-solving or adjustment. This change is in line with trends in other subjects.

Psychology

Like sociology, psychology permeates the social studies program in a variety of ways. Units of instruction contain concepts and points of view on learning, individual and group behavior, emotions, motivation, frustrations, personality, and a host of other topics in the broad

[84] Robert A. Feldmesser (Director), Sociological Resources for Secondary Schools, Dartmouth College, Hanover, N.H.

[85] *Op. cit.*

[86] *Op. cit.*

domain of psychology. On the other hand, little is done in the typical social studies program to provide for the direct study of psychology in depth except in the high school psychology course. In most schools, some psychology is included in the program of health education, particularly those aspects dealing with mental health.

Elementary schools

In addition to the references cited in Chapter 8, there are reports that deal with certain aspects of psychology in elementary schools. For example, Ojemann has headed a group which has produced a variety of materials and reports.[87] The preparation of behavioral digests is currently under way; these can be used as source materials for planning social studies programs.

Secondary schools

The outline of attitudes and skills, knowledge, understandings and abilities presented in *The Social Studies and the Social Sciences* is helpful in planning for the use of psychology in the social studies or in planning a separate course.[88] Attitudinal goals are detailed with specific reference to the limitations of existing knowledge, development of a healthy skepticism, the paucity of valid generalizations, sources of bias, creative imagination, objectivity in studying social problems, and sensitivity to the feelings of others. Understandings and abilities are discussed in relation to methods of inquiry that are used in psychology. The outline of concepts and generalizations is organized around biological backgrounds of behavior, perception, learning, motivation and emotion, personality, abilities and traits, and social psychology.

The essay in *High School Social Studies Perspectives* that deals with anthropology, sociology, and social psychology is indicative of

---

[87] For example, see: Alice S. Hawkins and Ralph H. Ojemann (Compilers), *A Teaching Program in Human Behavior and Mental Health.* Handbook for Third Grade Teachers (Iowa City: Preventive Psychiatry Research Program, State Univ. of Iowa, 1959); Ralph H. Ojemann and Bill C. F. Snider, "The Development of the Child's Conception of the Teacher," *Journal of Experimental Education,* 32:73–80 (fall), 1963.

[88] *Op. cit.,* pp. 171–190.

the many relationships among the behavioral sciences.[89] The sections on personality, learning theory, psychoanalytic theory, and culture and personality point up specific aspects of psychology of relevance to the social studies.

Recently published textbooks for use in a high school course in psychology reflect the current trend to emphasize psychology as a science of behavior.[90] Methods of inquiry are included along with key concepts and generalizations. The learning activities suggested in current texts should help students get a feeling for the styles of thought that are characteristic of psychologists.

Philosophy

Philosophy is a part of the social studies far more than is realized by some individuals. In both elementary and secondary schools, questions arise regarding the right or wrong of events, what is versus what ought to be, goals and values that should be emphasized, best ways to reach goals, the making of choices in the light of values, changes that should be made, differences between statements of fact and opinion, the meanings of terms in different contexts, and other matters calling for the use of philosophic modes of reasoning, criticizing, and judging. Philosophy also may contribute to the social studies by providing analyses of the values and ideals that are fundamental in our society and other societies.[91]

Elementary schools

A good example of the use of philosophy as one of the foundations of the social studies is contained in the program under development

[89] *Op. cit.,* pp. 29–51.

[90] For example, see: Albert A. Branca, *Psychology: The Science of Behavior* (Boston: Allyn and Bacon, 1964); and T. L. Engle, *Psychology: Its Principles and Applications,* 4th ed. (New York: Harcourt, Brace & World, 1964).

[91] For example, see: Thomas Berry, "The Spiritual Form of the Oriental Civilizations," in *Approaches to Asian Civilizations,* W. T. De Bary and A. T. Embree, eds. (New York: Columbia Univ. Press, 1964), pp. 73–85; Ralph H. Gabriel, *Traditional Values in American Life* (New York: Harcourt, Brace & World, 1963); Abraham Kaplan, *The New World of Philosophy* (New York: Random House, 1961); and Arthur Goodfriend, *Two Sides of One World* (Washington, D.C.: U.S. Commission for UNESCO), 1957.

in the Greater Cleveland Social Science Project.[92] Outlined in the teacher's manuals are basic generalizations related to the individual, moral and ethical principles, rational behavior, social conscience, patriotism, a free society, the family, institutions, the common good, and interdependency. For example, the generalization on institutions highlights "the right of free men to devise institutions which make possible" attainment of the common good; and the statement on the common good highlights the importance of legal justice, responsible freedom, and fulfillment of duties.

Secondary schools

An excellent source of information on principles and methods of philosophy applied to teaching in secondary schools is the short volume written by Hullfish and Smith.[93] Specific attention is given to beliefs, value judgments, inference and fallacy, meaning and language, reflective thinking in the classroom and other topics relevant to social studies instruction.

Helpful in thinking through basic curriculum issues and problems is the volume written by Broudy, Smith, and Burnett.[94] The philosophic analysis of knowledge and the differentiation between content as descriptive concepts and principles and content as valuative concepts and norms help to clarify problems that have plagued social studies curriculum planners for many years. The chapters on developmental studies and problem-solving strategies are directly relatable to the social studies.

Illustrative of how content on the philosophy of different societies may be included in the social studies are the units and teaching guides on world cultures developed in Pennsylvania.[95]

[92] Haig Babian (Director), Greater Cleveland Social Science Program, Educational Research Council of Greater Cleveland, Cleveland, Ohio. The example is taken from: *The Child's Expanding World,* Teacher's Guide K, Vol. 2, rev. ed., 1964, pp. a12–a14.

[93] H. Gordon Hullfish and Philip G. Smith, *Reflective Thinking: The Method of Education* (New York: Dodd, Mead, 1961).

[94] Harry S. Broudy, B. Othaniel Smith, and Joe R. Burnett, *Democracy and Excellence in American Secondary Education* (Chicago: Rand McNally, 1964).

[95] *World Cultures* (Philadelphia: Pennsylvania Council for the Social Studies, 1961); *India Today;* and *China Today* (Harrisburg: Department of Public Instruction, 1962).

Values, ideals, and religious beliefs are outlined for India, China, Japan, the Islamic World, and other areas. The position is taken that to understand other cultures one must understand significant philosophic components of each culture.

Other Projects

In this final section projects and activities are discussed which it did not seem appropriate to include under the preceding headings.

The Foreign Relations Project of the North Central Association has produced several bulletins for use in secondary school classes.[96] Historic, economic, geographic, political, and cultural data are included in brief reports on different countries and regions of the world. In addition to the bulletins, the project sponsors conferences and issues materials on topics of interest to teachers and curriculum specialists.

With assistance from the National Council for the Social Studies, the Glens Falls Public Schools have been involved in a project designed to improve the teaching of world affairs.[97] The project cuts across all subjects and all grades. The report on the project describes the origin and development of the project idea, steps that were taken to organize for action, examples of generalizations that were developed, activities that were used, and the program of evaluation.

A project aimed at developing materials that can be used in the analysis of controversial public issues has been set up under the auspices of the Cooperative Branch of the U.S. Office of Education.[98] The primary purpose is to develop teaching units organized around problems and conflicts and to bring social science, legal, and ethical concepts to bear upon them. The units are currently being tried out in the classroom.

[96] James M. Becker (Director), Foreign Relations Project, North Central Association, Chicago. The bulletins are available from Laidlaw Brothers.

[97] Harold Long (Director), *Improving the Teaching of World Affairs; The Glens Falls Story,* Bulletin No. 35 (Washington, D.C.: National Council for the Social Studies, 1964).

[98] Donald Oliver (Director), *A Social Science Curriculum for Grades Eight–Ten Focusing on the Analysis of Controversial Public Issues* (Cambridge: School of Education, Harvard Univ., 1963).

A social studies curriculum center has been set up to provide for the testing and evaluation of materials produced in current projects.[99] The center will attempt to coordinate research, demonstration, dissemination, evaluation, and training activities in the St. Louis metropolitan area.

Morrisett is working with a group to set up a consortium of mid-western universities that will develop an elementary and secondary social studies program based on social science concepts and structures.[100]

Three seminars have been held on social studies topics and two studies of interest to curriculum workers are under way. Sowards organized a seminar in which social scientists and social studies specialists examined current problems and needed research.[101] Price directed a conference on needed research in the social studies.[102] Morison headed a seminar on a curriculum reform program in social studies and history.[103] Davis is doing a study of the usefulness of graphic illustrations in the social studies.[104] Johnson and Dambach are making a survey of materials on conservation education.[105]

Mention also should be made of the Commission of Current Curriculum Developments of the Association for Supervision and Curriculum Development.[106] The purpose of this commission is to review and report on new developments in all areas of the cur-

[99] Shaplin, Judson T. (Director), *Development of a Model for the St. Louis Metropolitan Social Studies Center, Grades K-12* (St. Louis: Graduate Institute of Education, Washington Univ., 1964).

[100] Irving Morrisett (Secretary), *The Social Science Curriculum Consortium* (Boulder, Colo.: Department of Economics, Univ. of Colorado, 1963).

[101] Wesley Sowards, *A Working Seminar on the Improvement of the Social Studies Curriculum* (Stanford: School of Education, Stanford Univ., 1963).

[102] Roy A. Price, *Conference on Needed Research in the Teaching of Social Studies* (Syracuse, N.Y.: Department of Education, Syracuse Univ., 1963).

[103] Elting E. Morison, *Planning Seminars for a Curriculum Reform Program in Social Studies and History* (Cambridge: Department of History, Harvard Univ., 1963).

[104] C. L. Davis, *The Usefulness of Graphic Illustrations in the Social Studies* (Kent, Ohio: Kent State Univ., 1963).

[105] Carl S. Johnson and Charles A. Dambach, *Survey of Printed Materials on Conservation Education* (Columbus, Ohio: Ohio State Univ., 1963).

[106] Robert Gilchrist (Director), Commission on Current Curriculum Developments, Association for Supervision and Curriculum Development, National Education Association, Washington 6, D.C.

riculum. The 1963 report includes a review of twenty-three social studies reports and projects.[107] A second report is planned for publication in the summer of 1965.

A recently completed survey of social studies courses of study is helpful in identifying new and revised teaching guides, available materials, prices of materials, and curriculum studies under way in school systems.[108]

In order to make it possible for readers of this volume to keep up to date with new developments in current projects, a directory of current and related projects follows.

DIRECTORY OF SOCIAL STUDIES PROJECTS

BAILEY, WILFRED AND MARION J. RICE, Development of a Sequential Curriculum in Anthropology for Grades 1–7, Department of Sociology and Anthropology, University of Georgia, Athens, Ga. 30601.

BECKER, JAMES M., Foreign Relations Project, North Central Association, First National Bank Building, Suite 832, Chicago, Ill. 60603.

BROWN, RICHARD AND VAN R. HALSEY, History and Social Studies Curriculum Materials: Average Terminal, College Bound, and Adults, Amherst College, Amherst, Mass. 01002.

COLLIER, MALCOLM C., Anthropology Curriculum Study Project (Secondary), 5632 So. Kimbark Ave., Chicago, Ill. 60637.

ENGLISH, RAYMOND, Social Science Program (K-12), Educational Research Council of Greater Cleveland, Rockefeller Building, Cleveland, Ohio 44113.

FELDMESSER, ROBERT A., Sociological Resources for Secondary Schools, Bartlett Hall, Dartmouth College, Hanover, N.H. 03755.

FENTON, EDWIN, A High School Social Studies Curriculum for Able Students, Carnegie Institute of Technology, Pittsburgh, Pa. 15213.

FRANKEL, M. L., Economic Education Activities (1–12), Joint Council on Economic Education, 2 West 46th St., New York, N.Y. 10036.

HELBURN, NICHOLAS, High School Geography Project, Association of American Geographers, Montana State College, Bozeman, Mont. 59715.

HILL, WILHELMINA, Committee on Curriculum Guide (K-12), Geo-

---

[107] John U. Michaelis, "The Social Studies," in *Using Current Curriculum Developments* (Washington, D.C.: Association for Supervision and Curriculum Development, 1963), pp. 71–85.

[108] Curriculum Committee, *Clearing House of Reports on Curriculum Revision Programs in Social Studies, 1962–64* (Washington, D.C.: National Council for the Social Studies, 1964).

graphic Education, U.S. Office of Education, Washington, D.C. 20202.

LEE, JOHN, New Approaches to and Materials for a Sequential Curriculum on American Society, Grades 5–12, Social Studies Curriculum Study Center, Northwestern University, 1809 Chicago Ave., Evanston, Ill. 60201.

LEE, MARVIN, Economics Education Committee of the Southern States Work Conference, College of Education, West Virginia University, Morgantown, West Va. 26506.

LEPPERT, ELLA C., The First Three Courses in a Sequential Social Studies Program for the Secondary School, Department of Education, University of Illinois, Urbana, Ill. 61803.

LERNER, DANIEL, The Development of a Basic Social Science Course for Undergraduate Students in the Natural Sciences and Engineering (College), Massachusetts Institute of Technology, Cambridge, Mass. 02139.

LONG, HAROLD M., Improving the Teaching of World Affairs (K-12), Glens Falls Public Schools, Glens Falls, N.Y. 12801.

MAHER, JOHN E., Development of Economic Education Programs (K-12), Joint Council on Economic Education, 2 West 46th St., New York, N.Y. 10036.

MICHAELIS, JOHN U., Preparation of Teaching Guides and Materials on Asian Countries for Grades I–XII, Department of Education, University of California, Berkeley, Calif. 94720.

MORISON, ELTING E., A Program of Curriculum Development in the Social Studies and Humanities (1–12), Educational Services Inc., 108 Water St., Watertown, Mass. 02172.

MORRISETT, IRVING, The Social Science Education Consortium (1–12), Department of Economics, Purdue University, Lafayette, Ind. 47907.

OLIVER, DONALD, A Jurisprudential and Social Science Curriculum for Grades 8–10 Focusing on the Analysis of Controversial Public Issues, Graduate School of Education, Harvard University, Cambridge, Mass. 02138.

PATTERSON, FRANKLIN, The Lincoln Filene Center for Citizenship and Public Affairs (Secondary), Tufts University, Medford, Mass. 02155.

PRICE, ROY A., Identification of Major Concepts from the Social Sciences, Development of Materials and Techniques for Teaching Them, and Evaluation of Their Applicability and Utility in Grades V, VIII, and XI, Department of Education, Syracuse University, Syracuse, N.Y. 13210.

RADER, WILLIAM D., Elementary School Economics Program, Industrial Relations Center, University of Chicago, Chicago, Ill. 60637.

RIDDLE, DONALD H., Secondary School Project, Eagleton Institute of Politics, Rutgers University, Woodlawn, Douglass College, New Brunswick, N.J. 08901.

ROSWENC, EDWIN C., Basic Concepts in History and Social Science (Secondary), Department of American Studies, Amherst College, Amherst, Mass. 01002.

RUNDELL, WALTER JR., Service Center for Teachers of History (Secondary), American Historical Association, 400 A St., Washington, D.C. 20003.

SENESH, LAWRENCE, Elkhart Indiana Experiment in Economic Education (1–12), Department of Economics, Purdue University, Lafayette, Ind. 47907.

SHAPLIN, JUDSON T., Development of a Model for the St. Louis Metropolitan Social Studies Center, Grades K-12, Graduate Institute of Education, Washington University, St. Louis, Mo. 63130.

SHAVER, JAMES P., Development of Economic Curricular Materials for Secondary Schools, Ohio State University, Social Studies Curriculum Center, Columbus, Ohio 43201.

SPERLING, JOHN G. AND SUZANNE WIGGINS, Development and Evaluation of a 12th Grade Course in the Principles of Economics, Department of Economics, San Jose State College, San Jose, Calif.

STAVRIANOS, L. S., World History Project (Secondary), Department of History, Northwestern University, Evanston, Ill. 60201.

TOY, HENRY, Civic Education Project (1–12), American Heritage Foundation, 11 West 42nd St., New York, N.Y. 10036.

WEST, EDITH, Preparation and Evaluation of Social Studies Curriculum Guides and Materials for Grades K-14, College of Education, University of Minnesota, Minneapolis, Minn. 55455.

RELATED STUDIES

BARNACK, ROBERT S., The Use of Electronic Computers to Improve Individualization of Instruction Through Unit Teaching, School of Education, State University, Buffalo, N.Y. 14205.

BECKER, JAMES, Experimental Statewide Seminars in Teaching About Democracy and Totalitarianism, Foreign Relations Project, First National Bank Building, Chicago, Ill. 60603.

COLEMAN, JAMES S., Research Program in the Effects of Games With Simulated Environments in Secondary Education, Department of Social Relations, Johns Hopkins University, Baltimore, Md. 21203.

DAVIS, O. L., The Usefulness of Graphic Illustrations in the Social Studies, Kent State University, Kent, Ohio.

EASTON, DAVID AND ROBERT D. HESS, Study of Political Socialization, Department of Political Science, University of Chicago, Chicago, Ill. 60637.

JOHNSON, CARL S. AND CHARLES A. DAMBACH, Survey of Printed Materials on Conservation Education, Research Foundation, Ohio State University, Columbus, Ohio 43201.

JOYCE, BRUCE AND CARL WEINBERG, Sociology in Elementary Social Studies, Department of Education, University of Chicago, Chicago, Ill. 60637.

OJEMANN, RALPH H., Preventive Psychiatry Program, W 613 East Hall, University of Iowa, Iowa City, Iowa 52240.

SANDERS, NORRIS, Use of a Taxonomy of Questions to Increase the Variety and Quality of Thought in the Classroom, Manitowoc Public Schools, Manitowoc, Wis. 54220.

SHINN, RIDGWAY, F., JR., An Investigation Into the Utilization of Geography and History as Integrating Disciplines for Social Studies Curricular Development in a Public School System, Department of History, Rhode Island College, Providence, R.I. 02904.

TABA, HILDA, Thinking in Elementary School Children, Department of Education, San Francisco State College, San Francisco, Calif. 94127.

WING, RICHARD L., The Production and Evaluation of Three Computer-Based Economics Games for the Sixth Grade, Board of Cooperative Educational Services, Yorktown Heights, N.Y. 10598.

APPENDIX

~~~~~~

Generalizations from
the social sciences

EACH OF THE EIGHT SOCIAL SCIENCES CONTRIBUTES CERTAIN BASIC ideas or concepts to the social studies program. These are broad, central generalizations that should become progressively more meaningful, even though they are not specifically introduced, through organized learning experiences at the various grade levels.

To prepare the generalizations which are presented on the following pages, groups of social scientists throughout the state were asked to review the content of their particular discipline and to assess its contributions to competent citizenship in our modern, complex society. The findings of these groups were then studied and analyzed by educators and other interested citizens on a statewide basis. As the generalizations were developed, "goals of understanding" were formulated. These were appropriate for application to adults rather than to a particular grade. Therefore, the curriculum planner must decide what subgeneralizations, concepts, and factual information are appropriate for youth in each of the grades that comprise the elementary and secondary school programs. These subdivisions then become reference points for planning and organiz-

From State Curriculum Commission, *Social Studies Framework for the Public Schools of California* (Sacramento: California State Department of Education, 1962), pp. 89–109. Reprinted by permission.

ing instruction and for preparing courses of study and other classroom materials. The reference points need to be cumulative so that understanding in the social studies is moved in the direction indicated by the generalizations.

Although these goals for understanding will be invaluable in guiding school district personnel in the selection of specific units of instruction, in determining learnings to be stressed, and in appraising pupil progress, they must necessarily be supplemented by understandings applicable only to the local community.

It is also recognized that the content of the social studies does not come exclusively from eight social sciences. When children and youth study topics related to this aspect of the curriculum, they utilize information from additional fields. Such is particularly the case in the elementary school, where pupils sometimes need information about the natural and physical sciences, art, music, literature, health, and safety to comprehend the significance of what they are studying. Although a setting for the practical application of information from these fields is thus established in a way that enhances learning in the social studies, the fields also receive attention in other parts of the instructional program.

The social studies simply provide an opportunity to bring the contributions of related social disciplines into a meaningful context for children and youth. In so doing, they serve as an essential and central aspect of general education and as a background for successful living in our American society. Contributions of the eight social sciences, however, do more than indicate the basic sociocivic learnings that relate to general education. In addition, they reflect persistent contemporary problems. Influences of general trends in our society—such as population growth, increased mobility of the population, and changes in the pattern of family living—can be noted in a number of the ideas or concepts.

These social science generalizations should not be taught but should emerge as conceptualizations from what has been studied. Acquiring of new information is essentially training, but the discussion and relation of new facts to other knowledge from which generalizations may be drawn constitute education.

Curriculum specialists know that pupils can generalize only to the extent that the breadth and depth of their knowledge will permit and that limitations in this process cannot be overcome by pupils through learning to verbalize a mass of words that have little or no meaning to them. Children and youth acquire meaning only from a broad base of experience and learn to generalize at ever higher levels only through skillful guidance from informed teachers.

Generalizations From Geography

Overview

Geography deals with areal arrangement. Its principal orientation is toward the earth's surface and the varying distributional patterns created by nature and man. It seeks to define the earth's physical and cultural features, to show their distribution, to make them understandable by explaining the basic forces or factors that affect them, and to present the more fundamental of their interrelationships. Because of its dual nature, geography is both a natural and a social science and, as such, helps to integrate both. As part of its educational responsibility, geography seeks to help pupils become earth-minded (even universe-minded) and spatially oriented, to build a useful mental image of the world and its parts, and to develop the pupils' sense of space in a manner similar to the way in which history seeks to develop their sense of time.

Physical geography

It is the task of physical geography to describe and explain the distribution of surface features and to define natural regions that are caused by and continuously affected by forces and processes in nature.

1. Life on the earth is influenced by the earth's (global) shape, its size, and its set of motions.
2. The shape of the earth causes the unequal distribution of sunlight, or energy, from the sun, which in turn influences the circulation of the atmosphere and causes differences in climate and natural vegetation.
3. Earth movements of rotation and revolution are basic to understanding climate and time: rotation of the earth on its axis is a measure of time and causes night and day; seasons are caused by a combination of revolution, inclination, and parallelism of the earth's axis.

4. Earth movements and earth-sun-moon relationships also offer bases for the understanding of the geography of outer space.
5. Weather, climate, and earth crustal movements affect the surface of the earth and cause regional differences in landforms, minerals, drainage, soils, and natural vegetation.
6. Climate is determined by sunlight, temperature, humidity, precipitation, atmospheric pressure, winds, unequal rates of heating and cooling of land and water surfaces, irregular shape and distribution of land and sea, ocean currents, and mountain systems.
7. Because of various combinations of heat and moisture and the distributions of these two factors, the earth is divided into climatic regions, consisting of tropical, middle latitude, polar, and dry lands; each of these types has several subtypes. These classifications are a means of organizing information about the earth.
8. The crust of the earth consists of various types of rocks that influence topography. It contains useful mineral deposits and is the parent material of soils.
9. Soil, water, solar energy, and air are the natural resources most indispensable to man. The great source of all activity and life on earth is heat from the sun.
10. Soil and vegetation may be thought of as the cover over the nonliving surface configuration. This cover provides the landscape with character and color.
11. Major climatic regions coincide approximately with major vegetation zones because vegetation is related to climatic conditions. Natural vegetation is a great resource utilized by man.
12. Soils are altered by nature and man. Nature combines the action of climate, vegetation, and animals on parent materials to produce regional variations in soils.
13. The physical elements of the earth are a unit, and no part can be understood fully except in terms of its relationship to the whole.

Cultural geography

Cultural geography is concerned with the distribution of man and his activities on the earth's surface. Since man's occupation of an area is affected by the physical environment, cultural geography is also concerned with the adjustments that he must make to this environment. The nature of these adjustments depends upon man's stage of technology and on the controls of social behavior and nature.

Cultural geography involves not only population distribution but also settlement patterns; land-use activities; ethnic, linguistic, and religious characteristics; and features of political organization. Since cultural geographers are interested in the activities of people in relation to their spatial organization, they seek to interpret the various world, regional, and local patterns of economic, social, and political behavior.

1. Man constantly seeks to satisfy his needs for food, clothing, and shelter and his other wants; in so doing, he attempts to adapt, shape, utilize, and exploit the earth. Some aspects of the natural environment, however, are not significantly altered or utilized by man.

2. The significance of the physical features of the earth is determined by man living in his environment. The natural environment may set the broad limits of economic life within a region, but it is man who determines its specific character within the limits of his culture.

3. To exist, man must utilize natural resources. Groups develop ways of adjusting to and controlling the environment in which they exist. Human change, and even the whole structure of civilization, may depend upon the nature and extent of man's supply of energy and his ability to utilize and control it.

4. The extent of man's utilization of natural resources is related to his desires and to his level of technology.

5. The processes of production, exchange, distribution, and consumption of goods have a geographic orientation and vary in part with geographic influences. The nature of the organization of economic processes within an area (spatial organization) results from the kinds of resources, the stage of technology, and the sociopolitical attitudes of the population.

6. The location of production is controlled by the factors of land (natural resources of the physical environment), labor, and capital. In most cases, the attainment of maximum efficiency, as motivated by competition for the factors of production, de-

termines location of production. In some cases, the location is determined by political or other social controls rather than by economic efficiency.

7. Land is less mobile than the other basic factors of labor and capital and has a dominant role in determining the location of production. Since people, in general, prefer to live near their work, this location becomes significant in the distribution of the population.

8. The kinds of climate, soil, native vegetation and animals, and minerals influence the nature and extent of man's achievements within each region. The amount and the kind of food needed for health vary with climatic conditions and man's technology.

9. Factors of production, including technology, are subject to change. Therefore, geography is concerned with changing patterns of land use.

10. Understanding the location of political or other social institutions is contingent upon a knowledge of the economy of an area. Since understanding of this economy depends in part upon a knowledge of the natural environment, it follows that political and social institutions are related to this environment.

11. The sequence of human activities and culture patterns is related to geographic location and accessibility and to the particular time in which human beings live. People in different stages of civilization react differently to similar environments.

12. Man and animals may, by their activities, upset the balance of nature. Man is different, however, in that he may do something —such as undertake conservation—to regain the balance.

13. Competition for the acquistion of the earth's natural resources sometimes results in political strife, and even in war.

14. Political cooperation and strife between nations are related to their geographic locations.

Summary

Geography encompasses more than a description of the earth's surface. Its prime concern in the social studies is the way in which man utilizes the raw materials and resources of his natural environment. The study of geography, therefore, has a major role in the development of civic competence. The problems of mankind cannot be fully understood or successfully solved without a knowledge of the geographic factors involved. Man's geographic distribution and his utilization of the resources of nature are basic to understanding many contemporary problems that have local, regional, and international implications. Geography is also closely related to all the social, biological, and physical sciences.

Generalizations From History

Overview

History is the record of what has happened to man. It is the effort to grasp the whole of human experience within a chronological framework. History is interpretive, imaginative, and normative. It is the script of human drama and also the drama.

Because of the interpretive role of history, the principal ideas— or major generalizations relative to it—necessarily involve other social sciences. The social sciences deal with man and his experience, but history alone presents a chronology of human experience.

The past furnishes a base from which to understand the present and from which to project into the future. The maturity of men and women is built upon reflections from the past. We are thus continuously indebted to the past and to the historical record of human activities.

Chronology, sequence, and change in history

1. Space and time form a framework within which all events can be placed. All of man's experience has occurred within a space and time framework; however, the same relationship does not necessarily apply to events as they have occurred in various parts of the world.
2. Man's struggle for freedom and human dignity has occupied a relatively brief period of time, as compared with the total span of man's existence.
3. The past influences the present, and the present cannot be ade-

quately understood without knowledge of the past. Life goes on against the intricate tapestry of the past. History does not repeat itself, but events tend to occur in some sort of sequence. Events in nature usually occur uniformly. Human events are predictable, but to a lesser extent.

4. History contributes much to man's preparation for his social and political life. It is possible to derive basic principles and implications for thought and action in contemporary affairs from the historical backgrounds of our society.

5. Change has been a universal condition of human society. Change and progress are, however, not necessarily synonymous. Many civilizations have risen and fallen, but only some have contributed greatly to our present civilizations. The tempo of change has increased markedly in the recent past.

Main tendencies in the growth of civilizations

1. History reveals a degree of homogeneity in mankind during all periods of recorded time. Environments in many places and regions have been altered physically, but human motives or drives within them have remained nearly the same.

2. Brotherhood, in the sense of peaceful cooperation, is one of man's worthiest and earliest historical concepts. Conflict and hostility are also within man's experience. Men of all races have many basic physical similarities. Geographical variations and time variations in man's environments help explain his past actions and continue to influence his behavior in the present.

3. In the contemporary world, historical events may have a significance that reaches far beyond the limits of a state or province or the place of their origin. The worldwide implications of such events must be understood.

4. Although certain historical customs and institutions have characterized individual civilizations or nations in the past, men in every age and place have made use of basic social functions in adjusting themselves to their world.

5. Past and present civilizations represent our cultural heritage. The races, cultures, and civilizations in most areas of the world and of most historical periods, beginning with the dawn of

recorded history, have made some contributions to the growth of our present civilizations.

6. Interdependence has been a constant and important factor in human relationships everywhere.

Historical interpretation

1. Such factors as the passing of time and advances in the techniques of scholarship have brought new perspectives and understandings of history. New interests and controversies of our own day and of past centuries have also had marked effects on the interpretation of events and ideas. Use of the historical method in fact finding and problem solving has made possible the discovery and use of new data and perspectives.

2. Human motives, drives, and ideas of many kinds, whether correct or incorrect in terms of historical progress and human improvement, have markedly influenced local, national, and international actions. The interpretation of these motives is one of the most critical tasks of historical analysis.

3. There are various traditional and contemporary interpretations of historical processes and movements of a national and international scope that may illuminate the study of history. Such historical processes are sometimes referred to by such terms as action and reaction, rise and fall, and growth and decline as they are applied to civilizations, nations, and empires.

4. The efforts of people, great material achievements, and important ideas are delineated, assessed, interpreted, and placed in perspective by historians.

5. History demonstrates that mankind has been motivated by morals and ideals and by material wants and needs. The demand for moral standards has persisted throughout man's experience. The ideals of men in all parts of the world and in all ages have been rooted in the value systems of large and small groups.

Summary

History is especially responsible for pointing up and interpreting the similarities and differences within man's experience. It serves as a yardstick of evaluation for the actions, institutions, and events of men. History, together with other of the social sciences, should show the great basic and universal values that comprise man's efforts to reach the worthiest of human goals. The study of history thus provides contemporary man with a basis for intelligent action now and in the future.

Generalizations From Political Science

Overview

Political science is the study of government—of the theory and practice of man in organizing and controlling the power needed to formulate public policy and administer the public services. It is divided into several branches.

Political theory is that branch which seeks to formulate principles, conclusions, and valid generalizations concerning the state and man's many relationships to it. The political theorist attempts to synthesize and integrate existing knowledge about the state, utilizing data and analyses of specialists both within and outside the social sciences.

Political scientists have been concerned with such basic questions as the origin of the state; the purpose or justification of the state; the nature of law, justice, and liberty; where the authority of the state should be reposed (i.e., in a monarch, an aristocracy, the whole people, a dictator, an elite, the proletariat); and, especially in the twentieth century, how far the authority of the state should extend into the realms of business, social life, and individual conduct.

Other branches of political science are *public law,* which embraces constitutional law, international law, administrative law, and criminal law; *politics,* which encompasses the institutions, processes, and methods of governing; *public administration,* which deals with the theory and practice of the executive branch of government; *national, state, and local government,* which includes study of the Constitution and the functions and services of government; *comparative government,* which includes comparisons of institutional phenomena and of political behavior and political values of foreign political systems; and *international relations,* which encompasses diplomacy, international law, economic policies, ideological competition and propaganda, military power, and international organization.

315

The state or government

1. Throughout history, the peoples of the world have experimented with a wide variety of governmental forms. While Americans are engaged with their own governmental problems, the peoples of all other countries are endeavoring to resolve their problems of government.

2. Government is but one of the institutions serving society. The state or government is essential to civilization, and yet many human needs can best be met by the home, the school, the church, the press, and private business.

3. Two essential functions of government are to serve and to regulate in the public interest. The ultimate responsibilities of government are divided into five major categories: (a) external security; (b) internal order; (c) justice; (d) services essential to the general welfare; and, under democracy, (e) freedom. Perhaps the clearest indication of the importance of the state in the twentieth century lies in the fact that, although it has exclusive responsibility in none of these fields, it has residual responsibility in all.

4. In a democracy, government is the servant of the people; people are not the servants of government. Government is by right an institution made by man for man. The source of authority resides in the people.

5. It is the business of government to do for the people what they cannot do or what they cannot do as well for themselves. Philosophies of government range from laissez-faire, in which a minimum of services is provided, to totalitarian collectivism, in which every phase of the individual's life is dictated for him. Government is indispensable to assure internal order and external security. Since order is indispensable if freedom is to have any genuine meaning—indeed, if life itself is to be tolerable —its establishment and maintenance are prime tasks of government.

6. No one yardstick is adequate for comparing different political systems. It is particularly important for citizens in a free society to understand the ideas and techniques characteristic of authoritarian political systems and to develop attitudes that will

permit them to cope objectively with problems arising from the real or potential hostility of those systems.

7. When government is organized, it is essential that leaders be authorized power with which to act and that they be held responsible for its wise use.

8. Government cannot be effective unless it has the flexibility to cope with new conditions. Adaptation, social invention, and gradual change provide the best safeguards against political revolution. To fulfill its role in a democracy, government must be adaptable. The Constitution of the United States provides for flexibility to meet changing conditions.

9. Political parties and special interest groups perform certain necessary services in the governing process. The political parties of this country and of every free nation were formed so that citizens having common beliefs and interests may seek to mold basic policies and choose government leaders. Parties and interest groups both have a check-and-balance and force-and-counterforce role, which leads to evolutionary changes and growth. The politician generates interest and musters popular or legislative support necessary for formal approval or adoption of policy.

10. All nations in the modern world are part of a global, interdependent system of economic, social, cultural, and political life. The evolution of the international law of war has been paralleled by the effort to develop an international law of peace and by the attempt to devise and build international political institutions and organizations capable of making such laws effective. Consideration for the security and welfare of the people of other nations remains the mark of the civilized man and has now become the price of national survival as well.

Democracy

1. Democracy implies a way of life as well as a form of government.

2. Democracy is based on certain fundamental assumptions. Among these are the integrity of man, the dignity of the individual, equality of opportunity, man's rationality, man's morality, man's practicality, and man's ability to govern himself and to solve his problems cooperatively.

3. Man develops his fullest potential in a climate of freedom. Much of the progress of civilization can be traced to man's search for a larger measure of freedom. For the truly civilized man, no amount of material wealth can ever compensate for lack of freedom. A society benefits when its individual members are relatively free to develop their creative talents.

4. Human beings are creatures of self-interest. For democracy to function, however, self-interest must be curbed to a degree in favor of public interest.

5. A chief goal of democracy is the preservation and extension of human freedoms. Freedom is unworkable, however, unless it is balanced by corresponding responsibility. Freedom appears to range from legal to political freedom, and from political to genuine economic and social freedom.

6. Civil liberty—freedom of thought, speech, press, worship, petition, and association—constitutes the core of freedom. With civil liberty, all other kinds of freedom become possible; without it, none of them can have any reality.

7. Basic to democracy is belief in progress. A free society is hospitable to new ideas and to change and encourages the unfettered search for truth. Peaceful action rather than violence is one of its hallmarks.

8. Certain factors are necessary for democracy to succeed and survive. These include (a) an educated citizenry; (b) a common concern for human freedom; (c) communication and mobility; (d) a degree of economic security; (e) a spirit of compromise and mutual trust; (f) respect for the rights of minority groups and the loyal opposition; (g) moral and spiritual values; and (h) participation by the citizen in government at all levels.

9. Opportunity for the individual to choose his type of occupation voluntarily is a concept that has flourished under democratic philosophy and practice and the capitalistic system.

Citizenship

1. The well-being of the state is dependent upon the education of its citizens.

2. A citizen can do his part in making democracy work only if he is sufficiently informed to think intelligently on the issues of the

day. Information can best be provided by free and responsible mass media of communication.

3. The citizen has civic responsibilities as well as rights.
4. A democratic society depends on citizens who are intellectually and morally fit to conduct their government. Civic responsibility and moral courage are balanced wheels in a democracy. To fulfill their obligations of citizenship, individuals must be aware of the quality of service that must be performed by the government; they must also be willing to participate actively in community affairs. The capable citizen should evaluate objectively information received through mass media of communication in making political choices.

Summary

Political science helps individuals to become more keenly aware of their opportunities and obligations as citizens. It provides perspective for the study of such current problems as recruitment of personnel for civilian and military services, costs of defense and other public services, raising of revenues to underwrite these costs, and achievement of security. To be a capable and conscientious citizen, the individual needs (1) to understand the structure and function of government; and (2) to develop citizenship skills. These include knowing how to read newspapers, speak in public, and conduct meetings; and how to be an action-minded participant in the affairs of the school, community, state, nation, and world.

Generalizations From Economics

Overview

Economics is concerned with analyzing information, issues, and public policies connected with the production, distribution, and consumption of wealth and income. This discipline begins with the study of scarcity and unlimited wants and proceeds through specialized production, interdependence, exchange, markets, prices, costs, and public policy. Emphasized are economic stability and growth; the allocation of resources to their most important uses; an equitable distribution of income; and, in our economy, a wide range of economic freedom for workers to choose their jobs, consumers to choose goods, and investors and entrepreneurs to own property and choose their investments.

All problems that may properly be termed "economic" must be considered in these categories whether they originate in capitalist, socialist, fascist, or communist countries. Economic theory has been defined as "a method rather than a doctrine, an apparatus of the mind, a technique of thinking which helps its possessor to draw correct conclusions." The study of economics is thus important to the individual and society for both the knowledge which it provides and the thinking processes which it requires. Valid information about our economy and the ability to use it effectively are indispensable to effective citizenship in assessing many of the most pressing public issues of the day.

Consideration of specialized areas in economics must be based firmly on this approach. Included in economics are the study of money and banking, business cycles, public finance and taxation, industrial organization and public policies toward business, labor-management relations, accounting, finance, statistics, consumer economics, international trade and finance, economic growth and development, and comparative economic systems.

Economic ends and means

1. Economic welfare is a goal in most, if not all, modern societies. It is believed that it is beneficial for people to have more rather than fewer economic goods and that poverty *per se* is not desirable. Many economists believe that economic welfare is an important quality of society; that economic progress makes the other qualities of society more readily obtainable; and that the creative arts—such as painting, music, and literature—flourish more fully in a highly productive economy.

2. Productive resources are scarce, and human wants are unlimited. Since man cannot satisfy all of his desires for material goods, he must make choices. The essence of "economy" lies in making wise decisions with regard to such matters as saving, spending, purposes of expenditures, kinds of investments, and types of jobs to be undertaken. The "real cost" of any end product is

thus the alternatives sacrificed in producing it. This is known as the "opportunity cost principle."

The gross national product—a measurement of economic achievement

1. The size of the Gross National Product (consisting of the total value of all economic goods—products and services—produced annually) depends upon many conditions. Among these are (a) the extent and richness of natural resources; (b) the number, quality, and motivation of the working population; (c) the amount and nature of capital goods (factories, houses, bridges, roads, machines and tools of all kinds) created through saving and investment; (d) the effectiveness of investors and entrepreneurs in organizing and developing productive activity; (e) the existence of a large free-trade area, in which the free flow of goods permits each locality to specialize in the production of those goods in which it has the greatest relative advantage and to obtain other goods by trade (the "principle of comparative advantage"); and (f) the presence of political institutions that are conducive to and encourage creative and productive effort on the part of all people. To maintain the conditions upon which high productivity (and consequently our high standard of living) depend, conservation must be practiced.

2. The size of both the GNP and population greatly influences economic welfare. This welfare depends upon the balance between population growth and depletion of resources and upon improvements in production techniques and expansion of capital goods. When population growth exceeds the capacity of the land and capital goods, output per worker declines unless there are compensating improvements in technology. This principle is known as the "law of diminishing returns."

3. The full use of productive facilities directly influences economic welfare. Fluctuations tend to be more severe in industrially advanced nations than in those that are primitive. In the former, specialization and complexity are vastly greater, shifts in demand and changes in techniques are more frequent, a larger proportion of resources are devoted to the production of durable consumer

and producer goods, and substantial changes in the volume of investment expenditures are dependent upon the people's desire to save a fairly stable part of their incomes.

4. Government can contribute to the maintenance of high-level production and employment, rapid economic growth and progress, and the stability of the dollar by proper use of its authority through sound fiscal and debt-management policies.

5. High per-capita income is the result of high productivity of labor. The total income of a society is its total output of goods. Therefore, if American labor is ten times as productive as foreign labor, American wages can be ten times as high without curtailing the ability of American industry to sell its products in world markets. High wages thus rest on high productivity, not on tariffs.

The composition of income—the allocation of resources

1. Basic to sound economic organization is securing effective co-operation among specialized producers. The type of economic system determines how much of each commodity and service is to be produced and how each resource unit is to be allocated to its most important use.

2. In a competitive, private-enterprise system, prices indicate the relative value of goods and services. On the one hand, these prices reflect the willingness of buyers to buy and sellers to sell; and, on the other hand, they influence the decisions of both consumers and producers. A relatively high price tends to restrict present consumption and to stimulate production of a larger supply in the future. A relatively low price has the reverse effect. Raising or lowering a competitive price by artificial means, whether by private monopoly or governmental authority, is likely to aggravate the situation that the action is designed to alleviate, unless the change in price is accompanied by the power to affect directly future demand or supply in an appropriate manner.

3. A market price system works best when both buyers and sellers are highly competitive, well informed, and able and disposed to act in accordance with the information available (competition—knowledge—mobility). Thus, a free-enterprise system is sup-

ported and strengthened by government action designed to keep markets free (antitrust policy), buyers and sellers informed (prohibition of false advertising and laws against misrepresentation), and the system mobile. At the minimum, government must maintain order and justice, protect property, enforce contracts, and provide a sound money system in some fields if free enterprise is to be effective.

4. Because of special conditions in such fields as public utilities, government has been authorized to regulate prices to assure that they are not discriminatory. The quality of service rendered by electric power, gas, and telephone companies has also been regulated. In some cases, the government has directly undertaken the provision of services such as those required in the operation of post offices and distribution of the water supply.

5. There are many ways to organize economic activity. Most national economies in the world today, though differing in fundamental respects, make considerable use of the price system to ration goods, providing incentives for productive services, and allocate resources to their best uses. A free society provides opportunity and incentives for the individual to invest what he owns in an effort to make a profit.

The distribution of income

1. In a competitive system, the prices paid for productive services also serve to divide the total output of goods among those responsible for their production. Thus, the wages of workers, the dividends of investors, and the rents of landlords all provide the incomes that determine the size of each individual's claim to actual goods and services.

2. In a competitive market, each productive agent tends to receive as income a sum equal to the value of his productive contribution to society. The greater the demand of the public for the particular service or product and the smaller the supply, the larger is the income. Those possessing the grestest skills demanded by the public tend to receive the highest incomes. Inequality in the distribution of income thus is the result of unequal payments for services and of unequal ownership of property. At the same time, the opportunity to acquire a larger income furnishes an in-

centive to develop individual abilities, to save and acquire property, and to use resources most efficiently and productively.

3. Imperfections in competition create important public problems. The power of monopoly, whether exercised by buyers or sellers, management or labor, or private groups sometimes supported by government, usually distorts the allocation of resources and distribution of income.

4. The way to improve the standard of living for all the people is to increase productivity. Such has been the tremendous economic achievement in the United States. Industrial output per man-hour has increased six times since about 1850. Half of this gain has been realized in shorter hours (and more leisure) and half in more goods. Thus, the average length of the work week has been reduced 50 percent and, at the same time, real income per capita has tripled. The grinding poverty in which a large part of the world's population lives today is caused by the sheer un-productivity of human labor, not by deficiency in purchasing power or imperfection in the distribution of income.

Summary

Since the world's resources are insufficient to satisfy all wants, the study of economics, both theoretical and applied, is essential to the general education of all people. The individual makes economic decisions throughout his life. Through voting and other types of community participation, he helps to decide problems involving the economic welfare of all people.

Generalizations From Anthropology

Overview

Anthropology is the comparative study of man. It is concerned with his evolution and present characteristics as a biological form; with his various modes of organizing group life; and with his utilization of the natural environment. Thus, anthropology is a social science with a special relationship to the biological sciences.

Specialists in the field include physical anthropologists; anthropological linguists, who study the numerous unwritten languages of the world; archeologists who seek to understand the story of prehistoric man by unearthing and studying remains of his activities; and operate for the welfare of mankind and yet maintain as much respect for one another's cultural patterns as possible.

Human beings as members of homo sapiens

1. Since long before the beginning of written history, all human beings have been members of a single biological species, the *Homo sapiens*. For convenience of description and classification, anthropologists divide the species into "races," each of which has distinctive, observable *physical* traits. These traits, however, merge imperceptibly into one another so that most men possess characteristics of more than one race.

2. Populations have seldom remained isolated long enough, nor have they been subjected to sufficiently intensive natural selection, to become homogeneous races. Modern, worldwide interdependencies and rapid transportation and communication make it clear that such isolation cannot be expected in the future.

3. Anthropologists distinguish three main stocks or extreme limits of human biological variability: Mongoloids, Caucasoids, and Negroids. The great bulk of humanity is intermediate between the extremes.

4. Physically, all human beings are much more alike than different. Geneticists estimate that all human beings have more than 99 percent of their genes in common and that the most extreme variation results from genetic differences in less than 1 percent of the genes. Differences between members of the same main stock are frequently greater than differences between persons of different groups.

5. A common misconception is that groups can be identified as "races" on the basis of differences in language, religion, or nationality. These differences are cultural and nonbiological. So-called "ethnic groups" are generally regarded to have one or a combination of these characteristics. Even when biological traits are considered to identify a group, wide physical variations are likely to exist within it. Such an ethnic group is, in general, a minority, either in numbers or in power, whose culture differs to some degree from the majority group of the locality. If cultural differences are to be cherished for their enrichment of human life, ethnic groups should not suffer disadvantages or

cultural anthropologists, who investigate the cultures and modes of organization of extant societies to reconstruct prehistoric life and formulate generalizations about the essential characteristics of human social life.

Although anthropology may be primarily identified with the study of preliterate societies, many modern anthropologists devote all or part of their research to the study of major civilizations.

Anthropology has perhaps made its greatest contribution to social science by developing the concept of culture as its central theme, which has illuminated all the disciplines concerned with the study of human group life. Research method in anthropology is notable for its emphasis on long-term intimate observation and participation in the day-to-day life of the society under study.

Development through biological evolution

1. Many persons believe that man has developed to his present form through the same processes of biological evolution by which animals have developed, and that the process of man's evolution has involved approximately one and one-half billion years. During this period, it is believed that a multitude of plant and animal forms have also evolved.

2. Physical anthropologists generally believe that man's separate stem of evolution spans several million years; however, in the scale of biological time man is a relatively new phenomenon.

3. Fossil remains of early man illustrate the ultimate evolution of distinctively human characteristics. The most important include a large brain, upright posture, manipulative hands, keen vision, and mouth and throat structures that make speech possible.

4. Man attained essentially his present-day biological attributes many thousands of years ago; his development since that time has been overwhelmingly cultural. Man's survival no longer depends chiefly on further biological evolution but rather on cultural development.

Development of culture

1. Although man is identified with other living creatures, he differs profoundly by virtue of his development of culture.

2. Culture is a product of man's exclusive capacity to comprehend

and communicate by means of language. Culture is socially learned and consists of the knowledge, beliefs, and values which humans have evolved to establish rules of group life and methods of adjusting to and exploiting the natural environment.

3. The variety of cultures developed by human societies affords man more diverse ways of living than animals. At a specific time and place, every society has a culture to some degree different from that of any other society, past or present.

4. Culture can be altered rapidly to cope with new conditions, and a society can borrow ideas readily from another culture. The superiority of man's cultural adaptations is thus emphasized in contrast with the slowly developing and constrictive biological adaptations of animals. Man's superiority illustrates the desirability of encouraging the continuance of many different cultural streams and of fostering sympathetic understanding of them. Such diversity enriches all of human life.

Cultural heritage

1. No modern society has evolved more than a small fraction of its present cultural heritage. Each is deeply indebted to the contributions of other civilizations.

2. Man has left evidences of his presence in the Old World for at least the last 500,000 years. Paleolithic ("Old Stone Age") men invented and developed languages; made crude tools of chipped stone and probably less durable materials; eventually developed primitive clothing and learned to control fire; and still later domesticated the dog.

3. Some nine or ten thousand years ago, men living near the east end of the Mediterranean Sea first domesticated food plants and animals, thus beginning the Neolithic ("New Stone") Age. Such control of the food supply constituted one of the most far-reaching revolutions in human history. Populations increased rapidly where farming developed and permanent towns sprang up. The increased density of population and the additional security and leisure made possible by the relatively assured food supply gave man his first opportunity to develop those parts of culture which are the basis of civilization: writing, mathematics, and science; specialized technologies, such as weaving, pottery

making, and metallurgy; organized philosophy and religion; and legal, political, and economic organizations. These advances and their improvement began soon after the agricultural base was established.

4. No real break exists between the cultures of the ancient Neolithic farmers and the great civilizations of today. But the rate of cultural progress and the dissemination of new knowledge have accelerated tremendously. This speed-up—particularly in science and technology—has created new opportunities and new and pressing problems for man. How the great cultural advances are put to use is the most urgent problem in the modern world.

Culture as an influence on society

1. The culture under which a person matures exerts a powerful influence on him throughout his life.

2. Since the culture of a society has such an impact upon an individual's personality, he feels, thinks, and acts in accord with its imperatives, not only to be accepted by his fellows but also to maintain his self-respect and confidence. The world into which every individual must fit is defined by his culture.

3. Language is an essential, effective, and exclusively human tool for the invention and transmission of culture. Art, music, and other symbolic and aesthetic expressions are also effective means of transmitting culture.

4. Culture, the creation of human activities, may be altered by them. Norms of culture are derived historically but are dynamic and thus may be subjected to planned change.

5. All cultures provide for the essential needs of human group life but differ, sometimes markedly, in the means by which they fulfill these needs. Different cultures result in different modes of thought and action. People generally prefer the culture of their own society but should recognize that they would probably prefer another culture if they had been subject to its influences to the same degree.

6. Anthropologists have been unable to discover a scientific basis for evaluating cultures as absolutely inferior or superior.

7. A major problem in the modern world is to discover ways in which social groups and nations with divergent cultures can co-

discrimination merely because they vary culturally from the norm of the majority.

Cultural participation and contributions

1. Human beings, regardless of their racial or ethnic background, are nearly all capable of participating in and making contributions to any culture.
2. The environment in which a person lives and his opportunities for personal growth have profound effects upon the development of every individual. When these opportunities are limited by cultural poverty or repressive action, society loses as much as the individual.
3. So-called "race problems" are cultural problems arising from conflicts between ethnic groups or an ethnic group and the majority population. If the positive social value of cultural diversity is recognized, ethnic differences can add to the general richness of life.

Summary

The person who has gained some anthropological knowledge about the range of human variation, both physical and cultural, and who understands and accepts the anthropological viewpoint about the causes and positive values of such differences will understand more fully his own behavior and that of others. Study of a variety of cultures increases a person's understanding of his own culture and reactions to life situations. The study of anthropology can also increase a person's effectiveness in daily life by helping him to understand the viewpoints of others and to be more effective in adapting to, introducing, or controlling social and cultural changes. Through knowledge of anthropology, a person can learn to appreciate man's universal qualities.

Generalizations From Psychology

Overview

Psychology is the science of human behavior. Its aim is the understanding and prediction of behavior. Broadly speaking, psychology is concerned with the scientific study of all its forms, such as learning, growth and development, thinking, feeling, perceiving, social behavior, personality development, and atypical behavior; and with the physiological processes underlying behavior. Psychology is closely related to both the social studies and the biological sciences.

Individual psychology is concerned with the description and understanding of the patterns of behavior exhibited by the person. Included are the nature of growth and development, appraisal of personality characteristics, measurement of individual differences in various aspects of behavior, and the discovery of the pattern of influences producing given forms of behavior, such as aggression, withdrawal, delinquency, and creativity.

Social psychology is a bridge between sociology, which focuses attention on understanding large social settings and group structures, and psychology, which focuses attention primarily on understanding individual behavior and personality. Social psychology deals with such problems as the effects of social pressure on the behavior and personality of individuals, differences in the behavior patterns of individuals living in the same culture groups, and the processes through which the behavior of individuals is influenced by their culture groups.

Behavior

1. Behavior is caused and is not its own cause. Each form of individual behavior has a pattern of causes that are multiple, complex, and interrelated. Behavior is not capricious or random. The discovery of causes leads to an understanding of behavior.
2. Human behavior is purposive and goal-directed. The individual may not always be aware of basic purposes and underlying needs that are influencing his behavior. The study of psychology attempts to bring about a greater awareness of the underlying causes of behavior.
3. Behavior results from the interaction of genetic and environmental factors. Through genetic influences, all individuals have a potentiality for development and learning; yet these genetic factors produce differences among individuals. The character of

the physical and social environment promotes or limits the degree of realization of the individual's potentialities.

Influence of social groupings

1. As a biologic organism, the individual posesses at birth certain physiological needs, but the methods of satisfying these needs and their subsequent development are to a great extent socially determined by his particular cultural unit.
2. Through the interaction of genetic and social and physical environmental factors, the individual develops a pattern of personality characteristics. This pattern includes motives for action, the organization and development of self, values and standards of conduct, and relationships with other individuals.
3. Individuals differ from one another in personal values, attitudes, personalities, and roles; yet, at the same time, the members of a group must possess certain common values and characteristics.
4. Social groupings develop as a means of group cooperation in meeting the needs of the individuals. The basic unit of the family makes it possible for two individuals to cooperate in producing and training children. Similarly, other social groupings—such as communities, social organizations, and nations—enable individuals to work together toward satisfaction of common needs. The nature and structure of groupings tend to change and become more complex with the circumstances under which man lives.
5. Every individual is a member of several social groups, each of which helps to satisfy his needs. The child starts life as a member of a family but soon establishes additional memberships in school, neighborhood, church, and other groups. As he matures, he extends his membership into a greater variety of groups.

Society and the individual

1. Each of the social groups to which an individual belongs helps shape his behavior. Members of different societies learn different ways of acting, perceiving, thinking, and feeling. Groups exert pressures on their members so that they will accept and

follow group ways and mores. The behavior of any individual reflects in many ways the influences of group pressures.

2. Differences are important in the personality structure and behavior of individuals and make possible the infinite variety of work and recreation activities that characterize modern culture. Differences also furnish a basis for flexibility and creativity, which are essential to social change and development. In any social group, the range of differences among individuals is likely to be greater than the differences between any two groups.

3. Socialization processes, such as methods of child training, differ markedly in different social classes, groups, and societies. Personality structure and behavior are largely influenced by these processes. Individuals develop standards of values that reflect these influences as they seek to relate themselves to the group and to satisfy personal needs.

4. The satisfaction of social needs is a strong motivating force in the determination of individual behavior. Values placed on learning, as well as levels of aspiration, are largely attributable to the mores of the individual's "reference groups." What sometimes appears to be nonconforming behavior may be in reality conforming behavior in terms of a particular group in which an individual seeks status. The strong human tendency to conform to social pressures often prevents individuals from seeing reality. The stereotyping of individuals because of racial or cultural backgrounds is another example. In general, noncooperative, aggressive behavior indicates that the individual's need for social acceptance has been frustrated. The individual displaying such behavior usually has been forced, through repeated experiences of rejection, to develop an attitude of defeat and inferiority.

5. The behavior of individuals is related to the structure and organization of the group in which they are placed. A range of roles, such as leadership, followership, aggression, and submission, may be exhibited by the same individual in different groups. The "need-satisfying" quality of a group and the member-to-member relationship influence behavior.

6. For preservation of its identity, a social group resists change through the phenomena of cultural lag and conservatism. A social group also changes in various degrees to preserve its identity when new conditions arise.

Summary

Psychology contributes to the social studies through its content and method. Both are important to those who guide learning experiences. Generalizations that deal with relationships between individual behavior and group structure illustrate important considerations in the development of content and method.

Generalizations From Sociology

Overview

Sociology is a scientific study of the social relations which men develop in their interaction with one another. Sociologists analyze the basic structures and functions of societies and of associations and groups within societies to discover how they became organized, to identify the conditions under which they become disorganized, and to predict the conditions for reorganization.

Groups, society, and communication

1. The work of society is performed through organized groups. Group membership requires that individuals undertake varied roles involving differing responsibilities, rights, and opportunities. Groups differ because of their purposes, their institutions, heritage, and location. Nevertheless, they are generally similar in organization, structure, and properties. Every person belongs to many groups, and, therefore, groups overlap in membership. In an open-class society, an individual may move up or down in the social system and thus experience significant changes in group membership. An individual's participation in several groups may produce conflicting demands and involve him in several roles that have varying responsibilities and opportunities. Moreover, any group may change its membership and its objectives. Therefore, the individual needs to analyze his relationship to various groups to discern the conflicting demands made upon him and to recognize that he must identify himself as a person as well as a group member. There are differences in the

significance or importance of membership in various groups. Many stereotypes ignore their important characteristics.

2. Communication is basic to the existence of culture and groups. Individuals and groups communicate in many ways other than language. However, every type of communication involves symbolism of varying meanings. These differ from one group to another. Basically communication takes place between individuals. Therefore, the tools of communciation are vital to every individual. Stereotyping and ethnocentrism are serious distorting elements in the communication process.

Personality and the socialization process

1. The expression of man's biological drives is influenced by his social environment.
2. The realization of self is modified by contacts with others.
3. Socialization results from the methods of child training and the experiences of childhood. Social controls and pressures tend to lead to the child's acceptance of the folkways and mores of his culture.
4. Role is determined by the expectations of others. Nonconformity, for example, is perceived in one culture as leadership behavior. In others, it may be regarded as damaging to society. Man occupies different social roles as he moves from group to group.
5. Status within a culture is achieved by means of the prestige attached to natural and artificial differences, such as caste, vocation, class, age, sex, and individual traits.
6. Individual or group organization or disorganization reflects the presence or absence of coordinated and integrated behavior.

Social relations and culture

1. An established society, association, or social group gradually develops patterns of learned behavior accepted by and common to its membership. These patterns, together with their accumulated institutions and artifacts, make up the cultural "way of life" of the society and its associations and groups.
2. Social relations and their complexes are generally shaped by culturally defined rights and duties shared by members of a group.

3. Cultures vary from society to society. Any given culture changes in the course of time. Some behavior and institutions within a culture are universal while others vary widely, even during the same period.
4. Changes and variations may result from factors generated by the culture itself, such as the invention and use of machines, or contact with other societies and cultures.
5. Children growing up within a society tend to learn that its particular behavior patterns, folkways, and institutions represent the "right" values and that those of other societies are "wrong" values.
6. Within any large and complex society, subsocieties with varying cultures exist. Often, these subsocieties consist of peoples who have migrated and are regarded as minority groups in the larger society.
7. People with a common culture sometimes become grouped as social classes and think of themselves as having (a) status or position; and (b) roles or functions quite distinct from those of other classes. A society which becomes so rigidly stratified that it allows little, if any, significant interaction between classes is described by sociologists as having a social caste system.
8. Culture tends to standardize human behavior and to stabilize societies by developing many interrelated and elaborate institutions.
9. Societies that fail to evaluate continuously these institutions and modify them intelligently are subject to cultural lag. This is a maladjustment between parts of a culture that leads to social disorganization. Cultures that fail to make adjustments rapidly enough tend to be absorbed or exploited by more aggressive and rapidly developing cultures. Sometimes societies are eliminated in the process.
10. Internal cultural crises tend to provoke social revolutions. These purport to bring about sweeping changes in the old social order.

Demography and human ecology

1. Many individual, social, and physical problems are influenced by changes in population. These problems may involve considerations of old age, youth, migration, war, housing, famine, employment, government, transportation, recreational activities,

education, vocational opportunities, sanitation, social controls, living habits, and medical facilities.

2. National migration develops cultural diversity within a group and cultural diffusion among groups.

3. The environment influences man's way of living. Man in turn modifies the environment. As he becomes more technically efficient, man is less influenced by his environment and more able to modify his environment. The spatial and temporal distribution of populations and their institutions, as well as the processes that bring about their establishing of patterns, is called human ecology. This is the study of the reciprocal relationship between the community and its physical and social environment. It involves for example, climate, clothing and shelter, natural resources, water and food, social environment and institutions, and folkways and mores.

4. Individuals generally function as members of communities. A community has a fixed geographic location, but its essence lies in the interaction of the persons that comprise it. They are grouped in a locality to cooperate and compete with one another for sustenance, survival, and cultural values. Communities have been increased and developed by modern inventions.

Social processes

1. Societies develop in accordance with recurrent sequences of interaction called social processes. Social interaction and communication are the general processes through which more specialized processes evolve. These include association, dissociation, and stratification; cooperation and accommodation; competition and conflict; and assimilation.

2. In association, human beings in interaction continuously organize and join groups and "societies." Dissociation is illustrated by the fact that groups tend to dissolve in time, losing members to new groups. Stratification is the tendency of individuals, families, and groups to become ranked by society into a hierarchy of social classes based on heredity, wealth, education, occupation, group memberships, and other status factors.

3. Cooperation is illustrated by the way in which members of families and other more intimately related social groups tend to

work together in performing functions of community living and in attaining common goals. Those persons who cannot fully accept other members of their intimate groups, other groups, or the way of life of these groups, often make the necessary compromises or adjustments to remain in the groups or larger community and to enjoy their high priority values. This process is known as accommodation.

4. In competition, persons become rivals of other group members or groups. They may compete as well as cooperate. Conflict occurs when a rivalry precipitates a clash or struggle because either side feels it must defend its social institutions and values or impose them on the other side.

5. Assimilation is the process through which persons and groups migrating to a new environment lose previously acquired modes of behavior and gradually accept those of the new society.

Social control

1. Societies require a system of social control to survive. This control is based upon uncodified rules of behavior (mores and values). Infraction of the rules will bring ostracism or pressure to conform to the controls.

2. Some of the techniques of social control that are used by groups on individuals to secure conformity are shunning, ostracism, gossip, jeering, praise, approval, and acceptance. Informal social control is the strongest factor in securing conformity to group standards.

3. Social control, particularly in complex societies, is also partially secured by formal, codified rules of behavior (laws), infractions of which result in formal penalties. The formal, legal controls are imposed upon those areas of social life which are too important to be governed by informal controls. When a "power group" seeks an objective which cannot be reached by other means, it may attempt to impose legal controls.

Summary

The study of sociology reveals and clarifies the structure of groups, group phenomena, and the role of the individual in various kinds of groups. Sociologists endeavor to predict social behavior by use of the scientific method and social research. These means of investigation and the application of what is known about group processes help to solve social problems. Thus, sociology contributes directly to the social studies.

Contributions of Philosophy

Overview

Within the past two hundred years, fields which were once considered a part of philosophy have been developed as separate social sciences. Before their emergence, philosophy and history were the disciplines within which students of human behavior inquired into the conditions and consequences of institutionalized life. Philosophy continues to be concerned with questions, concepts, and valuations related to the study of man and appraisals of his conduct. Thus, it is similar in subject matter to other social sciences. Philosophy has an essentially critical role in the analysis and valuation of concepts and generalizations contributed by these fields. It is the responsibility of philosophers to explore methodology, foundations of theorizing, and judgment criteria concerned with man's activities and values.

Although philosophy is not studied separately in elementary and secondary schools, it contributes to all social studies undertaken in the spirit of *inquiry*. If the study is to enlist pupils as effective participants, they must acquire and employ intellectual skills requisite for following arguments, clarifying ideas, and submitting claims to tests. Social studies conducted to develop the spirit of inquiry must utilize these skills.

Logic, scientific method, and ethical analysis

1. Philosophy contributes to social studies the tools of logic, scientific method, and ethical analysis. It contributes also to social philosophy, political philosophy, and the philosophy of history. These tools and areas of study equip individuals to cope critically with questions, problems, concepts, theories, and value judgments that arise in discussion of race, private property, the family, the state,

human nature, obligation to others, socialism, free enterprise, civic responsibility, civil disobedience, classes and class conflict, self-government, the rights of man, and the relation of religion to morality.

2. Because of the influence of interests and emotionally charged words in discussions of human affairs, the teacher needs to make clear the "how" and "why" of requirements laid down for testing assertions on the basis of evidence and right reasoning and to point out the pitfalls that trap discussions that do not fulfill these requirements. By utilizing the requirements and developing respect for them, pupils learn to make intelligent choices and decisions as citizens. They learn how to face up to controversial issues through objective examination of ideas and arguments.

Ability to make judgments

1. The study of philosophy, either as a separate discipline or in conjunction with other social sciences, helps pupils to develop the ability to make well-considered judgments.
2. The processes by which sound conclusions are reached need to be emphasized to pupils continually and utilized in their oral and written discussion. Thereby pupils engage in the work of critical analysis essential to judgment. They will not be satisfied with ready-made answers or with the omission of issues that can stimulate the spirit and practice of inquiry.

Summary

For its own well-being, a free society must keep open the path of free inquiry and develop in its future citizens those habits of study which result in responsible commitments in thought and action. Conducted as an inquiry to which philosophy contributes tools and areas of investigation, the social studies can be expected to develop the ability of pupils to make well-reasoned judgments. Concepts, generalizations, and doctrines which pupils encounter will be subjected to questioning. Reasons for their acceptance or rejection will be reviewed, their applications investigated, and their implications explored. In this way, the examined life which Socrates declared to be the life most worthy to be lived by man will be developed and encouraged in the pursuit of social studies in all grades.

Index